Mark Powell

in company

Upper intermediate

MACMILLAN

Unit and topics	Communication skills and tasks	Reading and listening texts	Grammar and Lexis links	
1 Business or pleasure? p4 **Networking** Corporate entertainment Making conversation	Discussing corporate entertainment Sharing information to select appropriate corporate events for clients Avoiding saying 'no' Paying & receiving compliments Keeping up a conversation	R Information on four corporate events in the UK L People chatting at corporate events L People chatting at corporate events	Tense review	Conversation
2 Exchanging information p10 **Meetings** Providing accurate information	Describing attitudes to & content of meetings Paraphrasing information Pointing out discrepancies Saying complex numbers & figures Dialogue-building using the language of meetings Breaking bad news & writing a report	R Article on Harold Geneen L Extract from a meeting: problems with a product L Extracts from five meetings: discrepancies L Saying complex numbers & figures R/L Meeting: breaking bad news	Conditionals	Language of meetings
3 Material world p16 **Talking points** Success & failure Ethics & investment	Doing a quiz on the billionaire lifestyle Discussing what success means Discussing ethics & investment	L Radio programme on the collapse of Barings Bank R Article on the Vice Fund L People discussing investments		
4 Voice and visuals p20 **Presenting** Giving presentations	Doing a quiz on how to command attention Giving feedback on a presentation Using visuals in a presentation Analysing the voice in presentations Giving a speech	R Book extract on the Kennedy-Nixon debate L Voice mail L Presenters giving information in different ways L Radio programme: drama for business L Speeches from five films	Modal verbs	Language of presentations
5 Problems on the phone p26 **Desk work** Customer complaints Solving problems	Discussing phone usage & its usefulness Dealing with 'chatterers' Complaining & dealing with complaints Toning down 'flames' Speculating about a problem Solving problems on the phone	R Article on 'chatterers' L Someone dealing with a 'chatterer' L Someone dealing with a customer complaint L People discussing a problem L People solving a problem	Complex question formation	Phone, fax and e-mail
6 Leading meetings p30 **Meetings** Chairing meetings	Discussing dynamics of meetings Disagreeing diplomatically Chairing a meeting	L Radio programme: alternative approaches to meetings R Article on behaviour in meetings L Extracts from a meeting R Newspaper articles	Linking & contrasting ideas	Language of companies & capital
7 Information age p36 **Talking points** Information and disinformation	Discussing the reliability of information Discussing the truth behind news headlines Discussing the reliability of statistics Exchanging opinions on the information economy	R Book extract on the reliability of information L People talking about the truth behind newspaper headlines R Article on Enron L People giving their opinions on the information economy		
8 Promoting your ideas p40 **Presenting** Innovation Presenting new ideas	Discussing attitudes to public speaking Describing what makes a good talk Discussing innovation in your company Presenting an idea for a product or service	L Presenters talking about what makes them nervous L People comparing audience expectations of presentations R Website extract: *Intrapreneurs* L Presentation: a new idea	Passive	Phrasal verbs
9 Relationship-building p46 **Networking** First impressions Visiting a colleague's home	Discussing first impressions Completing a questionnaire on networking Practising networking skills Visiting a colleague's home	R Article: *First impressions* R Article on golf and business L People chatting at golf L Conversation extracts: visiting someone's home	Multi-verb sentences	Social English

1 Business or pleasure?

All things being equal, people will buy from a friend. All things being not quite so equal, people will still buy from a friend.

Mark McCormack, What They Don't Teach You at Harvard Business School

Discussion

1 Work with a partner and discuss the following questions.

a Is it easier to work with friends or more complicated?

b Would you be worried about doing business with a member of your family?

c How many of the people you work with do you mix with socially?

d When was the last time you had to attend an office party or business function? Did you have a good time?

e The Japanese spend $40 billion a year on corporate hospitality – almost as much as the country's annual defence budget! In what ways can entertaining clients and colleagues be good for business?

2 Complete the following extract from a corporate entertainment company's website using the words in the box. Are you persuaded by what it says?

service	team	experience	clients	seats	relationships
box	reception	setting	office	members	viewing

What better way to build and maintain (a) _____ with key (b) _____ and to reward star (c) _____ of your (d) _____ than to offer them a unique and unforgettable (e) _____ far away from the pressures and constraints of an (f) _____ environment? Whether it's front row (g) _____ at the Metropolitan Opera in New York, a VIP (h) _____ at the World Cup Final, a private (i) _____ at the Guggenheim Gallery in Bilbao or a champagne (j) _____ at the Paris Ritz, we can provide the ideal (k) _____ and first-class (l) _____ that will leave your guests simply saying 'Wow!'

3 Work in two groups. Group A read about corporate events **a** and **b**, Group B events **c** and **d**.

a   British Grand Prix, Silverstone

Engines roar, tyres squeal and sparks fly as two-million-dollar supercars accelerate from 0 to 250kph in under seven seconds. 200,000 spectators descend on Silverstone for this fabulous sporting occasion that attracts a worldwide TV audience of 350 million. From your trackside seat you'll soak up all the atmosphere of one of the most glamorous and spectacular events in the motor-racing calendar. VIP treatment; breathtaking action!

VIP box and hospitality tent: €1,000 per person

b   All England Lawn Tennis Championships, Wimbledon

Experience the nail-biting climax to the world's premier international tennis tournament as the true giants of the game clash in the men's Wimbledon final. All the tradition of vintage champagne and strawberries and cream combine with 140-mile-an-hour serves and awesome cross-court shots to make what many consider to be the greatest sporting event on Earth. Game, set and match!

Men's final, lunch, champagne, music: €3,000 per person

c   Banquet on board the Royal Yacht Britannia

Dinner on board Britannia is a once-in-a-lifetime experience – oysters and aperitifs, tables decorated with ice sculptures, waiters in white gloves and music played on the very piano Princess Diana used to practise on. You'll be seated in the state dining room where the Queen once entertained world leaders like Boris Yeltsin, Bill Clinton and Nelson Mandela. Why not really roll out the red carpet for your guests and make your corporate hospitality event a truly 'royal' occasion?

5-course dinner, military band, fireworks: €500 per person

d   London Eye and Private Tour of Tate Modern

Your evening begins 130 metres above London in your very own capsule on the London Eye. A waiter serves champagne. On a clear day you can see for 25 miles – all the way to Windsor Castle. You are then transferred to the Tate Modern for a private tour of one of the world's most cutting-edge contemporary art galleries, followed by a superb dinner in the tasteful surroundings of the Level 2 Café. High altitude; high culture!

London Eye, tour of Tate Modern, dinner: €1,600 per party of 20

Fluency   **4**   Team up with people from the other group. You all work in the PR department of a British engineering company. Using the information you read in 3, hold a meeting to decide which would be the best event to invite each of the following to:

a   your top fifty sales reps and their partners

b   six Finnish engineers with whom you have just completed a very successful two-year project

c   a delegation of twelve Chinese government officials with whom you are currently negotiating an $80 million contract

d   the CEO of your biggest Dutch customer, her husband and teenage son

Also think of a suitable gift you could give to each of your guests.

5   Which of the events would
a you **b** your partner **c** the people in your department
most enjoy?

Making conversation

1 [▶] **1.1** Listen to some business people chatting at two of the corporate events on page 5 and answer the questions.

Conversation 1

a What's the connection between Helen Keating, James McRae and Alan Sullivan?

_____

b When Helen asks James 'Mind if I join you?', how does he reply?

N_____ a_____ a_____. B_____ m_____ g_____.

c What excuse does Helen make for leaving the rest of the party?

_____

d Two of the following mean 'That can't be true.' Which two?

You're joking! ☐ You're fooling! ☐ You're kidding! ☐

e Helen and James use several expressions to refer to memories. Can you remember the first three words of each expression? Contractions (_it's, you're,_ etc.) count as **one** word.

1 _____ _____ _____ somewhere before?

2 _____ _____ _____ me to forget a face.

3 _____ _____ _____ recognised you.

4 _____ _____ _____ back to me now.

5 _____ _____ _____ remember spending most of the evening fighting off some creepy little guy called Alan.

Conversation 2

a How would you describe relations between Mr Ishida and Mr Thompson?

warm ☐ amicable ☐ cordial ☐ cool ☐ strained ☐ frosty ☐

b Mr Thompson uses the word 'so' five times during the conversation:

So, Mr Ishida, let me freshen your glass.

So, how are you enjoying the match?

So, tell me, have you been to one of these big tournaments before?

So, do you still play?

So, shall we return to our seats?

Why does he need to use it so often? _____

What's the equivalent word or expression in your own language?

c Mr Ishida says he's too old to play table tennis now. Mr Thompson replies 'Oh, I'm sure that's not true.'

Is he: paying Mr Ishida a compliment? ☐ calling him a liar? ☐

d Mr Thompson tries to use his background knowledge to keep the conversation going. Complete his remarks below.

1 I h_____ you're quite a tennis fan.

2 I u_____ the Japanese are world table tennis champions.

3 I s_____ the Nikkei's looking strong. That m_____ be good news for you.

4 I r_____ somewhere that things were improving. Or a_____ I mistaken?

e What word is Mr Ishida avoiding by saying the following? _____

Not at the moment, thank you.   Not really.   Not especially.
Not any more.   As a matter of fact, ...

2 Work with a partner. Practise avoiding saying 'no'.

Prepare
- Write down eight false (but believable) statements about yourself, your job, your family, your interests, your company or your country. When you are ready, swap lists with a partner.

Play
- Imagine the two of you are chatting at a conference or corporate event. Take it in turns to make wrong assumptions about each other using the lists as a starting point but adding remarks of your own if you can.
  e.g. *I hear* you're based in Rotterdam.
      I understand you're a keen golfer.
      I believe your company's about to be involved in a merger.
      I read somewhere that Russia will be joining the EU soon.
- Your objective is to get the other person to say 'no'. Their objective is the same. Use the expressions opposite to help you avoid saying 'no'.
- Whoever says 'no' first loses.

Useful expressions
- Not very.
- Not really.
- Not especially.
- Not exactly.
- Not yet.
- Not any more.
- Not at the moment.
- Not as far as I know.
- Actually, ...
- As a matter of fact, ...

3 ▭ 1.2 Listen to some business people chatting at the other two corporate events on page 5 and answer the questions.

Conversation 1

a What sort of people are the Hamiltons? Compare your impressions with a partner. _____

b Put the words in the following greetings and introductions in the correct order.

1 Dan call please me

_____

2 meet last to both pleasure at a you

_____

3 mentioned name Julian's course your of

_____

4 Fiona calling me mind do don't you you you?

_____

c It's common when someone joins a group at a party to tell them a bit about the conversation you've just been having. Complete the following:

talking	wondering	discussing	saying	trying

We were just

- _____ what a marvellous party this is.
- _____ these new tax laws they're bringing in.
- _____ about you – how are things?
- _____ what this pile of dirty laundry was doing in an art gallery.
- _____ to work out what this whole thing must have cost.

d Why does Dan say to Alistair 'I wonder if we could have a word?' when they're already talking? _____

e All the expressions below mean 'I'm going'. Which also mean 'but I'm coming back'? Some of them were in the conversation you just listened to.

It's been nice talking to you. ☐   Would you excuse me a moment? ☐

I'll have to be going. ☐   I'll be right back. ☐

If you'll excuse me. ☐   Is that the time? ☐

Don't go away. ☐   I'll catch you later. ☐

Conversation 2

a Do Tom and Ricardo do a deal? _____

b What expression does Tom use to switch from discussing motor racing to discussing business?

T_____ o_____ races, how's the South African bid going?

c Complete the expressions below. They were all in the conversation you just listened to. Contractions (*I'd, wouldn't, who's*, etc.) count as **one** word.

1 Glad _____ _____ make it.

2 I _____ _____ missed it for the world.

3 There's _____ _____ like you to meet.

4 Can't _____ _____ standing there with an empty glass.

5 So, _____ _____ person you wanted me to meet?

6 I _____ _____ two know each other already.

7 I'll _____ _____ two to chat. See you later.

d What do the following remarks tell you about Ricardo and Élise's relationship?

_____

Lexis link

for more on conversation see page 101

Long time no see.

You haven't changed a bit.

Neither have you. Charming as ever.

Ricardo and I go back a long way.

I'll have whatever you're having.

Fluency

4 Work with a partner. Practise paying and receiving compliments.

The mutual appreciation game

Prepare
- Spend a few minutes thinking of compliments you could pay your partner. Use the expressions opposite to help you.

Play
- When you are ready, start exchanging compliments with your partner. Respond to each compliment you receive in an appreciative but modest way. See who can give the most compliments in under two minutes!
- Join the rest of your group and report some of the compliments you've been giving.
  e.g.
  I was just saying how nice Alain's new haircut looks.

  I was just telling Yvonne what a marvellous tan she's got.

Useful expressions
- You're looking as ... as ever/usual today!
- What a brilliant/fantastic/fabulous ...!
- You know, that/those ... really suit(s) you!
- I (really) like your ...! Where did you get it/them?
- By the way, you did a great job in the meeting/presentation the other day.
- In fact, I must say you're one of the ...*est* people I've ever met. And I'm not just saying that. I (really) mean it!

Discussion

5 They say 'Flattery will get you everywhere.' How important is it in your culture to

a pay people personal compliments?

b compliment them on their work?

Does it depend on how well you know each other? Is it different for men and women?

6 According to Dale Carnegie, author of the all-time best-selling people skills book *How to Win Friends and Influence People*, 'You can make more friends in two months by becoming interested in other people than you can in two years by trying to get people interested in you.' Work with a partner to practise keeping up a conversation.

Speaker A see page 126. Speaker B see page 128.

The hot buttons game

Conversation starters

1 How are you enjoying ...?
Do you attend a lot of these things?

2 Isn't this weather ...?
Apparently, the forecast is for ...

3 How's business?
I hear ...

4 Have you heard about ...?
... news, isn't it?

5 I see the stock markets are ...
It's probably a good time to put your money into ...

6 Are you into (sport) at all?
Did you see the game/match on ...?

7 What kind of music are you into?
Have you heard ...'s latest album?

8 Do you know ..., by the way?
S/he's a bit/very ..., isn't s/he?

9 Have you seen any good films lately?
I quite liked that one with (actor) in ... oh, what was it called?

10 Do you get to do much travelling?
Have you ever been to ...? I've always wanted to go there.

11 Have you seen those new ...?
I wonder if they're any good? Because I heard ...

12 I like your ..., by the way. Where did you get it/them?
I suppose it/they must have cost you ...?

13 Have you been away on holiday this year?
Anywhere nice? I was/We were planning to go to ...

14 Shall we get ourselves ...?
What do you fancy? How about ...?

Topics

- the event
- the weather
- work
- recent news
- the economy
- sport
- music
- mutual friends
- movies
- travel
- gadgets
- clothes/jewellery
- holidays
- food/drink

Grammar link

for more on tenses see page 100

7 Have the conversation again – this time the situation has changed a little.
Speaker A see page 126. Speaker B see page 128.

Meetings are called by managers who get lonely. *Sue Gaulke, management trainer*

1 Roughly how much of your working week do you spend in meetings?

Discussion 2 Which of the following attitudes is closer to your own? Indicate your position on the scale below and compare with a partner.

Meetings: where the real work gets done! ◄──────────────► Meetings: a practical alternative to work!

3 Read the article below. Would you have liked to work for Harold Geneen? Is he anything like your boss?

Business Life magazine

THE MEETING MAN

Harold Geneen

The average executive spends half their life in meetings. If there was a king of meetings, it would have to be former ITT chief, Harold Geneen, a remorselessly driven workaholic who believed that facts and analytical rigour could – and surely would – conquer all.

Every month more than fifty ITT executives flew from all over the world to Brussels to spend four days poring over the figures. Clocks in the meeting remained resolutely on New York time. The room housed a 90-foot long table. The curtains were drawn and the executives survived on a diet of hamburgers and statistics.

The shareholders didn't complain. Between 1959 and 1977, when Geneen was chief executive, ITT's sales went from $745 million to nearly $28 billion.

Collocations 4 Some of the things you might discuss in an information-sharing meeting are listed below, but the second word in each collocation has been switched with another. Switch them back. The first two have been done for you.

production **margins**	quality **campaigns**	customer **budgets**
balance **appraisals**	sales **chains**	recruitment **setting**
market **channels**	advertising **control**	salary **support**
staff **sheets**	cost **development**	training **relations**
profit **methods**	supply **projections**	price **procedures**
distribution **trends**	product **cutting**	IT **reviews**

Discussion 5 Use the template below to help you talk about the meetings you attend. Use some of the phrases in 4 or choose others that are more relevant to your own line of business.

> Well, a lot of the meetings I go to these days tend to be about _____ and usually that will involve discussing things like _____. The most important figures we look at are _____. So I'll probably have to prepare _____ and issue copies before the meeting. If there's any real disagreement, it will generally be about _____. But, frankly, the worst thing about the meetings is _____.

Making things clear

Paraphrasing 1 In meetings, people are sometimes reluctant to say exactly what they mean – especially if they have bad news! Match the vague statements to their blunter equivalents.

Vague

a I'm sorry to report that the project has not been a complete success.
b Technically speaking, we have run into negative profit.
c I think there's a general lack of consumer confidence.
d You know we've always been a market-driven organisation.
e Now is not the time to expand, but to consolidate.
f There will have to be some restructuring of the department.
g We may also have to consider outsourcing production to cut costs.
h Of course, we won't be able to finalise anything today.

Blunt

1 Our assembly plant may be closed down too.
2 Sales are falling.
3 People are going to lose their jobs.
4 It's failed.
5 We'll have to hold another meeting!
6 We've made a loss.
7 Let's do nothing.
8 We've never had an original idea.

2 ▭ 2.1 A computer games company has had problems with its latest product. Listen to an extract from their meeting and check your answers in 1.

3 Work with a partner. Take it in turns to read out the vague statements in 1 in random order. The other person should respond in a more direct way using the expressions below.

> You mean … What you (really) mean is …
> In other words … So what you're (really) saying is …

Spotting discrepancies 4 ▭ 2.2 Listen to short extracts from five meetings. Each contains one piece of information that doesn't make sense. After each extract, turn to a partner and decide what the discrepancy is. Then listen again and check.

Fluency 5 Work with a partner to practise pointing out discrepancies. Speaker A see page 126. Speaker B see page 128.

Number crunching 6 ▭ 2.3 How do you say the following numbers? Compare with a partner, then listen and check.

a $12½bn	c ²/₃	e 4:1	g 298m³	i 400Gb
b €580,753	d $8,491	f 1.05km²	h ¥52–58m	j 0.0012%

7 Which of the figures in 6 is:

a six-figure sum? ☐   accurate to two decimal places? ☐

a round figure? ☐   just under 8½K? ☐

in excess of 12 billion? ☐   a fraction? ☐

expressed as a ratio? ☐   a negligible proportion? ☐

somewhere in the region of 300? ☐   a rough estimate/a ballpark figure? ☐

8 Write down some key figures in your job and explain their significance to a partner.

Queries and comments

1 Read the following extract from a meeting. A CEO is breaking some bad news to the board. Write in the board members' queries and comments using the notes in brackets to help you. The first one has been done for you.

A OK, everyone. It's bad news, I'm afraid. As you may have heard, the latest European sales figures are looking extremely disappointing.

B (say/fall short/projections again?) <u>Are you saying they've fallen short of projections again?</u> (a)

A I'm afraid so. In fact, we may be 30% down. Now, this will be the third quarter in a row we've missed our targets and, frankly, unless things pick up considerably next quarter, we may have to rethink our whole pricing strategy.

C (suggest/introduce/price cuts?) _____ (b)

A If we still can, Anna. Certainly if we'd done that a year ago, it might have stimulated demand. But do it now and we may end up running at a loss. As you know, we're barely breaking even on some of our product lines as it is.

D (surely/not say/time/phase them out!) _____
   _____ (c)

A No, no, of course not. At least, not yet. But what I am saying is that we need to keep production costs down somehow if we want to remain competitive.

B (this mean/should/invest more/new technology?) _____
   _____ (d)

A If only it was that simple, Erik. But right now we're not really in a position to invest in anything, even if we wanted to. No, I'm afraid the situation calls for more drastic action. It's clearly time for a major restructuring.

D (tell us/could be layoffs?) _____ (e)

A I don't see how we can avoid it, James – unless, of course, we can get some of our people to accept reduced hours.

C (mean some kind/job-share scheme?) _____ (f)

A Yes, either that or introduce a four-day week – providing the unions don't oppose it. Of course, it's not just a question of costs. It's also a question of product. The fact is, better products are coming onto the market all the time.

D (so/say/should/spend more/R&D) _____
   _____ (g)

A As I've said, capital investment is no longer an option for us. Pour any more money into R&D and we'll simply slide further into debt. And then there are all the problems we've been having with our overseas distributors.

B (this mean/think/centralise distribution?) _____
   _____ (h)

A Well, that's one option, yes. But even if we decided to do that, and it's a big if, it would take time to implement – time we simply don't have. As you know, our share price has fallen to an all-time low of just 85 cents. And I wouldn't be surprised if, by our next meeting, it's fallen even further. The fact is, we're selling old product at inflated prices in a volatile market through inefficient distributors.

D (hope/not suggest/situation/hopeless) _____
   _____ (i)

A Well, let's put it this way: we've cancelled the Christmas party!

2   ▭ 2.4 Listen to the meeting in 1 and compare your answers.

Collocations   **3**   Underline at least six collocations in 1 you may want to use yourself e.g. *fall short of projections, miss targets, run at a loss, break even, slide into debt.*

4   Explain your choice of phrases in 3 to a partner. How do they relate to your own job?

Conditionals   **5**   Look back at the meeting in 1 and answer the following:

    a   How many examples of conditional sentences and expressions are there?

    _____

    b   Apart from *if,* which three words are used to link the conditional to the main clause?

    _____, _____, _____

    c   Only one of the conditional sentences refers to the past. Which one?

    _____

    d   Why is the past tense used in the following example from the meeting?
    *Even if we **decided** to do that, and it's a big if, it would take time to implement.*

    _____

    e   ***If only** it was that simple* (line 18) means:
    I wish it was that simple. ☐   I doubt it's that simple. ☐

    f   *We're not really in a position to invest in anything, **even if** we wanted to* (lines 18–19) means:
    We don't want to invest in anything. ☐
    Wanting to invest would make no difference. ☐

> **Grammar link**
>
> for more on conditionals see page 102

The language of meetings

Lexis link

for more on the language
of meetings see page
103

1 ▣ **2.5** Complete the following extracts from meetings using the words in the box. Some of the expressions have already appeared in this unit. Then listen and check your answers.

point   question   answer   situation   fact   position   option   problem

a **A scheduling meeting**

A Right. Basically, the _____ is this: the contract is ours if we want it.

B But we're not in a _____ to take on another project right now, are we?

A I know. Jan, what's your _____ on this?

b **An IT meeting**

A Look, it's not just a _____ of software, Alessandro.

B Of course not. It's also a _____ of hardware. The entire system needs upgrading.

A But that's out of the _____ We can't afford that kind of capital outlay.

c **A marketing meeting**

A Sales are down. One _____ would obviously be to cut our prices.

B That's no longer an _____ for us. We're barely breaking even as it is.

A Well, then we've no _____ but to rethink our whole marketing strategy.

d **An HR* meeting**

A Well, there's no easy _____ to this, but how about voluntary redundancy?

B I don't think that's the _____ but maybe we could reduce people's hours.

A That might have been the _____ if we didn't already have a strike on our hands!

e **A strategy meeting**

A Now, let's not make a _____ out of this. What if we just pulled out of Sudan?

B Well, I've no _____ with that, but our partners won't be happy.

A No, but that's not our _____ is it? The political situation is just too unstable.

f **A CRM** meeting**

A I'll get straight to the _____ We're getting too many customer complaints.

B I agree with you. But the _____ is we don't have the staff to deal with them.

A That's beside the _____ We shouldn't be getting them in the first place!

g **A crisis meeting**

A I'm afraid the _____ is serious. And if the press get hold of the story, …

B Look, we'll deal with that _____ if and when it arises. Let's not panic just yet.

A You're right. What this _____ calls for is calm and careful planning.

h **A budget meeting**

A The _____ is, we're simply not spending enough on R&D.

B As a matter of _____ we've doubled our R&D budget this year.

C That may be so, but the _____ remains we're losing our technological lead.

* Human Resources
**Customer Relationship Management

Dialogue-building **2** Work with a partner to write a short dialogue using at least five of the expressions in 1. Read it out to the rest of the class. Can they write the next line of your dialogue using another expression from 1?

Breaking the bad news

Fluency **1** Your company was recently acquired by a former competitor in a hostile takeover. The new board of directors has decided it's time for a serious shake-up. Each of you has been chosen to announce at a special interdepartmental meeting some of the changes they would like to see implemented. After the meeting, you will be expected to report back to the board on people's reactions to the proposal(s) you submitted. Read the template below before you hold the meeting.

Interdepartmental meeting:

Executive Summary

I am
| delighted |
| pleased |
| sorry |
to report that at the interdepartmental meeting held at _____

on _____ the proposed changes
| got the full backing of everyone present. |
| were very well received by the majority of those present. |
| were broadly accepted, though with one or two reservations. |
| met with a certain amount of opposition. |

1 The proposal that _____

was
| particularly welcomed and the general feeling was that |
| eventually approved with the proviso that |
| considered impractical in view of |
| seriously questioned on the grounds that |
_____

_____

| Further |
| Alternative |
suggestions included: **a** _____
 b _____
 c _____

2 There was
| also |
| however |
| some |
| considerable |
| support for the proposal that |
| doubt as to whether |
| disagreement with the thinking behind |
_____

_____

Several other options were explored, including: **a** _____
 b _____
 c _____

We, therefore, strongly recommend the board to _____

---

2 Work in groups and turn to pages 126–127 to see the board's proposals.

3 Material world

You can't have everything. Where would you put it? *Steven Wright, surrealist comedian*

Quiz 1 Work with a partner to see how much you know about the billionaire lifestyle.

Who wants to be a billionaire?

1 How many dollar millionaires are there in the world?
a 720,000
c 72 million
b 7.2 million
d 720 million

2 How many dollar billionaires are there?
a 45
c 4,500
b 450
d 45,000

3 What's the world's most expensive neighbourhood to live in?
a Zürichberg, Zürich
b Eaton Square, London
c Fifth Avenue, New York
d Motoazabu, Tokyo

4 Where can you find the highest concentration of multimillionaires per square metre?
a Monte Carlo
c Nassau
b Santa Barbara
d Geneva

5 With $25,000 to spend, what *couldn't* you afford?
a your own Boeing 747 jumbo jet for an hour
b one night in the world's most expensive hotel room – the Bridge Suite at the Atlantis Resort in the Bahamas
c a Harvard MBA
d 50 hours of helicopter flying lessons

6 With $2 million to spend, what would still be financially out of your reach?
a the world's most expensive watch by Chopard encrusted with over 200 carats of multicoloured diamonds
b the world's most expensive dress, embroidered with 2,000 diamonds, by Maria Grachvogel
c a round of golf with the world's greatest golfer, Tiger Woods
d the Fender Stratocaster Sunburst guitar that Jimi Hendrix famously set fire to on stage

7 Who sold the world's most expensive yacht *Katana* (valued at $68 million) to buy something a little bigger?
a CEO of Oracle, Larry Ellison
b Michael Jackson
c the Royal Family of Qatar
d Media mogul, Rupert Murdoch

8 Who *doesn't* own an island?
a entrepreneur Richard Branson
b actor Nicholas Cage
c ex-prime minister Margaret Thatcher
d the Barclays Bank brothers

9 Who *didn't* own a Rolls-Royce?
a Vladimir Lenin
b Ayatollah Khomeini
c John Lennon
d Ronald Reagan

10 Which classic car was voted the most desirable dream machine ever?
a E-Type Jaguar
b Aston Martin DB5
c Ferrari Dino
d Porsche 911

11 A case of Chateau Le Pin cost £400 in 1983. When ready to drink in 1999, how much was it worth?
a nothing
b £400
c £12,000
d £36,000

12 The most expensive painting ever sold at auction was bought by Japanese businessman Ryoei Saito for $82.5 million. Who was the painter?
a Picasso
b Cézanne
c Van Gogh
d Rubens

Check your answers on page 128

2 According to Benjamin Franklin, 'Success is getting what you want; happiness is wanting what you get.' What does success mean for you? Complete the following using the pairs of words in the boxes. Then discuss their relative importance with a partner.

| making + money | being + thing | getting + career |
| enjoying + life | spending + family | making + world |

a _____ on in
my _____

b _____ the simple things
in _____

c _____ loads
of _____

d _____ quality time
with my _____

e _____ my mark
in the _____

f _____ free to do
my own _____

| running + business | achieving + goals | having + suntan | living + full |
| being + retirement | making + place | | |

g _____ life to the _____

h _____ all my personal _____

i _____ my own _____

j _____ able to take early _____

k _____ the dream house, the flash car and the year-round _____

l _____ the world a slightly better _____

3 Who's the most successful person you know? How did they become so successful?

4 The following sentences refer to either success or failure. Mark them S or F.

a It was a very fruitful meeting. ☐

b The whole thing came to nothing. ☐

c The investment paid off in the end. ☐

d It all went smoothly. ☐

e It was a total flop. ☐

f The deal went through. ☐

g The deal fell through. ☐

h The whole idea was a non-starter. ☐

i We pulled it off. ☐

j It was a major publicity coup. ☐

k We've blown our chances. ☐

l We tried in vain to reach agreement. ☐

5 Tell a partner about a situation in your own life to which one of the sentences in 4 could apply.

Nick Leeson in prison

Upward mobility

1   Work with a partner and discuss the following questions.

a   What do you know about the upwardly mobile whizzkids and yuppies of the 1980s and 1990s? What was business like in your country then?

b   Were you (or would you have liked to be) working during that period?

c   What do you know about the collapse of Barings Bank in 1995? Who was at the centre of the scandal?

2   🔲 3.1 Listen to the story of the collapse of Barings. Check your answers to **c** above.

3   What do the following figures in the story refer to?

a $10 million _____

b   10% _____

c   £50,000 _____

d   £150,000 _____

e $1.3 billion _____

f   6½ years _____

g   233 years _____

h   £1 _____

4   Who do you think was to blame for the disaster? Has anything similar happened at a bank in your country?

5   Match the halves of the following expressions you heard in 2.

a   land   hard
b   enjoy   the bottom
c   work hard and play   your touch
d   work your way up from   a U-turn
e   do   a job
f   lose   the high life

Which of the above mean:

1   rise from the lowest level in a company? ☐

2   completely change direction? ☐

3   put a lot of effort into having fun as well as into your job? ☐

4   partying, travelling, spending money on expensive things? ☐

5   no longer have the special ability that made you successful? ☐

6   get a job you really wanted? ☐

6   What noun can be preceded by these adjectives? Some of them were in 2.

a mounting **b** crippling **c** outstanding **d** heavy _ _ _ _ _

Which adjective means:

unpaid? ☐   damaging? ☐   increasing? ☐   large? ☐

7   🔲 3.2 Listen and find out what happened to Leeson after he got out of prison.

8 You've been talking about upward mobility. What do you think 'downward nobility' is? Read the magazine extract below. Do you agree?

> Want to show off? Walk into a room and say you're a happy person. Better yet, announce that you've been happily married for 25 years. Satisfaction and contentment are the status symbols of the future. That's downward nobility.

Watts Wacker in *Fast Company* magazine

Making money

1 Is there any connection at all between being moral and making money? Is it possible to do both? Look at the two opinions below. Where would you place yourself on the scale?

Being good is good for business.
Anita Roddick, founder of The Body Shop

←————————→

The surest way to remain poor is to be an honest man.
Napoleon Bonaparte, founder of the French Empire

Discussion

2 Work with a partner and discuss the following questions.

a Do you think ethical investment in greener, environmentally friendlier, less exploitative businesses makes the world a better place?

b Does it make sense financially for the individual investor?

c Are there any kinds of company you wouldn't like to see your money being invested in for moral reasons, even if they were a sound investment?

3 Read about an investment fund which takes a different view of ethics and investment. Would you be interested in investing in their fund?

WHEN VICE is capital

'When it is good, it is very, very good, but when it is bad it is better.' This is the motto of the Vice Fund, the first investment fund not afraid to describe itself as 'politically incorrect'.

Imagine that you are one of that ever-increasing number of investors who have lost a fortune on the stock exchange. Feeling depressed, you decide to drown your sorrows in alcohol. Then in the middle of a nervous breakdown you start smoking again. You try your luck at gambling with the few savings you have left, but this also goes wrong. In sheer desperation, you consider the possibility of buying a gun.

Without realising it, the solution to your problems lies in your very miseries. Or, at least, that is what the managers of the Vice Fund claim – an investment fund which was born in the USA and invests in all those areas which pick up in times of recession – arms, alcohol, gambling and cigarettes.

Translated from *La Vanguardia*

VICEFUND Risk/Return Summary

The fund is not appropriate for investors that have short-term goals.

Principal investment strategies

1 First, we look for companies that derive a significant portion of their revenues from products often considered socially irresponsible, and

2 then we select companies from this group based on their financial soundness and potential for growth.

Percentage return in investments compared to S&P 500 index, June 2001 – June 2002

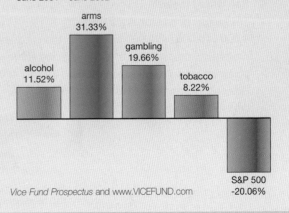

arms 31.33%
gambling 19.66%
alcohol 11.52%
tobacco 8.22%
S&P 500 -20.06%

Vice Fund Prospectus and www.VICEFUND.com

4 🔲 3.3 Listen to three people discussing the question in 3. Who do you agree with most?

4 Voice and visuals

I do not object to people looking at their watches when I am speaking. But I strongly object when they start shaking them to make certain they are still going.

Lord Birkett, British judge

Quiz 1 When you stand up to speak in public, what keeps an audience interested in what you're saying? Expertise or enthusiasm? PowerPoint or natural presence? Work with a partner and underline the answers.

How to command attention

1 Am I boring you?

The attention span of the average audience member is
2 ½ seconds / 12 ½ seconds /
2 ½ minutes / 12 ½ minutes.
(Clue: the attention span of a goldfish is about two seconds.)

2 Is anybody listening?

In a study carried out at UCLA, psychology professor Albert Mehrabian discovered that, of the total impression speakers make on an audience,
38% / 55% / 7% is visual (how we look)
55% / 7% / 38% is vocal (how we sound)
7% / 38% / 55% is verbal (what we say).

3 How low can you go?

Research shows that people generally prefer low voices to high-pitched ones. In a recent study at Wake University, North Carolina, which actor and actress were found to have the lowest and sexiest voices?
Bruce Willis / Mel Gibson / Michael Douglas /
Sean Connery
Gwyneth Paltrow / Michelle Pfeiffer
Nicole Kidman / Julia Roberts

4 See what I mean?

The human brain processes images
4,000 / 40,000 / 400,000 times faster than text and a presenter who uses visuals in their talk will improve audience recall on average by 100% / 200% / 400%.
Use of colour makes visuals 25% / 85% / 850% more memorable.

5 Not just a pretty face?

Although most people would deny it, we often judge others as much by their appearance as by their ability. Only one of the following statistics is false. Which one is it?

a A survey conducted by London Guildhall University claims unattractive Britons earn £3,000 less than better-looking colleagues.

b A UK report found that both male and female sales personnel earn at least 50% higher commission if they're good-looking.

c A study in America has shown that convicted criminals are twice as likely to avoid a jail sentence if they are attractive.

d Since 1900 the US presidency has been won by the taller (and usually better-looking) candidate in nearly 90% of the elections.

2 Check your answers on page 130. If these statistics are true, what are the implications? _____

_____

The television age

1 The televised debate between Richard Nixon and John F. Kennedy in the 1960 American presidential election was the classic case of verbal skills versus visual appeal. Read the full story below. Does image play as important a role in the politics of your country?

From *Artful Persuasion* by Harry Mills

Glossary

five o'clock shadow the hair on a man's face in the afternoon when he has shaved in the morning

grim serious and unfriendly

pallid pale-faced

The Kennedy-Nixon debate

A milestone in television broadcasting came on September 26, 1960, with the first ever US presidential television debate between Richard Nixon and John F. Kennedy.

5 The polls had Nixon and Kennedy neck and neck: Nixon 47 per cent, Kennedy 47 per cent. Nine out of ten American families now owned a television set, and the viewing audience would be the largest ever assembled. The television

10 confrontation was expected to be decisive.

Nixon knew he had problems with television. His five o'clock shadow made him look grim and pallid, even after shaving. Nevertheless, Nixon believed he could rely on his verbal skills. In

15 face-to-face debates he hardly ever lost.

Kennedy prepared diligently, spending hours answering possible questions prepared by his staff. Nixon refused to practice; no one could tell him

20 what he needed to know.

The signs were ominous for Nixon from the time he arrived at the television studio. The gathered photographers flocked to

25 take pictures of the young, good-looking Kennedy. When the moderator introduced the

30 two candidates, Richard Nixon looked, according to author of

35 *Kennedy and Nixon* Christopher Matthews,

like an 'ill-at-ease, unshaven, middle-aged fellow
40 recovering from a serious illness. Jack Kennedy, by contrast, was elegant in a dark, well-tailored suit that set off his healthy tan.'

Verbally Nixon handled himself well. Americans who tuned in to their radios rather
45 than their television sets later rated Nixon the clear winner. But this was the age of television, and the images – the non-verbal body language – that were projected across millions of television screens had an impact. According to Matthews:
50 'Each time Kennedy spoke, Nixon's eyes darted toward him in an uncomfortable mix of fear and curiosity.' In stark contrast, Kennedy's body language projected strength and confidence.

Nixon's close adviser Henry Cabot Lodge, watching the last few minutes of the debate, remarked despondently: 'That son of a bitch just lost the election.'

Kennedy won the great debate decisively: a total of 43 per cent of the viewers gave it to Kennedy, 29 per cent called it even, and only 23 per cent favoured Nixon. In the all-important opinion polls Kennedy pulled ahead. On election day, Nixon lost by just 103,000 votes out of more than 68 million votes cast. For the rest of his life Nixon would refuse even to look at the tapes.

2 The following words and phrases appeared in the text. Delete the incorrect definitions.

   a *A milestone* (line 1) is *a key stage/a terrible moment* in the development of something.

   b People who are *neck and neck* (line 5) are *equally placed/competing fiercely* in a race.

   c If you *prepare diligently* (line 16), you do it *with care and effort/because you have to.*

   d *Ominous* (line 21) means something *unexpected/bad* is going to happen.

   e People *flocked* (line 24) means they *fought each other/crowded round.*

   f If you are *ill-at-ease* (line 39), you are *not relaxed/not well.*

   g If you say something *despondently* (line 56) you feel *hopeless/angry* about it.

3 Read the extra information about the Nixon-Kennedy debate. Imagine you were Nixon's chief adviser Henry Cabot Lodge. What would you have said right after the debate? Complete the sentences below with your ideas.

> **Background to the story**
>
> Nixon had a lot of bad luck prior to his first debate with Kennedy. Exhausted after a tour of all 50 American states, he was suffering from a knee infection, had lost a lot of weight and was running a temperature. To add insult to injury, the TV studio had been painted an identical shade of grey to Nixon's suit, making him virtually invisible to the television audience!

   a What on earth were you thinking of? Do you realise you might have just …

   b If only you'd listened to me! I told you you should have …

   c Don't you think it might have been a good idea to …

   d I know there was nothing you could have done about …

   e And it probably wouldn't have made any difference even if you'd …

   f But surely you could at least have …

> **Grammar link**
>
> for more on modal verbs see page 104

Giving feedback

4 Work with a partner to practise giving and receiving feedback on a presentation. Speaker A see page 130. Speaker B see page 129.

5 ▭ 4.1 Listen to the voice mail from your Taiwanese client following the presentation in 4. Discuss his reaction with a partner.

Visuals

1 When you give presentations, what visuals do you use?

> overhead   handouts   PowerPoint   slides   flipchart   videos   websites

2 Read the book extract. Do you share the author's doubts?

> **Death by PowerPoint**
>
> Are you risking 'Death by PowerPoint'? This is when you inflict on your defenceless audience endless bullet-pointed slides, keywords and clipart that look pretty, yet cumulatively create a numbing effect and loss of impact. Beware of spending more time on the technology than on preparing yourself. Remember, you are the presentation.

Adapted from *The Ultimate Business Presentation Book* by Andrew Leigh

3 All the expressions below can be used to comment on a visual in a presentation. Complete them using the verbs in the box.

notice	give	point	learn	mention	have	put	draw
see	show						

Introduction _____ a look at this. As you can _____, …

Highlights One thing you'll immediately _____ is that …

I'd particularly like to _____ your attention to …

I'd also like to _____ out …

And perhaps I should _____ …

Context Just to _____ you some of the background to this …

To _____ this into some kind of perspective …

Conclusions Clearly then, what these figures _____ is …

The lesson we can _____ from this is …

Lexis link

for more on the language of presentations see page 104

4 Draw a simple graph or chart relating to an interesting aspect of the business you're in *or* the company you work for *or* your country's economy. Use some of the expressions in 3 to present it to the class.

"This is where things started getting really weird."

Voice

1 In a career spanning over 50 years, charismatic lawyer Gerry Spence has never lost a criminal case. Read what he has to say about the power of the human voice.

The sound and the fury

We speak with an instrument we call 'the voice'. Listen to the sounds people make when they speak – only the sounds – and you will discover something of the person who is playing the instrument.

I learned that the spaces between words were as important as the words themselves. A word could be emphasised and a thought underlined by silence, by space, whilst the rapid, close, unbroken delivery of words causes the ideas to become blurred and recede into noise.

The voice reveals who we are and how we are more than the words we choose. And the feelings communicated in the sounds of words are the only truth.

Adapted from *How to Argue and Win Every Time* by Gerry Spence

Delivery 2 ▭ 4.2 Listen to three presenters speaking in different ways. Decide which presenter sounds **1** fluent and confident **2** fluent but boring **3** hesitant.

    a There's a whole market in Eastern Europe just there for the taking. ☐

    b Quite frankly, the results we've been getting are absolutely incredible. ☐

    c Now, I'm sure I don't need to tell you just how crucial this is. ☐

    d Net profits are up ninety-seven per cent – yes, ninety-seven per cent. ☐

    e Would you believe that so far we've not been able to sell a single unit? ☐

    f Miss this deadline and we'll lose the biggest client this company's ever had. ☐

3 Why does the boring presenter sound so monotonous?

_____

4 What exactly is the hesitant presenter doing wrong?

_____

5 ▭ 4.3 Work with a partner. Listen again to the fluent and confident versions. One of you should mark the pauses like this: | The other should underline the stressed words. Compare your results. What's the connection between where we pause and what we stress? _____

6 ▭ 4.4 Deliver all the sentences in 2 in a fluent and confident way. Experiment with longer pauses and stronger stresses. Then compare your version with the recording.

Discussion 7 ▭ 4.5 According to Swedish businessman Jan Carlzon, 'All business is show business.' Listen to an extract from a radio programme on how several training companies have taken his opinion literally, and discuss the questions.

    a Would William Freeman's advice help you face a business audience?

    b What does Michael Lame think classically trained actors can teach business people? _____

    c According to Richard Olivier, what makes someone a brilliant speaker?

    _____

    d Which of the trainees' opinions would be closest to your own?

Fluency 8 Work with a partner. Choose one of the film speeches opposite and take turns to be the actor and director.

    • The speeches are unpunctuated. Decide where you are going to pause – mark short pauses like this: | , longer pauses like this: || and very long pauses like this: |||

    • Underline the words you are going to stress: usually nouns and verbs, but sometimes, for dramatic effect, you can stress pronouns and conjunctions.

    • Highlight in different colours parts of the text you really want to project, even shout, and parts you want to say quietly or perhaps whisper.

    • Try the speech a few times, the actor speaking, the director giving advice and feedback. When you are ready, perform it!

9 ▭ 4.6 Listen to the speeches in 8. How does your performance compare with the recorded version? If you were competing, who'd get the Oscar?

10 Prepare a one-minute presentation on a topic which is relevant to your work. Make your voice as powerful and dramatic as you did in the film speech.

Take 1: Clint Eastwood in *Dirty Harry*

A police detective tries to get a murder suspect to put down his gun after a shoot-out

I know what you're thinking did he fire six shots or only five well to tell you the truth in all this excitement I've kind of lost track myself but being as this is a point four four Magnum the most powerful handgun in the world and would blow your head clean off I guess you've got to ask yourself one question do I feel lucky well do you punk

Take 2: Demi Moore in *Disclosure*

The new boss in a software firm presents the company's latest product

What we're selling here is freedom we offer through technology what religion and revolution have promised but never delivered freedom from the physical body freedom from race and gender from nationality and personality from place and time communicating by cellular phone and hand-held computer PDA and built-in fax-modem we can relate to each other as pure consciousness

Take 3: Alec Baldwin in *Glengarry Glen Ross*

A sales manager is trying to motivate his team of sales staff to close more sales

The good news is you're fired the bad news is you've got all you've got is one week to get your jobs back have I got your attention now good because we're adding a little something to this month's sales competition first prize as you know is a Cadillac Eldorado second prize is a set of steak knives third prize is you're fired do you get the picture are you laughing now

Take 4: Cher in *The Witches of Eastwick*

A woman makes it clear she doesn't wish to see her lunch-date again

I think no I am positive that you are the most unattractive man I have ever met in my entire life you know in the short time we've been together you have demonstrated every loathsome characteristic of the male personality and even discovered a few new ones you are physically repulsive intellectually retarded you're morally reprehensible vulgar insensitive selfish stupid you have no taste a lousy sense of humour and you smell you're not even interesting enough to make me sick goodbye Darryl and thank you for a lovely lunch

Take 5: Mel Gibson in *Braveheart*

A Scottish rebel leader, outnumbered by an opposing English army, tries to motivate his men!

I am William Wallace and I see a whole army of my countrymen here in defiance of tyranny you have come to fight as free men and free men you are what will you do with that freedom will you fight aye fight and you may die run and you'll live at least a while and dying in your beds many years from now would you be willing to trade all the days from this day to that for one chance just one chance to come back here and tell our enemies that they may take our lives but they'll never take our freedom

5 Problems on the phone

No problem is so formidable that you can't walk away from it.

Charles M. Schulz, creator of the Peanuts cartoon

Discussion

1 It's been said that 'When the phone rings, there's usually a problem on the other end of it.' What problems do people phone you with at work?

2 How much of your working day do you spend on the phone? How much of that time is productive?

3 Complete the text below using the nouns and verbs in the boxes.

Glossary

chatterer person who can't stop talking about trivia

24/7 24 hours a day, 7 days a week

something	day	minute	point	line	thing	time
chatter	business	touch				

get	get	do	go	keep	say	listen	hear	continue	expect

HOW TO DISPOSE OF
CHATTERERS
ON THE PHONE

We are living in the age of telephony. One sixth of the planet now has a mobile. In Finland, where they have more mobiles per person than anywhere else on earth, 25% of the
5 country's exports are Nokia phones. Whenever we want, wherever we want, we can get in (a) _____.

But when we do, it seems we can never get to the (b) _____. Up to two hours in every working day are wasted in idle (c) _____ on the phone. And
10 great skill and determination are needed to escape the deadly game of social chit-chat – 'How are you? … Settling in to the new job? … How's Ellen? … And the kids? … Hasn't your eldest just gone to college? … How (d) _____ flies! … Oh, I (e) _____
15 you're moving house as well. … Did you have a nice holiday, by the way? … I suppose you haven't heard the latest, then? … Well, I'm not supposed to (f) _____, but there's a rumour going about …'

Of course, what you want to say in these
20 circumstances is 'Look, I haven't got all (g) _____. Either state your (h) _____ or kindly get off the phone,' but professional courtesy forbids it. Here, then, is the definitive executive guide to 'chatterer disposal'.

Getting down to business The most tactful way of
25 bringing the conversation round to the subject of business is to ask in a slightly louder than normal voice

'What can I (i) _____ for you?' If you know the caller, you could try 'I (j) _____ you're calling about …' and then mention anything you can think of.
30 They, hopefully, will reply 'Er, no, actually, it's about something else.' Should this strategy fail, you may have to resort to a sterner 'Was there (k) _____ you wanted to talk to me about?'

Ending the conversation Phone call termination is
35 more difficult. The trick is not to seem too abrupt. 'Anyway, …' – though a clear signal to most averagely perceptive people that you want to end the call – is much too subtle for chatterers. Try instead 'Well, I mustn't (l) _____ you', 'I'll let you (m) _____
40 on' or the more insistent 'I'll have to let you (n) _____ now.' If you feel that sounds a little too harsh, friendlier alternatives include 'Well, (o) _____, it's been great talking to you', 'We must (p) _____ together soon' or 'Oh, one last
45 (q) _____ and then I really must go.' Of course, with a hardened chatterer this last alternative may be asking for trouble.

Drastic measures In genuine emergencies the following may be used: 'Ah, someone's just this
50 (r) _____ stepped into the office. I'm afraid we'll have to (s) _____ this conversation later. Bye.' Or 'Oh, I've got an international call just come in on the other (t) _____. Can I call you back?' And, if all else fails, you can always try 'Hello? Hello? Are you
55 still there?' Of course the secret with this one is that when the caller says 'Yes, I'm still here,' resist the temptation to reply 'Well, I can't hear you!'

4 📼 5.1 Listen to someone trying unsuccessfully to get a caller off the phone. Underline the expressions they use in 3.

Fluency   5   Work with a partner to practise dealing with a chatterer. Speaker A see page 130. Speaker B see page 129.

Dealing with complaints

Discussion   1   When was the last time you made a formal complaint about something? Was it in person, in writing or on the phone? Were you satisfied with the way it was handled?

2   Put the following stages of handling a customer complaint into the most likely order:

- suggest possible solutions
- end on a positive note
- greet and reassure the caller
- get the details
- agree on a course of action
- listen and empathise

3   Which of the following expressions would be most inappropriate at each of the stages in 2? Delete one from each set of three below. Then underline which of the remaining two you prefer.

Stage 1
a   How can I help you?
b   What can I do for you?
c   What's the matter, then?

Stage 2
a   Can you tell me exactly what the problem is?
b   What exactly is your problem?
c   What seems to be the problem?

Stage 3
a   Tell me about it! I know just how you feel.
b   I can understand exactly how you feel.
c   I can understand how upset you must be.

Stage 4
a   Well, I suppose I could always send you a new one, but I can't give you a refund. Sorry.
b   I can't give you a refund, I'm afraid, but I can certainly send you a new one. How's that?
c   Unfortunately, we're not authorised to give refunds, but what I can do is send you a brand-new one. How would that be?

Stage 5
a   Is that all OK for you?
b   Are you satisfied now?
c   Are you happy with that?

Stage 6
a   I'm so pleased we've managed to sort this out. Was there anything else?
b   Glad to be of assistance. Is there anything else I can help you with?
c   Good, well, that's that, then. Is there anything else or is that it?

4 📼 5.2 Listen to a customer services adviser at iDeals, a computer supplies retail chain, dealing with a complaint and compare what she says with your choices in 3.

5 A 'flame' is an angry or insulting e-mail. Have you ever received or been tempted to write one?

6 Work with a partner. Read the flames you and your partner wrote below and take turns to hold the telephone conversations that might have followed. Caller, be as direct as you like. Receiver, calm the caller down and deal with their complaint.

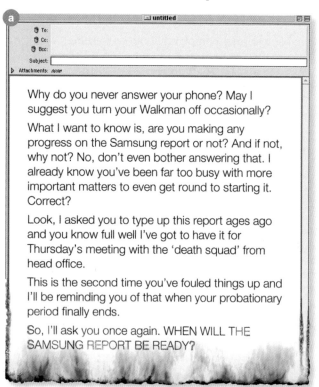

Why do you never answer your phone? May I suggest you turn your Walkman off occasionally?

What I want to know is, are you making any progress on the Samsung report or not? And if not, why not? No, don't even bother answering that. I already know you've been far too busy with more important matters to even get round to starting it. Correct?

Look, I asked you to type up this report ages ago and you know full well I've got to have it for Thursday's meeting with the 'death squad' from head office.

This is the second time you've fouled things up and I'll be reminding you of that when your probationary period finally ends.

So, I'll ask you once again. WHEN WILL THE SAMSUNG REPORT BE READY?

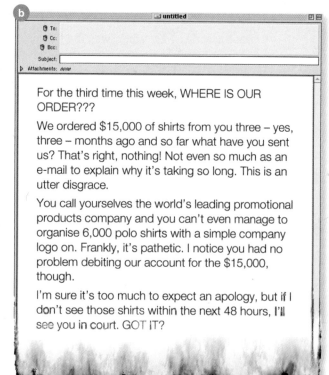

For the third time this week, WHERE IS OUR ORDER???

We ordered $15,000 of shirts from you three – yes, three – months ago and so far what have you sent us? That's right, nothing! Not even so much as an e-mail to explain why it's taking so long. This is an utter disgrace.

You call yourselves the world's leading promotional products company and you can't even manage to organise 6,000 polo shirts with a simple company logo on. Frankly, it's pathetic. I notice you had no problem debiting our account for the $15,000, though.

I'm sure it's too much to expect an apology, but if I don't see those shirts within the next 48 hours, I'll see you in court. GOT IT?

7 Rewrite the e-mail you sent in 6 to make it more polite but equally assertive. Use the prompts below to help you.

a Unfortunately / unable / reach / phone

Can / tell / managing / make / progress / Samsung report? // having / problems / please let / know / soon / possible // understand / been preoccupied / other matters / may not / even / made a start yet / although / hope / not / case

did ask / some time ago / this report / as you know / do need / urgently / Thursday's meeting / people / head office

not / first time / let me down / consequently / shall have / discuss / matter / when / probationary period ends

really must know today how / longer / going / take

b again writing / regard / order / ref no 099X

records show / order / $15,000 / shirts / placed three months / but so far / received anything // Nor / sent / e-mail explaining / reason / delay // afraid / quite unacceptable

You advertise / world's leading promotional products company // therefore / find / inability / take care / simple order like this both surprising / disappointing // notice / however / were more efficient / debiting / account / sum / $15,000

should like / delivery / 48 hours / together / apology // Otherwise / no alternative / hand / matter over / legal department // hope / made myself clear

Lexis link

for more on phone, fax and
e-mail see page 107

Fluency 8 Exchange rewritten e-mails with your partner and hold the two telephone
conversations again. How do these calls compare with the ones you had in 6?

Tackling problems

Discussion 1 ▭ 5.3 Listen to an overheard telephone conversation. Take notes and, with a
partner, try to work out what the problem is.

> It sounds like …
> It seems as though …
> There's been some kind of …, by the sound of it.
> I'm not (exactly) sure whether … or whether …
> It's definitely something to do with …

2 ▭ 5.4 Now listen to both sides of the conversation in 1 and check your ideas.

Idioms 3 You heard the following idiomatic expressions in 2. Can you remember the
missing words? The first two letters are given. Use the definitions in brackets to
help you.

  a I'm working fl_____ out. (I'm working as quickly and as hard as possible.)

  b It completely sl_____ my mind. (I completely forgot to do it.)

  c We're sn_____ under at the moment. (We've got too much work to deal
with.)

4 What would you do in Graham and Piotr's situation?

5 ▭ 5.5 Listen to Graham and Piotr's second conversation and compare your
solutions with theirs.

**Problem-solving
on the phone** 6 Match the halves of the following sentences. You heard them all in 5.

  a Can you get hold   of sending someone else out here?

  b I don't suppose   to have a phone number for the promotions people?

  c Do you happen   getting some brochures to me in Polish?

  d Is there any chance   of the organisers?

  e I'll check   what I can do, but I can't promise anything.

  f I'll see   with Liz and see if she can spare Kim for a few days.

  g Would you mind   you remembered to put another CD player in?

  h Is there any point   the minute I get off the phone.

  i Are you absolutely   if we got a local Polish interpreter in?

  j I'll look into it   to me.

  k Could I ask you   in sending the ones we've got in Russian?

  l Would it help   to that right away.

  m I'll get on   to hurry that up a bit, please?

  n Leave it   sure we didn't order a reprint of the Polish ones?

Grammar link

for more on complex
question formation see
page 106

Fluency 7 Work with a partner to practise solving problems on the phone. Speaker A see
page 135. Speaker B see page 133.

6 Leading meetings

Either lead, follow or get out of the way. Sign on the desk of Ted Turner, founder of CNN

1 How much influence do you have at the meetings you participate in? When it comes to meetings, would you rather lead, follow or simply get out of the way?

Discussion **2** Think about a regular meeting you attend and consider the following:

- Who is the most powerful person in the room? Does he/she actually lead the meeting?
- What are the seating arrangements – fixed or flexible?
- Does anyone tend to dominate the discussion? Is that ever a problem?
- Are there people who hardly speak at all? If so, why are they there?
- Who, if anyone, is the most 'dangerous' person in the room?

Explain to a partner how the meeting works. A simple diagram may help you.

Collocations **3** Combine one word from each box to make ten common problems encountered in meetings. Do you have similar problems in your meetings?

communication communication time point- hidden pulling inadequate late over group-	**+**	barriers wasting preparation breakdowns agendas rank scoring runs think starts

1 _____   6 _____

2 _____   7 _____

3 _____   8 _____

4 _____   9 _____

5 _____   10 _____

Which of the above mean:

misunderstandings? ☐

failing to finish on time? ☐

competition between colleagues? ☐

the need to agree at all costs? ☐

secret intentions or objectives? ☐

using your status to get what you want? ☐

things which make people reluctant to talk? ☐

4 Read the suggestion below. Does it strike you as a good idea? Which of the problems in 3 might it help to solve? Which would it probably make worse?

> **The power table**
> Suppose you removed the table from your conference room and replaced the seats with armchairs. Suppose you turned it into a living room. How much would this affect your meetings?
> That's how much your meetings are about power, not communication.
>
> David Weinberger, *The Cluetrain Manifesto*

5   Five alternative approaches successful companies have taken to the problem of meetings are listed below. What do you think they might involve?

    a the non-stop meeting   **d** the democratic meeting

    b the mobile meeting   **e** the virtual meeting

    c the recreational meeting

6   🔲 6.1 Listen to an extract from a business news programme and match the approaches in 5 to the companies that have adopted them.

Federal Express ☐   another.com ☐   Xerox Corporation ☐

Michaelides & Bednash Media ☐   St. Luke's Advertising ☐

7   Could any of the ideas in 6 work in your company? Would any be thought ridiculous?

Chairing skills

Discussion

1   Complete the following and compare with the other members of your group.

A meeting without a chairperson is like (a) _____ without

(a) _____ .

Collocations

2   Complete the collocations by writing the nouns and noun phrases in the right-hand boxes. They are all things the leader of a meeting might do.

the agenda   points of view
the final decision   the main goals
the participants   the meeting

areas of conflict   follow-up tasks
an action plan   the key issues
other speakers   troublemakers

open / close		bring in / shut out	
welcome / introduce		anticipate / avoid	
set / stick to		identify / discipline	
ask for / summarise		work out / draw up	
establish / define		prioritise / assign	
deliberate over / take		explain / focus on	

Which of the skills above are mostly about managing
• the content of the meeting?   • the people present?
Write C or P.

3 What, in your opinion, is the single most important task of a chairperson? Read the article below. Does the author agree with you?

Adapted from *Fast Company* magazine, www.fastcompany.com

You have to start meeting like this!

We work, therefore we meet. But why do so few of our meetings meet our expectations?

Michael Begeman is a *leading authority* on one of the business world's most *universal rituals*: the meeting. An anthropologist and computer scientist by training, he is manager of the 3M
5   Meeting Network.

So what's the most effective meeting that Begeman has seen lately? He says that it didn't take place in a *high-rise* office building or at a *cutting-edge* chip factory. In fact, it took place in a
10   tepee – in a scene from 'Dances with Wolves', the Oscar-winning film featuring Kevin Costner. The scene takes place after a group of Native Americans discover Costner not far from their camp. Between 20 and 30 members of the tribe
15   gather around for a meeting. There's one big question on their agenda: what should they do with this mysterious white man?

What follows, claims Begeman, is a *masterclass* in
20   good meeting behaviour.

'People actually listen to one another,' he *marvels*. 'There are some genuine disagreements, but everyone recognises *merit* in everyone else's
25   position and tries to *incorporate* it into his thinking. The chief spends most of his time listening. When the time comes to make a decision, he says something like 'It's hard to know what to do. We should talk about this some
30   more. That's all I have to say.' And the meeting ends! He is honest enough to admit that he's not ready to make a decision.'

How does Begeman compare that with what takes place inside most conference rooms today?
35   'Do you want to know the truth?' he asks. 'Here's my *mental image* of what happens at most business meetings: you could take the people out and replace them with radios *blaring* at each other, and you would not have changed very
40   much. That's what most meetings are like. People wait for the person who's speaking to *take a breath*, so they can jump into the empty space and talk. The quality of communication in most meetings is *roughly comparable to* the quality
45   of the arguments that you used to have with your ten-year-old brother.'

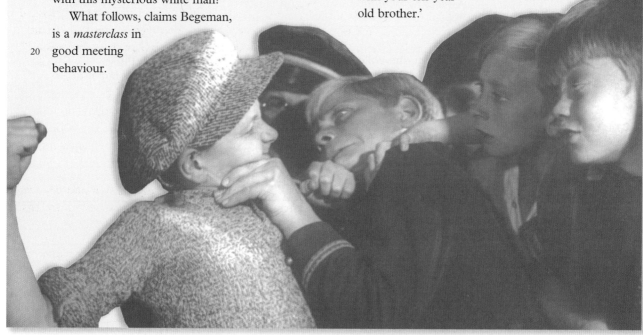

Glossary

tepee tent used by Native Americans

tribe ethnic or cultural group

4 How do you think Michael Begeman would describe the ideal meeting? You may want to refer to some of the terms in the box.

| listening | patience | decisions | consensus | diplomacy |
| disagreement | teamwork | respect | authority | |

5 With a partner, work out the meaning of the words and phrases in *italics*.

HW

6 In the article, Begeman points out that although 'there are some genuine disagreements' in the meeting, 'Everyone recognises merit in everyone else's position and tries to incorporate it into his thinking.' How can you avoid upsetting people you disagree with? How important is it in your culture for people to 'save face'?

7 Match the examples on the right to the disagreement strategies they exemplify.   *HW*

1 `e` and ☐   2 ☐ and ☐   3 ☐ and ☐   4 ☐ and ☐   5 ☐ and ☐

Disagreement strategies

1 Show support before you disagree

2 Disagree but ask for more detail

3 Check you've understood correctly

4 Be specific about your disagreement

5 Disagree but offer an alternative

Examples

a I think I'm going to go with Janine's idea, **but tell me more about your idea first.**

b That's not quite how I see it, **but how about looking at this a different way?**

c I'm not so sure, **but maybe I'm missing something here. Run me through it again.**

d I'm not against your whole idea, **just the part about** pricing.

e **While I agree with a lot of what you say,** I think you may be exaggerating the problem.

f I don't quite agree with you there. **However, you've given me another idea.**

g I'm not so sure I'm going to agree with this. **I'd like to hear more about it, though.**

h Before I answer that, **let me just check I understand what you're saying.**

i **I can understand exactly how you feel,** but at the moment it's just not an option.

j **It's not so much** your actual plan **I have a problem with as** how you intend to implement it.

8 In informal meetings with people you know well, you can use simpler expressions to show you disagree, but if there are problems it is usually better to be more formal and explicit. Match the informal expressions below to the strategies in 7.

Go on. I'm listening. ☐   Yeah, but … ☐   *HW*

Hm, well, how about this instead? ☐   I'm not with you. ☐

OK, but just one thing. ☐

Grammar link

for more on linking & contrasting ideas see page 108

Managing meetings

1 ▭ **6.2** A venture capital firm is discussing the start-up company it had talks with last week. Listen to three extracts from their meeting and answer the questions.

a Who's absent from the meeting and why?

_____

b What are the main goals of the meeting?

_____

c What's the main area of conflict in the meeting?

_____

d Who do you think the main troublemaker is?

_____

e What follow-up tasks are assigned?

_____

Lexis link

for the language of companies & capital see page 108

f Does timeofyourlife.com's business plan sound good to you?

g In your opinion, how effective was the chairman of the meeting?

2 The following expressions are all useful in chairing meetings. Complete them by filling in the missing letters.

Opening the meeting

a O_, le_'_ g_t st_ _ _ _d, th_ _, sh_ _ _ w_?

b Th_ _k_ f_ _ c_m_ _g, ev_ _ _b_ _y.

Setting the agenda

c A_ I s_ _d i_ m_ e-m_ _l, th_ p_ _p_se o_ th_ _ m_ _t_ _g i_ t_ ...

d B_ th_ e_d o_ th_ _ m_ _t_ng I'_ l_k_ s_m_ ki_ _ o_ d_c_s_ _n o_ th_ _.

Managing the discussion

e P_ _h_ps w_ c_n c_m_ b_ _k t_ th_s l_t_r.

f Le_'_ m_v_ o_ t_ th_ n_x_ it_ _ o_ th_ ag_ _ _a.

g W_ s_ _m t_ b_ g_tt_ _g s_d_-tr_ck_d h_r_.

h C_n w_ g_ b_ _k t_ wh_ _ w_ w_r_ d_s_ _ss_ _g e_rl_ _r?

i P_ _h_ps w_ c_ _ld sp_ _d th_ _g_ u_ a l_tt_ _.

j O_, s_ j_s_ t_ s_mm_ _ _s_ w_ _t w_'v_ s_ _d s_ f_r.

k M_yb_ w_ sh_ _ _d t_k_ a sh_ _t br_ _k a_ th_ _ p_ _ _t.

Managing other speakers

l Luis i_ g_ _ _g t_ f_ll u_ i_ o_ th_ b_ckg_ _ _ _d. Luis?

m Jack, c_ _ld Luis j_s_ f_ _ _sh w_ _t h_ w_s s_y_ _g?

n H_ _d o_ a m_n_te, Jack – y_ _'ll g_t y_ _r ch_ _ _e i_ a m_m_ _t.

o O_, O_! Le_'_ a_ _ j_s_ c_lm d_ _n, sh_ _ _ w_?

p D_ _s a_yb_ _y h_v_ a_yt_ _ _g th_ _' l_k_ t_ a_ _?

q Tania, wh_ _'s y_ _r p_s_t_ _n o_ th_ _?

r Luis, I th_ _k wh_ _ Tania i_ t_y_ _g t_ s_y i_ ...

Assigning follow-up tasks

s Luis, c_n I l_ _v_ th_ _ o_ _ w_ _h y_ _?

t Tania, c_n y_ _ g_t b_ _k t_ m_ o_ th_ _?

Closing the meeting

u I th_ _k th_ _'s ab_ _ _ _a_ f_r a_ w_ c_n g_ a_ th_ _ st_ _ _.

v I'_ af_ _ _ _ _ w_'_ _ h_v_ t_ st_ _ i_ th_ _e.

3 Listen to the meeting in 1 again and tick the expressions as you hear them. Which two are not used? _____

In the chair

Fluency

1 Work in groups of three. Take it in turns to lead three short meetings. Prepare for each meeting separately by reading the information at the back of the book and the related article below. Speaker A see page 131. Speaker B see page 132. Speaker C see page 134.

Meeting 1
Should genetic tests decide job prospects?

What if you were faced, at a job interview, with a test that would tell whether you could expect to develop Alzheimer's or Parkinson's disease? What if you were turned down because of that tiny bit
5 of your DNA?

This scary scenario is coming closer to reality with the development of a technology that will allow employers to carry out genetic tests and get the results in the time it takes to stroll to the
10 canteen and have a cup of coffee.

Would it be ethical? Would it be legal? Would it be acceptable to recruiters, let alone society at large? The moral debate lags behind the scientific advances. A technology that will identify DNA
15 electronically has been developed by Dr John Clarkson and his colleagues at the company Molecular Sensing. They plan to miniaturise it and build a hand-held device that will produce results in less than 30 minutes.

20 Simon Barrow, chairman of The Recruitment Society, opposes such genetic screening for illnesses, but would welcome tests for behaviour. And Professor Robin Plomin of the Maudsley Hospital's Institute of Psychology confirms that
25 genetic associations have been reported for reading disability, hyperactivity, personality and drug abuse.

Adapted from The Sunday Times

Meeting 2
Employers spy on workers

Big Brother is watching. And it's increasingly likely to be your boss.

She might be recording the casual conversations between you and your co-worker,
5 or tracking e-mails on your company computer, or watching the goings-on in the staff lounge.

Sounds like an invasion of your privacy? Think again. Most employee monitoring in the workplace is perfectly legal, and it happens more
10 than most people realise.

Two-thirds of US businesses eavesdrop on their employees in some fashion – on the phone, via videotape and through e-mail and Internet files – according to a survey by the American
15 Management Association International.

In fact, employers can trace everything from deleted e-mails and voice mails to the exact computer keys a worker strikes. Special software can follow employees' paths across the Internet
20 and high tech employee badges even let bosses track their workers' movements within an office building. Wireless video cameras are small enough to fit in pagers.

Businesses have lots of good reasons to
25 monitor workers: to deter workplace crime, to protect business secrets and to make sure employees aren't calling Timbuktu! Those worried about the Internet sites that employees are surfing can buy software that watches employees' screens.

Adapted from *Knight Ridder Newspapers*

Meeting 3
Creative way to better management

From Chopin to Schubert and jazz to jive, music, along with theatre, film, drawing and painting, is now widely used in UK business schools to help executives improve their management skills.

5 It may all be great fun, but does it work? Opinion is divided. Strongly against is David Norburn, director of Imperial College Management School, London. He says that after a few drinks he could probably make a case for
10 any human activity having managerial relevance. 'Weber's clarinet concerto and emotion; jazz and chaos theory; sex and timing.'

His argument is that when executives and MBAs invest time in business school programmes
15 they want rigorous and relevant training.

But staff at many of the UK's leading business schools, such as Patricia Hodgins at the London Business School, disagree. 'The key to creativity is being relaxed and being able to think laterally.
20 Using arts, music and theatre helps us to find that.'

Gay Haskins, head of executive training at LBS, defends the techniques. 'We are highly geared towards capitalist values,' she says.
25 'Everyone in business needs to understand that there are other ways of seeing the world.'

Adapted from the *Financial Times*

7 Information age

There is nothing so deceptive as an obvious fact.

Sir Arthur Conan Doyle, The Adventures of Sherlock Holmes

Discussion

1 Work with a partner and discuss the following questions.

a Is it important in your job to have access to the most up-to-date information? Why (not)?

b Where do you get most of the information you need to do your job?

c Which of the following sources of information are the most reliable?

> the Internet   newspapers   magazines   trade/academic journals
> TV news   company reports   specialist news agencies like Reuters
> opinion polls and surveys   end-of-year accounts   market research
> TV viewing figures   government statistics   scientific studies   the grapevine

2 You are going to read an extract from *Great Myths of Business* by the journalist and self-made millionaire William Davis. First match the following words and expressions to what they mean.

a a mixed blessing

b a spin doctor

c get the wrong end of the stick

d have a vested interest in *...ing*

e hearsay

f a myth

something believed by many but in fact untrue ☐

completely misunderstand something ☐

something that has disadvantages as well as advantages ☐

something you've heard people say which may or may not be true ☐

someone whose job is to make people or organisations look as good as possible ☐

want things to happen in a particular way because it will benefit you ☐

3 Now read the extract. How far do you go along with the argument it's presenting?

Information – A mixed blessing

Many people seem to find it difficult to accept that the information they get may be unreliable. It does not come out of nowhere: someone, somewhere, has had to put it together. That someone
5 may have got the wrong end of the stick, or made use of hearsay, or deliberately set out to mislead.

Public relations people, for example, often put out press releases, which are little more than sales promotion. They can easily create a false impression.
10 Information is slanted, twisted, misrepresented. Achievements may be exaggerated and awkward facts may be suppressed. In politics, 'spin doctors' are experts in dissembling. In business too, there are many specialists who have a vested interest in
15 ensuring that everything a company does is presented in a favourable way.

My own profession is not without blame. Journalists frequently print stories which turn out to be inaccurate and TV programmes give a distorted
20 picture of what is happening in various parts of the world. It is dangerous to read newspapers casually. That's how the germ of a myth is planted. The next thing you know, it has grown into a fact. A glance at a headline, a swift scan of the introduction, a note of the
25 picture caption, and you are on your way to a firmly held misconception.

from Great Myths of Business by William Davis

The language of deception

4 Look back at the text in 3 and find words or expressions meaning:

a make someone believe something which is untrue (paragraph 1) _____

b embarrassing pieces of information (paragraph 2) _____ _____

c hidden from the public (paragraph 2) _____

d present something inaccurately (paragraphs 2 and 3)

_____ a _____ _____

_____ a _____ _____

e a wrong belief or opinion (paragraph 3) _____

Headline news

Discussion

1 Work with a partner. Complete the headlines below using the words in the box. Do you believe them? Divide them into facts, half-truths and myths.

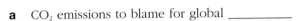

world	failure	countries	crime	warming	species
deforestation	toll				

a CO_2 emissions to blame for global _____

b It's official – 83% of company mergers end in _____

c G7 _____ account for 67% of global GDP

d Cost of _____ – 120 million km² of trees disappear every year

e Latest police figures show rise in violent _____ amongst under-25s

f Free market economics bring prosperity to developing _____

g 110 _____ become extinct every day

h Spread of famine – annual death _____ climbs to 40m

2 ▭ **7.1** Listen to the surprising facts behind the headlines. Take notes and discuss your reactions after listening to each one.

> It's good news that …   It's reassuring to hear that …
> I'm astonished that …   I had no idea that …   It's debatable whether …
> I can hardly believe that …   It's not what I've heard.
> I'm appalled that …   I think it's scandalous that …

THE TIMES

No 62,904   TUESDAY OCTOBER 20 1987   (25p)

Dow Jones crashes 508 points: City wipes £50bn off shares

Wall Street's blackest hours

● Share prices on Wall Street plunged by nearly a quarter in one day, a far steeper drop than in the crash of 1929

● In London, the FT-SE 100 share index fell 250 points, cutting more than £50 billion from share values

● The dollar dropped sharply. Mr James Baker, US Treasury Secretary, went into urgent talks with the West German Finance Minister

● British Petroleum shares plunged 34p down at 316p. The Government's offer price is 330p, but the Treasury said the sale would go ahead

By Kenneth Fleet

President Reagan, after "watching with great concern" Wall Street's blackest day, sought last night to reassure apprehensive and frightened Americans that "the underlying economy remained sound".

His words were echoed by other senior figures in Washington and New

In the foreign exchange markets the dollar wilted before the West German mark, while the pound remained firm but largely on the sidelines.

At the weekend the Germans seemed determined to raise their interest rates. This provoked a pained reaction from Mr James Baker, the US Secretary of the Treasury, who declared that this was "not in

Yuppies aghast at end of boom

From Charles Bremner New York

Crowds of dazed young brokers milled around Wall Street yesterday evening trying to come to terms with the unthinkable – the roaring Eighties, the years of easy prosperity, could be over.

As Mr John Phelan, chair-

3 Match the words and phrases below to summarise the information in 2. All the expressions were in the recording.

a	Contrary to popular	not the case that,	in a recent study, which puts the figure at 83%.
b	Nor is there	to be some truth	that the G7 earn 67% of global GDP.
c	It's impossible	opinion	the planet is not getting significantly warmer.
d	But there does seem	thought	that global warming is caused by heavy industry.
e	It's a sobering	any real evidence	as some claim, the number of trees has halved.
f	It's simply	to quote	an exact figure for the number of mergers that fail.

g	Statistically	the matter	90% of them are happy, self-confident individuals.
h	Surveys	vary widely	today's teenagers are committing fewer crimes.
i	The truth of	truth is	is that IMF loans have not helped a single country.
j	Estimates	perspective,	that 40 million people die from hunger every year.
k	The shocking	speaking,	as to exactly how many species there are.
l	To put that in	show that	it's the equivalent of 300 jets crashing every day.

Lies, damned lies and statistics

Discussion

1 According to American writer Ray Stout, 'There are two kinds of statistics – the kind you look up and the kind you make up.' Which do you think makes up more statistics: companies or governments?

2 What do you understand by the term 'creative accounting'? Can you think of any companies who have been guilty of it in recent years? How common do you think it is?

3 Work with a partner. What do you know about Enron? You are going to read an article about the financial scandal that damaged the company in 2001. The following words and phrases are in the article. Use them to predict what it says.

> seventh-biggest corporation   steady growth   phenomenal share price
> huge debts   creative accounting   cash flow situation   tax losses
> shareholders   collapse

4 Now read the article on page 39 and check your ideas in 3. Do you think Enron really did anything wrong, other than get caught?

5 With a partner, work out the meaning of the words and phrases in *italics*.

6 To whom do you think a company is most accountable? Put the following in order of importance.

the government ☐
the general public ☐
the board of directors ☐
its employees ☐
its shareholders ☐
its customers ☐

THE FALL OF ENRON

Enron was once the star of the new economy. As well as its traditional businesses, such as gas lines and power plants, it was also involved in Internet bandwidth operations and several obscure e-commerce ventures.
5 *At its peak* the company was worth $70 billion and was the USA's seventh-biggest corporation.

Of course, *the Internet boom* didn't last. On April 14th 2001 more than one trillion dollars in market capitalisation was *wiped out* in six and a half hours of *panic selling* on Wall
10 Street. *Dot.com fever* was over. But, miraculously, Enron survived. In fact, it seemed stronger than ever.

Enron's accounting system was always complex and obscure, but Wall Street trusted the company's steady record of growth and asked very few questions about just how it was
15 achieving it. The speculators loved Enron, especially when its share price reached a phenomenal $90. All the management gurus pointed to Enron as the model modern company.

But what the stock market investors didn't know was that the company had been *cooking the books*, inventing partner
20 companies that didn't really exist to hide huge debts and even huger losses. In 2000 Enron reported a net income of $979 million, even though it actually only earned $42 million. And by employing some of the most brilliant creative accounting ever, Enron managed to make $2 billion in tax savings, even
25 claiming some tax losses twice. In so doing, its cash flow situation was transformed from a $154 million outflow to a $3 billion inflow.

But by 2001 the authorities were closing in. Sensing disaster, in the weeks preceding its collapse, Enron's top 200
30 executives were paid $56.6 million in *bonuses*, $172.6 million in salaries and $1.1 billion in *stock options*, most of which were very swiftly sold. But for the company's many thousands of employees, shareholders and pension fund members, it was a different story.
35 In what has been called the greatest corporate failure of modern times, on December 2nd 2001 Enron was officially declared bankrupt. The court ruling also *spelt disaster* for the main accounting consultancy Enron had employed, the equally famous Arthur Andersen, which was fined a *staggering*
40 $500 million.

Both Enron and Arthur Andersen are still in business.

The information economy

Discussion 1 Work in groups to exchange opinions on the three issues below.

- Information overload: These days we are all suffering from having access to too much data.

- Knowledge is power: The intellectual capital of a company is more important than its financial capital.

- Human error: The weakest link in any computer network is the people who operate it.

2 ▶ 7.2 Listen to three business people discussing the issues in 1 and compare your views.

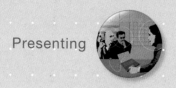

Presenting

8 Promoting your ideas

We had snakes in Raiders of the Lost Ark and bugs in Indiana Jones and the Temple of Doom. But supposedly man's greatest fear is public speaking. That'll be in our next picture. *Steven Spielberg, film director*

Discussion

1   How important is it in your line of business to be able to present your ideas professionally? Do you enjoy giving presentations or generally try to avoid them?

2   8.1 Listen to five experienced presenters talking about what still makes them nervous every time they give a presentation. Underline the speakers whose worries you share.

Speaker 1   Speaker 2   Speaker 3   Speaker 4   Speaker 5

3   Complete the following expressions from the extracts in 2 using a single verb.

a   Your mind   blank.
b   Your mouth   dry.
c   Your mike   funny.
d   The audience   quiet.
e   Everything   wrong.

4   Which of the expressions in 3 means:

you can't think of anything? ☐   your microphone doesn't work properly? ☐

Phrasal verbs

5   Complete the expressions from the extracts in 2.

up   up   up   down   down   out   about   over   of   to

a   You dry _____ completely.
b   Your equipment breaks _____.
c   You run _____ _____ time.
d   You run _____ schedule.
e   You pace _____ and _____.
f   You wave your arms _____.
g   Your heart speeds _____.
h   Your legs turn _____ jelly.

6   Someone once observed: 'There is nothing wrong with having nothing to say – unless you insist on saying it.' Read the text. Can you think of any less extreme ways of achieving the same objective?

Keep it short and simple!

According to ancient custom, the elders of a remote African village have to stand on one leg while addressing their audience at council gatherings. As soon as their second foot touches the ground, they must stop speaking immediately.

Audience analysis

1 ▭ 8.2 Listen to six business people comparing audience expectations of presentations in different countries. Which are they talking about? Give your reasons.

Country	Extract	
USA	☐	_____
Germany	☐	_____
Japan	☐	_____
UK	☐	_____
France	☐	_____
Kuwait	☐	_____

Check your answers on page 132.

2 In an increasingly global economy do certain national stereotypes still hold true?

Phrasal verbs   3 Match the phrasal verbs in these sentences. They were all in the extracts in 1.

a	Wisecracks – that's what they tend to **go**	1	**off** altogether.
b	The one thing you can't **do**	2	**across** as a person.
c	The audience may **switch**	3	**up** a certain level of formality.
d	They'll want you to **go**	4	**for.**
e	Anecdotes and amusing stories seem to **go**	5	**without** is a sense of humour.
f	What matters is how you **come**	6	**off.**
g	Be too techno and they'll think you're **showing**	7	**down well.**
h	You have to **keep**	8	**through** all the main points again.

4 Match the phrasal verbs in 3 to the meanings below.

a present yourself _____   e like _____

b lose interest _____   f repeat _____

c be appreciated _____   g maintain _____

d try to impress _____   h manage without _____

Lexis link

for more on phrasal verbs see page 111

5 In your experience, what sort of thing do audiences in your country tend to go for? What doesn't go down so well?

Idioms   6 You heard the following idiomatic expressions in 1. Complete them by filling in the missing letters. Use the words in brackets to help you.

a You should have all the technical information at your fi_____. (easily available)

b Give your presentation the personal to_____. (aim it directly at your audience's needs)

c You'll get loads of interruptions, but just go with the fl_____. (let things happen)

d Don't get too carried aw_____. (be overenthusiastic)

e Have a few gimmicks up your sl_____. (plan some clever surprises to attract attention)

f It really is essential that you do your ho_____. (prepare very carefully)

7 Which piece of advice in 6 do you think is the most important?

Innovation

1 How much of your company's business depends on innovation? Give a few examples.

2 Look at the extract from a web page below. What do you think the title means? Now read the text. Does your company encourage this kind of initiative?

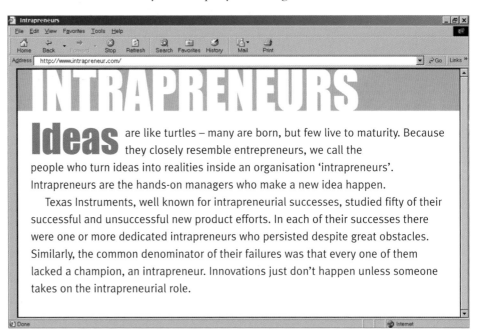

INTRAPRENEURS

Ideas are like turtles – many are born, but few live to maturity. Because they closely resemble entrepreneurs, we call the people who turn ideas into realities inside an organisation 'intrapreneurs'. Intrapreneurs are the hands-on managers who make a new idea happen.

Texas Instruments, well known for intrapreneurial successes, studied fifty of their successful and unsuccessful new product efforts. In each of their successes there were one or more dedicated intrapreneurs who persisted despite great obstacles. Similarly, the common denominator of their failures was that every one of them lacked a champion, an intrapreneur. Innovations just don't happen unless someone takes on the intrapreneurial role.

Gifford and Elizabeth Pinchot, www.intrapreneur.com

3 Find the words and phrases in the text which mean:

   a people who don't just talk about it, but do it _____

   b giving a lot of time and energy to something _____

   c kept on trying to do something _____

   d things that make progress difficult _____

   e the only thing in common _____

   f someone who supports and fights for an idea _____

4 What new ideas within your company or department have you been closely involved with recently?

23

5 🔊 8.3 Two managers for MaxOut, an American chain of fitness centres, are presenting a new business idea to their board of directors. Listen to four extracts from their presentation and answer the questions.

Extract 1

a Put the stages of the first part of the presentation in chronological order.

quote statistics ☐   build up expectations ☐   pose a problem ☐
introduce themselves ☐   thank the audience ☐   set a challenge ☐
share corporate vision ☐

b Are the presenters successful at arousing the curiosity of their audience? Why (not)?'

c The following figures were quoted. What do they refer to?

1,000 _____

35 _____

250,000 _____

$^{7}/_{10}$ _____

$^{4}/_{10}$ _____

61% (122m) _____

d On a scale of 1–5, how confident did the presenters sound? _____
Would their presentation style be popular in your company?

Extract 2

a What do these figures refer to? Do you find them surprising?

a mere 13% _____

a staggering 92% _____

b What do you think 'mere' and 'staggering' mean? _____ ,
_____

c Complete the following extract from the presentation.

We did a nationwide su_____ of people who had previously shown an
in_____ in joining a MaxOut club and then changed their mi_____.
Full de_____ are in the re_____ in front of you, but this chart hi_____
our main fi_____.

d Complete the chart, which shows the results of the survey referred to in **c**.

Nationwide survey
Reasons given for not becoming a
member of MaxOut Health Clubs

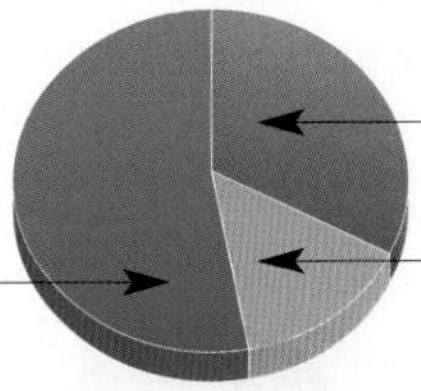

e What product do you think the speakers are about to present?

Extract 3

a What is the product? _____

b How much of the project budget was spent on making the prototype?

_____

c How long has it taken to develop?

_____

d Complete the product features chart.

e What's the main selling point?

_____
_____

f In what ways do you think the product would benefit MaxOut's main business?

Main product features

weighs just over _____

fits easily into _____

assembles in _____

35 different _____

settings _____

Extract 4

a Complete the extract below using the verb phrases in the box. The first one has been done for you.

> might easily be sold   are currently being considered   has been suggested
> would probably be priced   is included   are all itemised
> ~~has been fully costed~~   is still being carried out   could be recorded

OK, to wrap things up. The Micro-GYM (1) **has been fully costed** – a complete breakdown (2) _____ in the report. Estimated costs of manufacturing, packaging and advertising (3) _____. Product testing (4) _____, but we would obviously need the go-ahead from you before we proceed much further with that. The Micro-GYM (5) _____ at around $35: well within the reach of most people. It (6) _____ that exercise demonstrations (7) _____ on video and that the product (8) _____ online. Both these suggestions would incur extra costs, but (9) _____.

Grammar Link

for more on the passive
see page 110

b If you were on the board of MaxOut, would you give the new product idea the go-ahead? If not, what other information would you need before you were persuaded?

Fluency **6** Work with a partner to give a team presentation.

Step One: Brainstorm

Your job is to come up with an innovative idea for a product or service that could be developed by your company or a company you know. If you and your partner work for different companies, you could consider how the two firms could collaborate.

Step Two: Plan

Make sure the new product or service:
- is a new departure for your company or companies
- complements the products and services currently on offer
- meets a need not catered for at present.

Be as original and alternative as you like!

Step Three: Rehearse

Use the presenters' prompt cards opposite to help you structure your talk. Most of the key language on the cards was in the presentation you listened to. Create any visuals you need.

Step Four: Deliver

Give the presentation, handing over to your partner after each phase of the talk. Invite questions at the end.

Open	Good morning, everybody, thanks for coming. I'm (*name*) and this is (*partner*).
	As some of you already know, (*partner*) and I have been working on this project for some time.
	By the end of this morning's/afternoon's presentation,
	we hope/think/feel confident you'll be as excited about this idea as we are.
Arouse interest	As the world's leading provider/a major player in the world of ..., we pride ourselves on ...
	For us, ... is not just a business – it's ... Figures recently published by ... show that ...
	That's a very worrying/somewhat alarming/quite staggering statistic.
	But it's also a tremendous marketing opportunity. The question is, how do we reach that market?
Refer to consumer research	A recent report claims that ...
	So we did a nationwide survey of/distributed questionnaires to/set up focus groups to find out ...
	Full details are in the report in front of you.
	But this chart highlights our main findings. As you can see, ...
Discuss potential	So, what does all this mean? We think the implications are clear.
	There's obviously a huge/substantial/growing/largely untapped market for ...
	And this represents a golden/an ideal opportunity to expand the company/stretch our brand
	and develop an exciting new product/service to complement our existing business.
Introduce product/ service	OK. And now the moment you've all been waiting for!
	Ladies and gentlemen, the new ... It's taken (*time*) to get this far with the concept/design/project.
	What you're looking at is the ultimate/world's first ...
	and, we believe, a significant part of this company's future.
Describe product/ service	The main features/benefits/selling points are ... And, as you'd expect ...
	Now, I know what you're thinking: how can ...?
	So, let me reassure you. We've really done our homework on this one.
	As far as the competition is concerned, our ... compares very favourably indeed.
Close	We really do believe the ... could be a bestselling product/first-class service
	and an excellent addition to our current range of .../enormously successful sideline to our main business.
	OK, to wrap things up. The ... has been fully costed. A complete breakdown is included in the report.
	What we need now is the go-ahead from you. Thank you very much.
Open Q&A session	Thank you, (*partner*).
	OK, we'd like to throw this session open now for questions and suggestions.
	As (*partner*) said, we need your authorisation to move on to the next stage. So, over to you!

9 Relationship-building

Adapted from *The Guardian*

One of our ironclad rules is 'Never do business with anybody you don't like.' If you don't like somebody, there's a reason. *Henry Quadracci, CEO of Quad/Graphics*

Discussion 1 They say 'You never get a second chance to make a first impression.' Read the text and underline anything you disagree with. Then compare with a partner.

First **impressions**

Creating a positive first impression is essential in a competitive job market. Most of us recognise that when we meet people for the first time we make all sorts of judgements about them, consciously or subconsciously – how successful they are, how capable, how credible, how creative, how sharp, how professional, and so on.

In fact, studies in this area show that we judge people within five seconds of meeting them, and then add another 50% to that judgement in the subsequent five seconds. Staggeringly, it can then take another twenty experiences with that person to change our initial impression.

Collocations 2 Match the nouns and noun phrases in the box to the adjectives below to make 30 things we usually notice about someone on first meeting them.

voice	sense of humour	clothes	manner	handshake	laugh

  a firm/limp/aggressive _____

  b casual/shabby/smart/designer/expensive-looking _____

  c high-pitched/irritating/sexy/pleasant-sounding/soft/deep _____

  d authoritative/confident/relaxed/cold/hostile/abrasive _____

  e good/great/no/dry/weird _____

  f great/loud/infectious/annoying/nervous _____

3 When you meet someone for the first time, which of the above do you find most:

  a appealing?

  b reassuring?

  c off-putting?

  What else do you tend to notice?

Discussion 4 Have you ever:

  a felt an instant rapport with someone you've only just met?

  b taken an immediate dislike to someone you've just been introduced to?

  c misjudged someone by taking too much notice of the way they looked or sounded?

Questionnaire 5 How good are your networking skills? Complete the questionnaire opposite using the pairs of verbs in the boxes. Then circle your answers. Compare your answers with a partner and then read the analysis on page 129.

Are you an effective networker?

talk + catch	relax + let	look + say	hover + wait	moan + bitch	crack + break

1 You meet a group of business people for the first time. Do you:

a _____ them in the eye, smile and _____ hello?

b _____ in the background and _____ to be introduced?

c _____ a joke to _____ the ice?

2 You meet up with some colleagues after work. Do you:

a _____ shop and _____ up on all the latest gossip?

b _____ about work and _____ about the boss?

c _____ and _____ your hair down?

introduce + slip	feel + mingle	make + escape	try + draw	persevere + find	stick + ignore

3 You meet a fascinating person at a cocktail party. Do you:

a _____ to them like glue and _____ everyone else?

b _____ and _____ other people into the conversation?

c _____ obliged to go and _____ with other people?

4 You're stuck with a bore at a conference. Do you:

a _____ in the hope you'll _____ something in common?

b _____ some kind of excuse and _____?

c _____ them to someone else and _____ away?

exchange + get	get + mention	go + make	cut + get	give + keep	look + pretend

5 You see someone you don't get on with at a function. Do you:

a _____ the other way and _____ you haven't seen them?

b _____ over and _____ the effort to speak to them?

c _____ them a polite nod, but _____ your distance?

6 You're introduced to a potential client. Time is short. Do you:

a _____ the preliminaries and _____ straight to the point?

b _____ to know them a bit before you _____ business?

c _____ business cards and say you'll _____ back to them?

Fluency 6 Work with a partner to practise your networking skills. Speaker A see page 135. Speaker B see page 133.

1 Is the golf course or tennis court a good place to do business? Read the article and think about the questions on the right. Then discuss them with a partner.

Golf and business
A PERFECT COUPLE

Adapted from Business Week Online

What better way to get to know somebody, commune with nature, work a deal and improve your swing – all at the same time. US president Calvin Coolidge once remarked that 'The business of America is business.' He didn't quite get it right. As any CEO
5 will tell you, the business of America is golf.

Golf and business have been *inextricably linked* for more than a century, and most executives seem to be as comfortable conducting business against the *serene backdrop* of a rolling emerald fairway as they are within the controlled confines of the office. Not everyone can play tennis, but everyone
10 thinks they can play golf. In an age of health and *enlightenment*, golf has replaced the three-martini lunch as the preferred vehicle for *sealing deals*. The ability to play golf, understand its *etiquette*, and respect its traditions can *boost a career*.

John D. Rockefeller played every day of his life until his mid-90s. Today,
15 the *titans* of high tech are no less enthusiastic. Sun Microsystems CEO Scott McNealy is a scratch golfer and Bill Gates is devoted to the game. Then there's Tiger Woods, readily identified with some of the biggest brands in business – American Express, Nike and Buick.

So why is golf the preferred sport of business? In a word, relationships.
20 No other sport lends itself to developing *lasting professional bonds* like golf does. 'How else can one get outside for four hours in such a relaxed, quiet and beautiful setting?' asks Jim Henry, a business development executive with Deloitte Consulting. 'There is *ample time* to build or renew relationships.'

25 That is a key differentiator between golf and other sports. 'Four to five hours on the golf course, and you get to know the *character traits* of your golfing partners – honesty, humility, ability to handle success and failure, approach to risk, desire to have fun, etc.,' says Miller Bonner, a public relations veteran. 'That translates into a successful business relationship.'

30 Marketing director Derek Van Bronkhorst has his own test of character on the links. 'Do they cheat?' he asks. 'If they cheat in golf, would you want to do business with them?'

Golf glossary
swing the movement you make with your arms when you hit the ball
fairway the long part of a golf course that leads to the green
scratch golfer a player without a handicap
links a golf course by the sea

a Are you a golf fan? Or do you agree with the writer Mark Twain that 'golf is a good walk spoiled'?

b Why is golf so popular with the business community?

c Do you wish you could get out of the office more?

d What's the best way to get on in your company?

e Tiger Woods's contract with Nike alone is worth $100m. Can that sort of money really be justified?

f What are the risks of playing sport against the people you do business with?

g What might your opponent do in a game of golf that would tell you something about their personality?

h Are you a good loser?

2 With a partner, work out the meaning of the words and phrases in *italics*.

3 📼 **9.1** Listen to a group of oil company executives chatting during a game of golf and answer the questions.

Extract 1

a Why doesn't Stella immediately accept Craig's offer? _____

_____

b Why are they only playing nine holes? _____

_____

c How would you describe the men's attitude to the game? _____

Extract 2

a How's Craig playing today? _____

b What do Craig and Stella disagree on? _____

_____

c What do you think Craig has to do if he wants the job? _____

Multi-verb sentences

4 Reorganise the words in **bold** to make correct sentences. They were all in the conversations in 3.

a We **be should thinking making probably of** a move quite soon.

_____

b We **count staying can't weather fine the on** at this time of year.

_____

c I **have have arranged lunch us to for** at the clubhouse.

_____

d We **be get should able to around** the course in a couple of hours or so.

_____

e You **be teamed been had must wishing you with up** Max.

_____

f I **have have meaning been word you a with to about** this disposal operation.

_____

Grammar Link

for more on multi-verb sentences see page 112

g I **get would was mentioning wondering you when round to** that.

_____

Visiting someone's home

Discussion **1** What are the advantages and disadvantages of inviting a client or colleague to your home? Is it common practice in your country?

2 📼 9.2 Listen to some people entertaining at home and answer the questions.

Extract 1

a Did Magda have a problem finding Anne's house? _____

_____

b What do you think 'Martin's still **slaving away** in the kitchen' means?

_____

c What has Magda brought as a present? _____

Extract 2

a What do you think 'The whole place was **an absolute wreck** when we moved in' means? _____

b What does Magda have in her drink? _____

c What do you think Martin means by 'I had to **rescue** the starter'?

_____

Extract 3

a What do you imagine Anne and Martin's apartment to be like?

elegant ☐ comfortable ☐ spacious ☐ light & airy ☐ old & tatty ☐ ultra-modern ☐ tastefully furnished ☐ full of antiques ☐ dark & gloomy ☐

b When Magda sees the chairs, she says 'I **could do with** some of those for my place.' What does she mean? _____

Extract 4

a How does Magda describe the duck? crispy ☐ tasty ☐ tender ☐ juicy ☐

b Who raises the subject of business? Why? _____

_____

c How does Martin excuse himself? _____

d How many times does Magda signal she's going to leave soon? _____

Social English **3** All the remarks below were in the conversation in 2. See who can remember the most in just three minutes!

Arrival
L__t me take your coat. → You m_____d to find us OK, then? → Oh, I b_____t you this. → You shouldn't h__e. → Come on t_____h. → Oh, w__t a fabulous apartment! → Now, what can I g__t you to drink? → I'll be right b__k. → Make y_____f at home.

The apartment
I was j__t looking at some of your oil paintings. → You've got q__e a collection, haven't you? → And I love the w__y you've done the fireplace. → Was that here when you m__d in? → Look at t____t view!

The meal
Dinner's r__y when you are. → Sit w_____r you like. → I thought we'd have a nice Spanish r_d. → Now, there's more duck if you w__t it. → And help y_____f to vegetables. → Mm, this is a_____y delicious! → I'm g__d you like it. → You m__t let me have the recipe. → A l____e more wine? → I s_____t really. I'm driving. → Oh, go on. You've o__y had one. → Just a d__p, then.

Farewells
Well, I o__t to be making a move soon. → You don't have to r__h off just yet, do you? → How a__t some more coffee? → OK, j__t half a cup. → And then I really must be g__g. → Thank you b__h for a lovely evening. → Next time you must come to my p____e. → T__e care now.

Lexis link

for more on social
English see page 113

A dinner invitation

Fluency   **1**   Work with a partner. Act out the situation of a business person (the guest) visiting the home of a colleague (the host) from arrival to departure. The host is the guest's immediate boss. Before you start, establish:

- what company you work for (name, location and main business activity)

- exactly what your roles are at work

- how business is doing and what problems or opportunities your company currently has.

You both have an ulterior motive for the dinner. Guest see page 135. Host see page 133.

Step 1   **This is the host's living room.**
Guest, make some positive comments, ask questions, show interest in the answers and try to keep the conversation going. Host, make up any information you like about your house to answer your guest's questions.

Step 2   **This is the view from the host's apartment.**
Guest, comment on what you see. Host, make up any information you have to.

Step 3   **This is the dinner.**
Guest, compliment your host on the meal. Host, explain what the food is.

Step 4   Guest, take your leave, thank your host. Host, say goodbye to your guest, thank them for coming. Conclude any business you discussed during the evening or arrange to meet to discuss it again.

10 Taking decisions

Standing in the middle of the road is very dangerous – you get knocked down by the traffic from both sides. *Margaret Thatcher*

Discussion

1 When was the last time you were faced with a difficult decision and were unable to make up your mind? How did you decide in the end, or was the decision made for you?

Glossary

curves unpleasant surprises

2 You may be a cool-headed decision maker in the office, but would you know what to do in a real life-and-death situation? Read the following extract from an unusual website and discuss the questions.

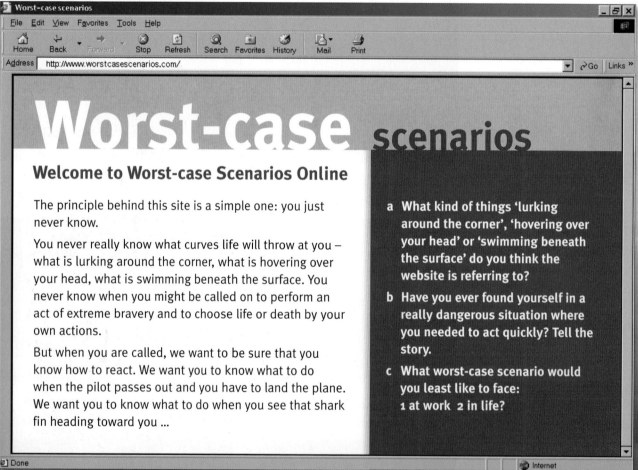

www.worstcasescenarios.com

Worst-case scenarios

File   Edit   View   Favorites   Tools   Help

Home   Back   Forward   Stop   Refresh   Search   Favorites   History   Mail   Print

Address   http://www.worstcasescenarios.com/   Go   Links »

Worst-case scenarios

Welcome to Worst-case Scenarios Online

The principle behind this site is a simple one: you just never know.

You never really know what curves life will throw at you – what is lurking around the corner, what is hovering over your head, what is swimming beneath the surface. You never know when you might be called on to perform an act of extreme bravery and to choose life or death by your own actions.

But when you are called, we want to be sure that you know how to react. We want you to know what to do when the pilot passes out and you have to land the plane. We want you to know what to do when you see that shark fin heading toward you ...

a What kind of things 'lurking around the corner', 'hovering over your head' or 'swimming beneath the surface' do you think the website is referring to?

b Have you ever found yourself in a really dangerous situation where you needed to act quickly? Tell the story.

c What worst-case scenario would you least like to face:
1 at work 2 in life?

Done   Internet

www.worstcasescenarios.com

Life-and-death decisions

1 On a driving holiday in the Pyrenees you lose control of your hire car travelling downhill at 70 miles per hour on a mountain road. You've no brakes and there's a 300 metre drop to the valley below. Do you:

a try to jump out of the car and roll to safety?

b steer away from the cliff edge and into the mountainside to stop the car?

c steer into the crash barriers on the cliff edge to slow down?

2 On a trek through the Chilean Andes you get cut off from the rest of your group and become hopelessly lost. Just as you begin to work out which direction to take, you are confronted by a hungry mountain lion. Do you:

a lie down and play dead?

b shout and flap your coat at the animal?

c run and hide (maybe find a tree to climb)?

3 Whilst walking over a frozen lake in Norway, which you were assured was perfectly safe, you fall through the ice and are in danger of drowning. Do you:

a attempt to pull yourself out?

b move about in the water to generate body heat?

c stay calm, conserve energy and call for help?

4 While on business in Paris, you wake up in the middle of the night to find your hotel is on fire. Your way down is blocked and you end up on the roof. Your only hope of escape is either to jump onto the roof of the next building – a distance of some four and a half metres – or to leap onto a truck carrying soft insulation material parked six floors directly below. Do you:

a take a long run-up and jump onto the next building?

b somersault straight down into the truck and land on your back?

c leap well away from the building to clear obstructions and land in the truck?

5 On a business trip to Amsterdam your taxi skids on a patch of oil and plunges off the road and into a canal. In seconds you are half-underwater. Do you:

a force open the door and swim to safety (taking the driver with you)?

b wind down the window fully to let the water in?

c wind the window up to trap air inside the car in case you sink?

6 You agree to do a parachute jump for charity with a group of friends. But as you free-fall from 14,000 feet at 120 miles per hour both your parachute and emergency chute fail to open. Do you:

a keep struggling with your emergency chute? It must work, damn it!

b grab hold of the nearest member of the group before they open their chute?

c take valuable time to attach yourself to the chest straps of another parachutist?

7 Whilst snorkelling off the Great Barrier Reef in North-Eastern Australia, you suddenly see a large shark swimming swiftly towards you from the depths. Do you:

a try to attack the shark's eyes?

b punch the shark on the nose?

c splash about and make a noise to frighten it away?

8 During a flight over the Grand Canyon in a single-engined private plane, your pilot collapses unconscious and you're forced to take over the controls. You manage to find the emergency radio channel, but lose contact just as you are about to land. Do you:

a keep the nose of the plane pointing above the horizon as you descend to the airfield?

b slow down to about 60 miles per hour as you touch down and then hit the brakes?

c keep the plane at a steady altitude of 500 feet as you approach the beginning of the runway?

4 🔲 10.1 Listen to some advice on how to survive the situations in 3. How many lives did you lose?

5 Put the following expressions on the scale below according to how likely they are. Most of them were in the advice in 4. The first one has been done for you.

a You've a good chance.
b You don't stand a chance.
c There's a 50-50 chance.
d Your chances are slim.
e You're in with a chance.
f The chances are remote.

g You've blown your chances.
h There's a fair chance.
i There's an outside chance.
j It's a million-to-one chance.
k You haven't got a cat in hell's chance.

a

←————————————————————————+————————————————————————→

more likely   possible   less likely

6 Complete the following expressions using the nouns and verbs in the boxes. They were all in the advice in 4.

mistake	bet	idea	point	circumstances	thing	move

forget	think	make	take	put	resist	do

a Don't even _____ about jumping from a moving vehicle.

b _____ the temptation to run from a mountain lion.

c _____ any ideas of playing dead out of your mind.

d Your best _____ is to shout and flap your coat at the animal.

e Do not in any _____ try to stand up on the ice.

f _____ care to land on your back to avoid breaking it.

g There's not much _____ trying to force the door open.

h _____ about trapping air inside a sinking car.

i By far the most sensible _____ to do is to open the car window.

j Just grabbing on to the nearest person with a parachute is not a smart _____.

k It's a common _____ to think the shark's nose is the best area to target.

l You'd _____ much better to strike at the eyes or gills.

m _____ sure that the nose of the plane is six inches below the horizon.

n It's a good _____ to brake as soon as you've gained control of the steering.

7 Work with a partner. Practise using some of the expressions in 5 and 6 by giving advice on how to handle *one* of the following situations. Don't worry if you can't give expert advice!

Worst-case scenarios
- on a round-the-world cruise the ocean liner you're on hits an iceberg and starts to sink
- during a bungee jump from the Golden Gate Bridge your cord snaps mid-jump
- a poisonous snake has crawled into your sleeping bag
- you've been abducted by aliens

Workplace dilemmas
- your boss is working you to death
- a colleague is taking the credit for all your ideas
- a computer virus is destroying your hard disk and you've had no time to back things up
- you've been passed over for promotion – again!
- there's a rumour your company is about to be downsized

The decision-making process

1 Read the anecdote about Alfred P. Sloan, the man who built General Motors into the biggest company in the world. What point is being made about group decisions? _____

2 🔲 **10.2** Listen to extracts from three different decision-making meetings and answer the questions.

    1 An industrial dispute

        a Why is Dan so concerned about a strike? _____

        b Who's the calmest person at the meeting? _____

    2 Political instabilities

        a What's Hans's objection to the proposal? _____

        _____

        b What's Andrea worried about? _____

    3 A product recall

        a Whose side is Laura on? _____

        b Do you think Simon has already made up his mind? _____

The language of decisions

3 The following remarks were all in the meetings in 2. Complete them using the pairs of words in the box. Listen again, if necessary.

> agreement + priority   minds + options   anything + consideration
> option + backing   input + action   time + heads   cons + decision
> data + instinct

a Look, _____ is short. So let's put our _____ together and see what we can come up with.

b OK, we've weighed up the various pros and _____. Now it's time to reach a _____ and stick to it.

c I don't want us rushing into _____. This whole issue requires long and careful _____.

d I take it we're all in _____ that our first _____ is to safeguard the well-being of our personnel.

e Well, then, I don't see we have any _____ but to give this proposal our full _____.

f I'd like your _____ on this before committing us to any definite course of _____.

g I'm in two _____ about it. At this stage I think we should keep our _____ open.

h Well, in the absence of more reliable _____, I think I'm going to have to go with my gut _____ on this one.

Idioms

4 You also heard the following idiomatic expressions in 2. Can you remember the missing words? The first two letters are given. The meaning of the idioms in brackets may help you.

    a the ball is in their co_____ (we're waiting for someone else to make a decision)

    b jump to co_____ (decide too quickly without considering all the facts)

    c when it comes to the cr_____ (when a decision finally has to be made)

    d sit on the fe_____ (refuse to support either side in an argument)

Crisis management

Discussion **1** What sort of crises can companies be faced with these days? Can you think of recent examples of any of the following?

> accusations of fraud   a lawsuit   a hostile takeover bid
> an environmental disaster   a product recall   a consumer boycott
> an anti-globalisation protest   mass redundancies   sabotage
> insider trading   an investigation by the monopolies commission

Articles **2** Work in two groups. Group A read about a crisis at McDonald's; Group B at Mercedes. Twenty-five articles (*a*, *an* and *the*) are missing from each text. Write them in. If you do the exercise correctly, both groups should have the same number of *a*'s, *an*'s and *the*'s.

McDonald's crying over spilled coffee

In 1994 Stella Liebeck, New Mexico grandmother, ordered coffee at McDonald's drive-through restaurant. Minutes later, sitting in her car in car park, she accidentally spilled coffee – heated, in response to customer preference, to scalding 180°F – and suffered severe burns requiring surgery. Crisis was about to unfold.

When McDonald's refused to take responsibility for paying woman's medical bills, she went to attorney and sued company. At trial jury found McDonald's liable and awarded $200,000 in compensatory damages (less $40,000 for negligence on Liebeck's part) and massive $2.7 million in punitive damages because of what they saw as McDonald's unacceptably dismissive attitude.

One might have expected bad publicity to ruin McDonald's, but instead newspapers leapt to company's defence, declaring what nonsense court's verdict was. 'America has victim complex,' announced *San Francisco Chronicle*. Punitive damages were later reduced by judge to $480,000 and, while awaiting appeal, parties made out-of-court settlement for undisclosed sum. But by then 'three million dollar coffee-spill' had already passed into corporate legend.

Mercedes on a roll

In automotive industry trend for many years has been towards smaller, more economical vehicle. So in autumn of 1997, Daimler-Benz introduced new economy model, Mercedes 'A Class'. It was car designed to compete with ever-popular Volkswagen Golf. But just before November launch, disaster struck.

Swedish auto magazine had conducted what they called 'elk test' on new car. Test is standard in Sweden to make sure cars can steer to avoid large deer crossing road. But at just 60kph 'A Class' overturned, injuring both test drivers. Storm immediately blew up in press and on TV, as buyers waiting to take delivery cancelled their orders. For Mercedes it was not only financial but image crisis too.

Daimler responded quickly, adding wider tyres, electronic stability mechanism and stronger anti-roll bars – all at no extra cost to customer. Highly successful advertising campaign and public support from Niki Lauda, ex-formula one racing champion, helped to restore consumer confidence in 'A Class' but at cost of hundreds of millions of dollars.

Lexis link

for more on marketing &
legal English see page 114

Grammar link

for more on articles see
page 114

Discussion

3 Summarise the story you read in 2 to a member of the other group. What lessons can be learned from how the companies behaved?

4 What is the best thing a manager can do in a crisis? Match the following. Which do you think are good advice?

a	deny	someone	**g** admit	honest
b	stay	time	**h** take	data
c	delegate	calm	**i** make	charge
d	buy	decisive	**j** act	quickly
e	blame	everything	**k** collect	nothing
f	be	responsibility	**l** be	promises

Case study

5 Work in groups to act as crisis management consultants to the Coca-Cola Company. It is May 1999 and the world's most famous brand is in trouble …

Step 1 ▭ **10.3** Listen to the first part of the case and answer the questions.

a How many Cokes are sold each day? _____

b How would you describe Coca-Cola's advertising strategy? _____

c What has just happened? _____

d Which markets are directly involved in the crisis? _____

_____

e Calculate how much those markets are worth in annual sales. _____

Step 2 ▭ **10.4** Listen to the second part of the case and answer the questions.

a What do the following figures refer to?

+25% _____   –13% _____

b What is the significance of these figures? _____

_____

c What have the inspectors at the Belgian bottling plant found? _____

d What is the toxicologist's verdict? _____

e Who is benefiting from Coca-Cola's current problems? _____

Step 3 Hold a meeting to decide what recommendations to make to your client. As well as the information you have just heard, consider the following:

Strategy Meeting
Client: Coca-Cola Co.

- Should there be an immediate product recall in spite of the lack of solid evidence?
- In the absence of any proof of contamination, should Coca-Cola appeal to the four European governments to lift their ban? Or even threaten legal action against them?
- Should any decision be postponed until the final results of the tests become available? Or will this just give the competition time to increase its market share?
- How should the company persuade the public that there's no real threat?
- Should there be an official apology? Or would that look like an admission of guilt?
- Should Coca-Cola put the blame firmly on its Belgian bottling plant and their shippers, whilst exporting Coke directly to Europe from the USA?
- What kind of public relations exercise would restore confidence in the world's number one brand?

Step 4 Each group should present its recommendations to the class.

Step 5 ▭ **10.5** Listen to the final part of the case and find out what really happened. How do your recommendations compare with the action Coca-Cola actually took?

11 Branded planet

I am irresistible, I say, as I put on my designer fragrance. I am handsome, I say, as I pull on my Levi's jeans. I am a merchant banker, I say, as I climb out of my BMW.

John Kay, British economist

1 How 'brand-aware' are you? Make a list of all the well-known brands you're wearing or carrying right now. Use the suggestions in the box if you like.

clothes	shoes	mobile	palmtop/organiser	briefcase/handbag
belt	cigarettes	lighter	watch	pen	tie/scarf	(sun)glasses
perfume/aftershave/cologne				

2 Compare with the rest of the class. Who are the most 'branded' people in the room?

3 Read the book extract and answer the questions.

The **surplus** society

This is the age of more. More choice. More consumption. More fun. More fear. More uncertainty. More competition. We have entered a world of excess, an age of superabundance. Shop till you drop.

Overcapacity is the norm in most businesses: 40% in automobiles, 100% in chemicals, 140% in computers.

Major label record companies launched 30,000 albums in the US in 1998 and the number of grocery product launches increased from 2,700 in 1981 to 20,000 in 1996. Disney's CEO Michael Eisner claims that the company develops a new product – a film, a comic book, a CD – every five minutes!

Funky Business, Jonas Ridderstråle and Kjell Nordström

a Do you agree with the authors that we are living in 'the age of more'? Is it just 'more of the same'?

b Find four words in the text which mean *more than is needed*.

_____, _____, _____, _____

c Is overcapacity the norm in *your* business? How can companies deal with the problem of supply exceeding demand? You may want to refer to some of the things below.

1	brand loyalty	4	price sensitivity	7	product positioning
2	market segmentation	5	product development	8	strategic alliances
3	stock control	6	customer service	9	advertising budgets

d Which six things in **c** involve:

collaborating with competitors? ☐

customers sticking to the names they trust? ☐

working out how much you can spend on promotion? ☐

dividing up the market into sectors? ☐

deciding whether your product is up- or downmarket? ☐

customers shopping around for the cheapest option? ☐

Calvin and Hobbes © 1995 Watterson. Reprinted with permission of Universal Press Syndicate. All Rights Reserved.

Branding

1 ▭ **11.1** You are going to listen to a radio news feature entitled *Branded!* First, discuss the questions below.

a Roughly how many advertisements do you think you are exposed to in the press, on TV and the radio, in the street and on the Internet in a typical day? 20? 50? 100? More?

b Which are the most effective forms of advertising: TV commercials, press ads, billboards, Internet ads, direct mail ('junk mail') or e-mail ('spam')? Which just annoy you?

c Work with a partner. How many of the terms below are you familiar with?

> celebrity endorsements   corporate sponsorship   product placement
> branded content   cool hunters   adbusters

Now listen to the programme.

2 Listen again, if necessary, and answer the questions below.

a In what context were the following people mentioned?

Britney Spears _____

Michael Schumacher _____

Tom Cruise _____

b What do the following figures refer to?

7 million _____

$9 million _____

30 times _____

November 29 _____

c Are you shocked by the statistics mentioned in the *Adbusters* commercial? Does 'Buy Nothing Day' sound like a good idea to you?

Discussion

3 There seem to be no limits to what the world's biggest companies will do to raise brand awareness. Five of the following are facts and three are hoaxes. Which are which? Mark them F or H.

a Swiss watchmaker Swatch has suggested replacing hours and minutes with their own global branded time system called 'Swatch beats'.

b McDonald's is negotiating with the city of New York to replace the Statue of Liberty with a similar-sized statue of Ronald McDonald for 18 weeks.

c Taking the idea from the Batman comics, Pepsi-Cola is proposing to project its logo onto the surface of the moon.

d Toy manufacturers Mattel celebrated 'Barbie Pink Month' by painting an entire street in the UK bright pink – houses, cars, trees, even dogs.

e Nike has been given the go-ahead by the Greek government to place a neon sign of its famous 'swoosh' logo on top of the Acropolis in Athens.

f In Kazakhstan a Russian rocket due to dock with the international space station was launched with the Pizza Hut logo displayed on its side.

g Gordon's Gin fills selected British cinemas with the smell of juniper berries when its commercials are being screened to get the audience in the mood for a gin and tonic.

h Calvin Klein is proposing to 'clothe' the twin Petronas Towers in Kuala Lumpur in a giant pair of CK jeans.

Check your answers on page 129.

Globalisation

1 Naomi Klein is the author of the world's bestselling book on brands and globalisation *No Logo*. Read the article about her. How would you counter some of the points made?

LOGO**MANIA**

From the age of six, Naomi Klein was obsessed with brand names and what she could buy. She used to stitch little fake alligators to her T-shirts so they would look like Lacoste, and her biggest fights with her
5 parents were over Barbie and the price of designer jeans.

But, aged 30, Klein wrote a book, *No Logo*, which has been called 'the *Das Kapital* of the growing anti-corporation movement'. The former teenager
10 fixated on brand names has become a campaigner against our overbranded world.

In *No Logo*, Klein shows how globalisation has hit the poor the most. She writes that Nike paid Michael Jordan more for endorsing its trainers ($20 million)
15 than the company paid its entire 30,000-strong Indonesian workforce for making them.

Klein's argument starts with what we all recognise. Logos, she says, are 'the closest thing we have to an international language'. Most of the world's six billion
20 people could identify the McDonald's sign or the Coca-Cola symbol – we are united by what we are being sold.

Furthermore, advertising today is not merely about selling products; it is about selling a brand, a dream, a
25 message. So Nike's aim is not to sell trainers but 'to enhance people's lives through sport and fitness'. IBM doesn't sell computers, it sells 'solutions'.

And while the corporations are busy doing what they think is important – branding a way of life –
30 someone, somewhere, has to make the stuff. Very often, it seems, it is produced under terrible conditions in free-trade zones in Indonesia, China, Mexico, Vietnam, the Philippines and elsewhere. In some of the sweatshops Klein visited they have rules
35 against talking and smiling. There is forced overtime, but no job security – it's 'no work, no pay' when the orders don't come in.

Anti-corporate activism is on the rise precisely because branding has worked so well, believes Klein.
40 Multinationals such as Nike, Microsoft and Starbucks have sought to become the chief communicators of all that is good in our culture: art, sport, community, connection, equality. But the more successful this project is, the more vulnerable the companies become.
45 When in the US a group of black 13-year-olds from the Bronx – Nike's target market and the one exploited by it to get a street-cool image – learned that the trainers they bought for $180 cost $5 to make, it led to a mass dumping of their old trainers
50 outside New York's Nike Town. One boy, reports Klein, looked straight into the TV news camera and said, 'Nike, we made you. We can break you.'

Adapted from *The Guardian*

2 Find the words and phrases in the article you've just read which mean:

a always thinking about (paragraph 1) _____

b improve (paragraph 5) _____

c factories where people work hard in terrible conditions (paragraph 6)

_____

d easily harmed or damaged (paragraph 7) _____

3 When *No Logo* was first published a long reply was published in *The Economist*. Read the extract. Are you convinced by what it says?

From *The Economist*

Pro Logo

Opponents of globalisation claim that poor countries are losers from global integration. A new report from the World Bank demolishes that claim with one simple statistic. If you divide poor countries into those that are 'more globalised' and those that are 'less globalised' – with globalisation measured simply as a rise in the ratio of trade to national income – you find that more globalised poor countries have grown faster than rich countries, while less globalised countries have seen income per person fall.

4 📼 **11.2** Listen to two people discussing the articles in 1 and 3, and the whole issue of globalisation. Take notes. Who do you agree with more?

5 Discuss your reactions to the discussion in 4.

> I'd no idea that …   It doesn't surprise me in the least that …
> I'm not sure I believe that …   I totally agree with the idea that …
> I think I'd go along with the point that was made about …
> I think both speakers have missed the main point, which is …
> Frankly, the person who said … clearly doesn't know what they're talking about!

The name game

Fluency

1 In a highly competitive marketplace, thinking up distinctive names for new companies and their products is a specialist business. Lexicon Naming, who gave us 'Pentium' and 'Powerbook', designed the following Name Game to test people's branding skills.

Work in groups. You are Lexicon Naming. Hold a meeting to choose the brand name that best matches the image the four client companies below would like to project.

Client 1 This cutting-edge video game company targets young males with its fast, fun, action-packed titles.
a Zule **b** Zyex **c** Mimem **d** Lura

Client 2 This environmentally progressive cosmetics company manufactures comforting, healing and improving products for women aged 18–34.
a Tromos **b** Vaxlaz **c** Dartu **d** Ios

Client 3 This manufacturer specialises in miniature high tech gadgets like cellphones and PDAs. Their products are powerful, reliable, advanced, yet also lightweight and user-friendly.
a Parmeon **b** Semsa **c** Areon **d** Zytos

Client 4 This prescription pharmaceuticals firm develops and manufactures innovative precision drugs for the traditional marketplace and for biotech applications.
a Sylag **b** Tura **c** Zantis **d** Bagnum

See page 134 for suggested answers.

2 Report your decisions to the class.

12 E-mailing

The beautiful part of writing is that you don't have to get it right the first time, unlike, say, a brain surgeon. *Robert Cormier, author*

Discussion 1 Work with a partner and discuss the following questions.

a How important is e-mail in your job? If you did what this businessman did, do you think you might find the same thing?

> A friend of mine, a merchant banker, decided that for one month he would turn off his e-mails. When he switched back into gear he found that out of 753 e-mails, ten were really useful. Out of the ten, two were vital – so vital that the senders all took the precaution of ringing to confirm, just in case their e-mails were missed. *Business Life* magazine

b According to the Electronic Messaging Association, around seven trillion emails are sent annually. How many of them end up in *your* inbox? And how do you deal with the following problem?

> When everybody has e-mail and anybody can send you e-mail, how do you decide whose messages you're going to read and respond to first and whose you're going to send to the trash unread? *Tom Peters in Fast Company* magazine

c Is e-mail a time-saver or does it distract you from more important business? Does this company's idea sound like it could work?

> Signs are that the first rush of enthusiasm for e-mail may be waning. One big company in the computing industry is considering banning e-mails in the afternoon. It found that its people had stopped talking to one another. *A Freethinker's A–Z of the New World of Business*

d The Institute of Management puts working with computers amongst 'The Top Ten Stress Factors at Work'. Have you ever resorted to the following?

> A survey by Mori reveals that three quarters of computer users shout and swear at their machines. A similar study by IT support company Sosmatic shows that 43% of them have slapped, smacked and even kicked their computer. The mouse is the most maltreated piece of equipment, coming in for 31.5% of the punishment, followed by the monitor, the printer, the hard drive and the keyboard. Over a year such outbursts of 'computer rage' can cost companies up to £25,000 in lost earnings and damaged hardware.

Writing e-mail

1 According to the novelist Ernest Hemingway, 'All good writing is rewriting.' Do you ever rewrite your e-mails? Do you attach the same importance to them you would to a business letter or is the important thing just to fire them off as quickly as possible?

Adapted from the *London Evening Standard*

Bad spelling is the key to success

Forget how to spell, never bother to check your grammar, and within a few short years you will have e-mailed your way to *the top of the corporate ladder* (1).

According to a new study into the dynamics of e-mailing by David
5 Owens, Associate Professor of Management at Vanderbilt University in Nashville, someone who sends messages that could have been written by a small child probably *has all the makings of* (2) a chief executive.

'High-status people in a company send short, *curt* (3) messages and they have the worst grammar and spelling in the firm,' he said. 'This
10 isn't because they are the least educated; they're probably the best educated, but they just don't have time to waste on *the small stuff* (4).'

Part of the reason top employees in a firm take so little care over e-mails is that they actually get their own way by 'face-mail': meetings with *underlings* (5) and clients. The *classic* (6) signs of a worker who
15 will go no further than middle management are a tendency to write long, overcomplicated messages, and send e-mails instead of talking to someone in person.

People who *aren't cut out for* (7) the top are more likely to resort to *sneaky* (8) tactics such as carbon copying (cc-ing) and even blind
20 cc-ing their bosses on correspondence with other workers. In contrast, confident power e-mailers rarely cc anyone on their e-mails because they want to give the impression they are giving the recipient their undivided attention.

Anyone who uses office e-mail to forward jokes or electronic
25 greetings cards, or uses happy symbols like ☺ is *destined* (9) never to see the inside of the executive dining room, warns the study. According to Professor Owens, company jokers *play an important role as social glue* (10), but if staff even have to ask whether forwarding 'amusing' e-mails is a bad move then their
30 career *is a lost cause* (11).

The professor advises keeping e-mails brief but *pouring every ounce of charm and intelligence you have into them* (12). Before you press the send button make sure you'd be happy to see what you've written stuck on
35 the company noticeboard or appear in the newsletter.

a Do you use grammar- and spell-checks on your e-mails?

b If Owens is right, are you writing the kind of e-mails that will get you promoted?

c Is your English better than your boss's?

d Isn't more business conducted by e-mail than 'face-mail' these days?

e Who sends you the longest e-mails?

f Have you ever blind cc-ed your boss on an e-mail? Did you have a good reason?

g Have you committed 'professional suicide' in any of these ways (lines 24-30)?

h Is there a joker in your office?

i How can you inject your personality into an e-mail?

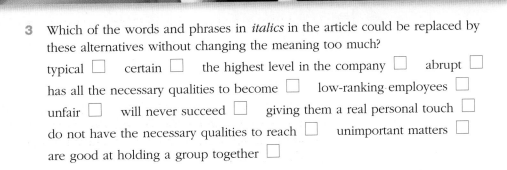

3 Which of the words and phrases in *italics* in the article could be replaced by these alternatives without changing the meaning too much?

typical ☐   certain ☐   the highest level in the company ☐   abrupt ☐

has all the necessary qualities to become ☐   low-ranking employees ☐

unfair ☐   will never succeed ☐   giving them a real personal touch ☐

do not have the necessary qualities to reach ☐   unimportant matters ☐

are good at holding a group together ☐

asap /ˌeɪ es eɪ ˈpiː/ as soon as possible
BTW abbrev by the way: used in e-mails and text messages for adding additional information
FYI abbrev for your information: used in e-mails and text messages as a way of introducing a useful piece of information

4 Look at the two e-mails below. From what Owens said in the article in 2, which do you think was written by a junior manager? _____

5 Correct the grammar, spelling and punctuation mistakes in the first e-mail. There are 18. Break up the text into short paragraphs and add a suitable subject line.

6 Were the mistakes in the first e-mail mainly language errors or mainly typos? _____ Do e-mails like this create a bad impression or doesn't it matter as long as the message is clear and the tone friendly?

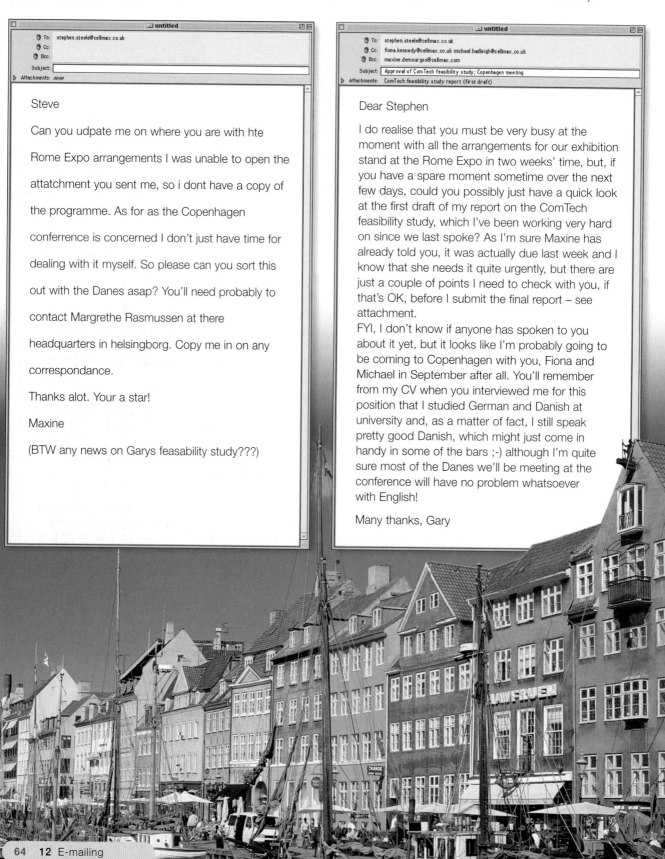

Email 1

To: stephen.steele@cellmax.co.uk
Cc:
Bcc:
Subject:
Attachments: *none*

Steve

Can you udpate me on where you are with hte Rome Expo arrangements I was unable to open the attatchment you sent me, so i dont have a copy of the programme. As for as the Copenhagen conference is concerned I don't just have time for dealing with it myself. So please can you sort this out with the Danes asap? You'll need probably to contact Margrethe Rasmussen at there headquarters in helsingborg. Copy me in on any correspondance.

Thanks alot. Your a star!

Maxine

(BTW any news on Garys feasability study???)

Email 2

To: stephen.steele@cellmax.co.uk
Cc: fiona.kennedy@cellmax.co.uk michael.hadleigh@cellmax.co.uk
Bcc: maxine.demourges@cellmax.com
Subject: Approval of ComTech feasibility study; Copenhagen meeting
Attachments: ComTech feasibility study report (first draft)

Dear Stephen

I do realise that you must be very busy at the moment with all the arrangements for our exhibition stand at the Rome Expo in two weeks' time, but, if you have a spare moment sometime over the next few days, could you possibly just have a quick look at the first draft of my report on the ComTech feasibility study, which I've been working very hard on since we last spoke? As I'm sure Maxine has already told you, it was actually due last week and I know that she needs it quite urgently, but there are just a couple of points I need to check with you, if that's OK, before I submit the final report – see attachment.

FYI, I don't know if anyone has spoken to you about it yet, but it looks like I'm probably going to be coming to Copenhagen with you, Fiona and Michael in September after all. You'll remember from my CV when you interviewed me for this position that I studied German and Danish at university and, as a matter of fact, I still speak pretty good Danish, which might just come in handy in some of the bars ;-) although I'm quite sure most of the Danes we'll be meeting at the conference will have no problem whatsoever with English!

Many thanks, Gary

7 Make the second e-mail shorter and simpler by deleting as many words as you can without changing the basic message or sounding too direct.

8 Now make the shortened second e-mail friendlier by adding a few personal touches. Use some or all of the following information to personalise it in your own way.

Stephen Steele
- has just become a father for the first time
- has put in for a promotion
- is under a lot of pressure because three people in his department are off sick
- has never been to Denmark (Gary knows it well)
- is a keen squash player (so is Gary).

E-mail style

1 How you write an e-mail largely depends on who you are writing to, but, in general, a friendly, neutral style will work best – neither too formal nor too familiar. Avoid unnecessary acronyms, abbreviations and slang which may confuse, date or sound silly. Underline the best option in each section of the e-mail below.

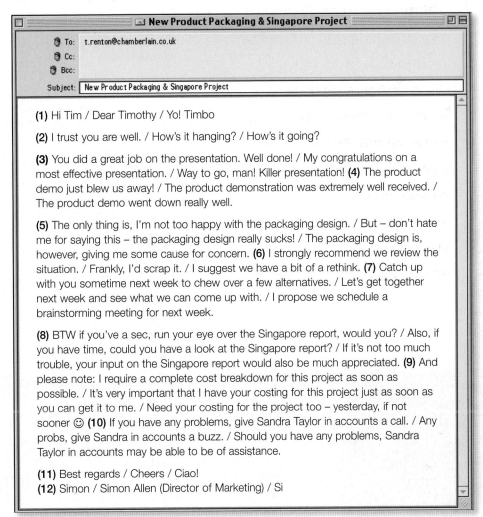

2 Write a short e-mail in reply to the one above using the prompts below.

glad / enjoyed / presentation / also pleased / response / product demo //
disappointed / hear / not keen / design // thought / quite stylish // let / know /
free / discuss / alternatives // around / most / next week // happy / go through
/ report // costing / ready / within / few days // may need / check / few things
/ Sandra // happen / have / extension number? / thanks

E-mail expressions

3 The following expressions are all useful in e-mails. Complete them using the prepositions in the boxes. Some of them have already appeared in this unit.

at	against	out	of	to	down	through	in	back
off	off	up	up	on	on	on	with	with	with
with	with	with	with					

back + to	through + to	up + on	in + on	up + to
out + with	on + to	out + on		

a Have a quick look _____ these figures and get _____ _____ me asap.

b Let me know if you need any help _____ the Koreans. And copy me _____ _____ any correspondence _____ them.

c Could you get _____ _____ our suppliers and sort something _____ _____ them? I'll leave the details _____ you, but keep me _____ the loop.

d BTW, you did a great job _____ the presentation. It went _____ really well _____ the Belgians. We'll just have to wait and see what they come _____ to us _____.

e Can you update me _____ where we are _____ the Expo arrangements? I'm a bit _____ of touch. Can I leave it _____ _____ you to contact the speakers?

f I'd like to sound you _____ _____ this new packaging idea. Let's meet _____ to discuss it sometime next week. BTW, I still can't seem to get _____ _____ Monica.

g I know you're _____ to your neck in work at the moment and probably don't want to take _____ any more, but could you take this Milan thing _____ my hands? THNQ

h I haven't had time to read _____ the whole report and I'll probably need to check some of these figures _____ the computer, but leave it _____ me.

i Thanks for your offer _____ a beer. If I can finish this report _____ by 7, I may just take you _____ _____ it! I could certainly do _____ one!

Lexis link

for more on prepositional phrases see page 117

The biggest e-mail blunders ever made

Discussion **1** Work with a partner and discuss the following questions.

a There are an estimated 50,000 computer viruses out there in cyberspace. Have any of them found you yet?

b What kind of things do people use their office computers for which are not strictly business? Have you ever been tempted to do any of these things yourself?

c Have you ever sent an e-mail and later regretted it? How dangerous is it to send business e-mails (even internally) without considering the possible implications?

2 ▶ 12.1 Listen to the story of some of the biggest e-mail blunders ever made and number the following in the order they are mentioned.

Netscape ☐   Merrill Lynch ☐   Dow Chemical ☐   Cerner ☐
the Love Bug ☐   Western Provident ☐   AOL ☐   Norwich Union ☐
Microsoft ☐   Norton Rose ☐

The 'I Love You' e-mail virus known as the 'Love Bug'

3 Work with a partner. Without listening again, can you remember:

a how much the Love Bug cost businesses worldwide? _____

b how much the two insurance companies settled out of court for? _____

c whose love life reflected badly on Norton Rose? _____

d how many people lost their jobs at Dow Chemical? _____

e whose stock fell by 28%? _____

f how much Merrill Lynch had to pay out because of Blodget's e-mail?

_____

g who regretted sending e-mails in the Microsoft antitrust trial?

_____

Answering your e-mail

Fluency **1** Work with a partner to practise exchanging e-mails.

Stage 1 Write an e-mail (maximum 150 words) to a real colleague on **one** of the subjects below. Use the suggested phrases to help you, but change and add anything you need to.

Subject: Change of plan

I was/we were originally hoping to …, but I'm afraid that won't be possible now because …, so what I'm/we're planning to do is …

Sorry it's a bit short notice, but do you think you'll be able to … or is that going to be a problem? I'll wait to hear from you.

Subject: Urgent request

I've got an important meeting/presentation coming up on … and I'm going to need … Can I leave it to you to …? I expect I'll also be needing …

I know you're probably up to your neck in work at the moment, but if you can get … to me before next …, it'll be a real help. Thanks.

Subject: Update please

Sorry to be a pain about this, but I'm still waiting for … Can you let me know how much longer it's likely to be? Do you think you'll have it finished it by … because …?

If you anticipate any problems, let me know. I'll … tomorrow to see how you're doing. Cheers!

Subject: Can you do me a favour?

I've had an e-mail/phone call from someone called …, who wants … Can I leave this one with you? I'm sure you'll know a lot more about it than I do. But keep me in the loop.

BTW a few of us may be … on … Are you going to be around? Fancy joining us? Should be fun.

Grammar link

for more on future forms see page 116

Stage 2 Exchange e-mails with your partner. You are standing in for the person they e-mailed while that person is off sick / on holiday / on maternity/paternity leave / away on a long business trip (you decide which). Write a reply (maximum 100 words) explaining the situation and asking for clarification or any details you need. Mention that you are new to the department.

Stage 3 Exchange replies and continue the correspondence as long as necessary to complete your business.

Feedback **2** Give your partner your impressions of the e-mails they wrote in 1.

- Do they sound friendly but businesslike?
- Is the style neutral?
- Have they kept their messages short and to-the-point?
- Have they made any important spelling, punctuation or grammar mistakes?

13 Making an impact

Speech is power: speech is to persuade, to convert, to compel.

Ralph Waldo Emerson, American writer, philosopher and orator

Opening

The opener to any business presentation is nearly always important, establishing the tone for the rest of the event. It's that vital moment when you take charge, gaining people's close attention.

People tend to remember openers more than any other part of a presentation, except perhaps for the closing remarks. You waste a wonderful opportunity if you resort to trivia like: 'Good evening, ladies and gentlemen, it's a great pleasure to be here today.'

Adapted from *The Ultimate Business Presentation Book by* Andrew Leigh

1 How important is it to make an impact right at the beginning of a presentation? Read the book extract on the left. Do you agree with the author?

2 With a partner, make a list of ways you can attract people's attention when you start a presentation. Could any of them be risky?

3 ▭ 13.1 Listen to the openings of six business presentations. Do the speakers use any of the techniques you listed in 2? What other techniques do they employ? _____

_____

4 How effective are the speakers in 3 at capturing your attention?

5 The openers below were all used in 3. Can you remember the first three words of each? Contractions (*I'd, I'm, it's*, etc.) count as **one** word.

a _____ _____ _____ that of the world's one hundred biggest economies only 49 are actually countries?

b _____ _____ _____ favourite lawyer jokes is: this guy's having a quiet drink in a bar when a drunk starts shouting …

c _____ _____ _____ start off by thanking Dr Jensen, Dr Tan and Dr Martinez for inviting me to speak today.

d _____ _____ _____ was Thomas Edison who said: 'I have not failed. I've just found 10,000 ways that don't work.'

e _____ _____ _____ through the appointments pages the other day and came across this unusual job advertisement.

f _____ _____ _____ about Total Quality, I think of the story of the American steel magnate, Andrew Carnegie.

Presence and performance

1 For many people the magic ingredient great presenters have is charisma. What's the equivalent word in your language?

2 ▭ 13.2 Listen to extracts from four famous political speeches. Rank them in order of how charismatic they sound. Compare with a partner.

Extract 1 ☐   Extract 2 ☐   Extract 3 ☐   Extract 4 ☐

3 Can you remember the following extracts from the speeches?

Extract 1

a I d_____ n_____ shrink from this responsibility – I wel_____ it.

b I do not believe that a_____ of us would ex_____ places with a_____ other people or a_____ other generation.

c The en_____, the faith, the devotion, which we bring to this endeavour will li_____ our country and all who serve it.

d And so, my fellow Americans, a_____ n_____ what your co_____ can do for you – a_____ what you can do for your co_____.

Extract 2

a I st_____ have a dr_____. It is a dr_____ deeply rooted in the Am_____ dr_____.

b I have a dr_____ that one day on the red hills of Georgia the sons of form_____ slaves and the sons of form_____ slave owners will be able to sit down tog_____ at the table of bro_____.

c I have a dr_____ that my four little ch_____ will one day live in a na_____ where they will not be judged by the col_____ of their skin but by the content of their char_____. I have a dream today.

Extract 3

a What are our chances of su_____? It depends on what kind of pe_____ we are.

b What kind of pe_____ are we? We are the pe_____ that in the past made Great Br_____ the workshop of the wo_____.

c … the people who pers_____ others to buy Br_____, not by begging them to do so, but because it was be_____.

Copyright Margaret Thatcher. Reproduced with permission from the official website of the Margaret Thatcher Foundation, margaretthatcher.org

Extract 4

a We und_____ it still that there is no easy road to fre_____. We know it well that none of us acting al_____ can ach_____ success.

b Let ea_____ know that for ea_____ the body, the mi_____ and the so_____ have been fr_____ to fulfil themselves.

c Ne_____, ne_____ and ne_____ again shall it be that this bea_____ land will again experience the opp_____ of one by another.

4 The speakers in 2 used a number of rhetorical techniques. The main ones are listed below. Complete them using the words in the box.

| questions | language | words | threes | points | sounds | opposites |

The **seven rules** of rhetoric

1 Repeat _____
I still have a dream. It is a dream deeply rooted in the American dream.

2 Repeat _____
We are the people ... who persuaded others to buy British, not by begging them to do so, but because it was best.

3 Use contrasts and _____
Ask not what your country can do for you – ask what you can do for your country.

4 Group key points in _____
We must therefore act together as a united people, for national reconciliation, for nation building, for the birth of a new world.

5 Ask rhetorical _____
What are our chances of success? It depends on what kind of people we are.

6 Accumulate supporting _____
We are the people who, amongst other things, invented the computer, the refrigerator, the electric motor, the stethoscope, rayon, the steam turbine, stainless steel, the tank ...

7 Use metaphorical _____
To lead our country out of the valley of darkness.

Lexis link

for more on metaphor
see page 119

5 Look back at the extracts in 3 and find more examples of the rhetorical techniques listed in 4.

6 🔊 13.3 Look at the following extracts from ineffective business presentations and rephrase them to give them more impact. Then listen and check.

a Cash flow is the main problem we're facing.

What's the _____ _____ _____ facing? The _____ _____ _____ cash flow.

b It's critical to our success, even though it's so risky and problematic.

It's _____ risky, _____ problematic, _____ yet _____ critical to our success.

c It's faster, cheaper, more reliable – that's the most important thing – and easier to use.

It's _____, _____ and _____ _____ _____. But, above _____, it's more _____.

d We can still be the best, but we can't ever be the biggest again.

Even _____ we can _____ again be the _____, we _____ still _____ _____ _____.

e Fewer jobs are being fought over by more graduates, that's the point.

The point _____, more and _____ graduates _____ _____ over fewer _____ _____ _____.

f We're number one in Latin America now, not just Brazil.

Not _____ _____ we number one in Brazil. We're _____ _____ _____ in Latin America.

g There isn't a company that's ever outperformed us in this market.

In this _____, no _____ has _____ us, not _____ – _____!

h We've had no complaints in over thirty years of business.

Not _____, in over _____ _____ _____ _____, have _____ _____ had a complaint – not a _____ _____!

7 Look carefully at word order and the order of clauses in the rephrased extracts in 6. What information tends to come last? _____
_____

Grammar link

for more on rhetorical techniques see page 118

8 Practise delivering the rephrased extracts to make as big an impact as possible.

Closing **9** 🔊 13.4 The last few minutes of a presentation are your final chance to make a lasting impression. Listen to the closing remarks of four presentations and number the techniques in the order you hear them. Which is the most effective?

the sum up ☐   the call to action ☐   the famous quotation ☐
the emergency stop ☐

10 Choose one of the closes below and use it as the basis for closing a presentation you have given in the past or may give in the future.

a Ladies and gentlemen, we are on the brink/threshold of … I'm reminded of the words of …, who said … And I'd like this company/this department/us to be able to say …

b Well, that just about brings me to the end of my presentation, except to say … And if there's one central message I'd like to get across to you this morning/afternoon/evening, it's this …

c So, how do you sum up …? I could tell you that …, that … and that … I could also mention … But all that would fail to do it justice. For the fact is, that … It is, quite simply, …

The last paradise on earth?

1 If you wanted to escape from it all for a while, where would you go?

2 Read the article and information on Bhutan. Does it sound like your idea of paradise?

Gross national happiness

'Gross national happiness is more important than gross national product.' That's the official government policy of King Jigme Singye Wangchuck of Bhutan, ruler of what some have called 'the last paradise on earth'. Indeed, his programme of careful economic development and gradual change has so far ensured that Bhutan, completely isolated from the rest of the world until 1961, has managed to balance the need to progress into the 21st century with the need to preserve its cultural heritage. But there's trouble in paradise.

Tiny Bhutan lies in the Himalayas, squeezed between the world's two most densely populated countries, China and India. Roughly the same size as Switzerland, Bhutan is a country of dense forest and breathtaking mountain ranges – at 22,623 feet, Gangkhar Puensum is the highest unclimbed peak in the world. This haven of peace and natural beauty is home to a multitude of exotic wildlife, including the endangered red panda and almost mythical snow leopard. Brightly coloured prayer flags fly from every hillside. The people here follow the Buddhist Middle Way, a philosophy based on pacifism, paternalism and egalitarianism. Time itself is measured differently in Bhutan – not in hours and minutes, but in *kalpas*, a unit of time equivalent to several million years.

At least, that's how it used to be. For now technology has finally come to this remote farming community. Foreign investment has helped build up the country's infrastructure, improve health and education and create a growing tourist industry. Cybercafés have opened in the capital, Thimphu, and the television aerials rising from the rooftops may soon outnumber the prayer flags. But the traditional way of life, upon which so much of Bhutan's 'national happiness' has depended, is under threat.

In 1998 the king of Bhutan decentralised power and appointed a central cabinet. The country now has a seat at the UN. But the Bhutanese themselves seem divided over their country's future. Should they continue to reap the many benefits progress has already brought or try to regulate the accelerating pace of change while there's still time?

- **Location** SE Asia
- **Area** 47,000 square km
- **Capital** Thimphu
- **Population** 657,000
- **Population density** 14.1 people per square km
- **Industry** farming, forestry, timber, limestone, food processing, chemicals, cement, hydroelectric power, tourism
- **GDP** US$2.1bn
- **GDP per capita** US$1,060
- **Inflation** 9%
- **Economic growth** 7%
- **National languages** Dzongkha (official), Nepali, English
- **Currency** ngultrum (Nu) of 100 chetrums, US$1 = Nu42.85

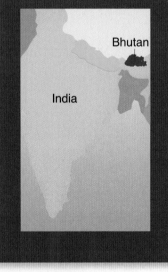

3 Work in two groups. Group A is the Bhutanese Preservation Party (BPP) and Group B the Progress Party of Bhutan (PPB). Read the introduction to your party's manifesto opposite.

Bhutanese Preservation Party

To the outside world we are Bhutan, a tiny Himalayan kingdom of scenic beauty and scientific interest, but little economic importance. But in our own ancient language we are Druk Yul, 'the Land of the Thunder Dragon', a land steeped in history and legend.

We in the BPP have never stood in the way of progress, so long as it is in harmony with the natural order and cultural traditions of our country. But we believe it is essential to protect the unique way of life we have enjoyed for over a thousand years from the worst excesses of the 21st century.

Will you join us in our campaign to preserve those qualities the rest of the world most envies about Bhutan – its simplicity, its tranquillity and the contentment of its people? Vote BPP.

Progress Party of Bhutan

For over a thousand years Bhutan has stood still. But the rest of the world has not. King Jigme Singye Wangchuck himself has said: 'Change is coming' and there is nothing in the teachings of the Buddha that tells us to resist change – rather the reverse. Change is not to be resisted, but to be embraced. It is time to end centuries of isolation and poverty.

The PPB has no wish to damage either our environment or our rich cultural traditions. Indeed, these priceless treasures are the basis on which we seek to build a better future for Bhutan.

Support our programme of culturally sensitive and environmentally aware development, and provide your children and your children's children with the opportunity and prosperity they deserve. Vote PPB.

Fluency   4   Work in your group to produce a ten-minute party political broadcast to the people of Bhutan. To help you prepare, Group A see page 136 and Group B see page 138. Use the rhetorical techniques you have studied to add impact to your speech. Your aim is to determine the future of what may well be 'the last paradise on earth'.

Take a little of home with you, and leave a little of yourself at home.
Mark McCormack, founder of IMG sports agency

Discussion

1 When packing to go on a business trip, apart from your travel documents, what are the absolute essentials? A good book? Swimming things? A decent hairdryer? An air pillow? Compare with a partner.

2 In the film *The Accidental Tourist*, travel guidebook writer Macon Leary gives advice on how to pack for a trip. Read the extract and discuss the questions.

THE BUSINESS Traveller

From The Accidental Tourist

'The business traveller should bring only what fits in a carry-on bag. Checking your luggage is asking for trouble. Add several travel-size packets of detergent, so you won't fall into the hands of unfamiliar laundries. There are very few necessities in this world
5 which do not come in travel-size packets.

'One suit is plenty if you take along travel-size packets of spot remover. The suit should be medium-grey. Grey not only hides the dirt, but is handy for sudden funerals.

'Always bring a book as protection against strangers.
10 Magazines don't last and newspapers from elsewhere remind you you don't belong. But don't take more than one book. It is a common mistake to overestimate one's potential free time and consequently overpack. In travel, as in most of life, less is invariably more.

'And most importantly, never take along anything on your journey so valuable or dear that its loss would devastate you.'

a Do you tend to travel light or do you bring along everything but the kitchen sink?

b Have you ever had any bad experiences with lost luggage or hotel laundries?

c Is grey your colour? Are you a practical or power dresser?

d What's the best way of avoiding unwanted conversations with strangers?

e Is it important to allow yourself some free time on a business trip?

f Have you ever lost something valuable on a journey? Tell the story.

3 What kind of person is Macon Leary? Tick the correct answers. Would you want to sit next to him on a flight?

sociable ☐   outgoing ☐   lonely ☐   private ☐   sarcastic ☐

practical ☐   dull ☐   fussy ☐   witty ☐   gloomy ☐   bitter ☐

well organised ☐   antisocial ☐   overserious ☐   a bit paranoid ☐

Discussion

4 Do any of following passenger types sound familiar? Match them to their typical behaviour. Which two would you least like to sit next to on a long-haul flight?

Space invaders ...

a	the sprawler	1	wants to tell you their life story from the very beginning; may bring out family photos
b	the bawler		
c	the discman	2	will smooch and giggle throughout the flight: two's company, three's a crowd
d	the workaholic		
e	the chatterer	3	spends the entire journey glued to their laptop, spreadsheets scattered everywhere
f	the sleeper		
g	the lovebirds	4	quiet at first, but may end up snoring like a bull elephant with their head on your shoulder
		5	under five years old, but can make a sound like a police siren for hours on end; may be sick
		6	bobs their head around to mindless music so loud that you can hear it through their headphones
		7	would be much happier on a sofa since they seem to need your seat as well as their own

a	b	c	d	e	f	g
7						

5 Read the following extract from *The Accidental Tourist*, where Macon Leary finds himself sitting next to an overweight man on a plane. What coincidence links the two men? _____

From The Accidental Tourist

Traveller: I'm sorry I'm so fat. *Name's Lucas Loomis.*

Leary: Macon Leary.

Traveller: *You a Baltimore man?*

Leary: Yes.

Traveller: Me too. *Greatest city on the earth.* One of these seats is not really enough for me. And the stupid thing is, I travel for a living. I demonstrate software to computer stores. What do you do, Mr Leary?

Leary: I write travel guidebooks.

Traveller: Is that so? What kind?

Leary: Well, guides for businessmen – people just like you, I guess.

Traveller: 'Accidental Tourist'!

Leary: Why, yes.

Traveller: Really? Am I right? Well, what do you know? Look at this. Gray suit – just what you recommend, appropriate for all occasions. *See my luggage?* Carry-on. Change of underwear. Clean shirt. Packet of detergent powder.

Leary: Oh, good.

Traveller: You're my hero. You've improved my trips a hundred per cent. I tell my wife, going with The Accidental Tourist is like going in a cocoon.

Leary: Well, this is very nice to hear.

Traveller: *Times I've flown clear to Oregon and hardly knew I'd left Baltimore.*

Leary: Excellent.

Traveller: I see you have your book for protection there. *Didn't work with me, though, did it?*

Glossary

cocoon warm, safe place

You're my hero I really admire you/your work

6 Find expressions in the conversation which mean:

a That's interesting. _____

b I suppose. _____

c How did you know that? _____

d What a coincidence! _____

Conversational English

7 In natural conversation certain words are sometimes omitted. Look at the sentences in *italics* in 5 and decide which three types of word are missing.

_____ , _____ , _____

8 The following things were said at different times during a business trip. Delete any unnecessary words to make them more conversational.

a A: Is everything OK with your meal, sir?

  B: It's delicious. It couldn't be better.

b A: Do you need anything else, sir?

  B: I don't think so, thanks.

c A: I like your laptop. It's a Sony, isn't it?

  B: Yeah. I haven't quite got used to it yet.

d A: Are you ready to start?

  B: Yeah, I'm just coming.

e A: Do you mind if I switch the reading light on?

  B: It doesn't bother me. I think I'll get another coffee. Do you want one?

f A: I saw you earlier in the fitness centre. Have you been here long?

  B: No, I just got here yesterday. Are you here on business too?

g A: Have you got a light?

  B: Sorry, I don't smoke.

Striking up a conversation

9 What are the advantages of having someone to chat to on a long journey? Do you find it easy to start conversations with people you don't know?

10 The most common ways of starting a conversation with a stranger are:

a make an observation
b pay a compliment
c make a request
d ask for information
e offer assistance
f make an apology

Categorise the following conversation starters by writing **a**, **b**, **c**, **d**, **e** or **f** in the boxes.

You couldn't help me with my bag, **could you?** ☐

Do you mind swapping seats? ☐

Looks like we're in for a bit of turbulence, doesn't it? ☐

Sorry about my kids. **Let me know if** they're bothering you. ☐

I couldn't help noticing you speak Dutch. ☐

Do you think I could borrow your paper if you've finished with it? ☐

Is this row 17, **do you know?** ☐

I like your PalmPilot. **Is that one of the new ones?** ☐

Let me help you with that. ☐

I'll get someone to come and help you. ☐

I see you're flying on to Caracas. ☐

Nice camera. **I used to have one like that**. ☐

I'm sorry, is that getting in your way? ☐

Are you from Lima, **by any chance?** ☐

Fluency

11 Work with a partner to practise holding short conversations with fellow passengers on planes. Speaker A see page 136. Speaker B see page 138.

Travellers' tales

1   ▭ **14.1** Listen to four business people talking about their worst flying experiences and answer the questions.

    a   What was all the noise about on Emma's flight?

    _____

    b   How might Enrique's flight have ended in disaster?

    _____

    c   What surprised Joe on his flight to London?

    _____

    d   Who got lost on Joe's flight to Frankfurt?

    _____

    e   What was the strange request on Selina's flight in Asia?

    _____

    f   How did the Nigerian army solve the overbooking problem?

    _____

Narrative tenses   2   Read this extract from the first conversation and underline the best grammatical choice.

    B: After a while, some of the passengers **were starting/had been starting** to get nervous, me included!

    A: I'm not surprised.

    B: Anyway, eventually, after **we were sitting/we'd been sitting** there for about ten minutes with no announcement and the plane still not moving, **I said/I'd said** something to one of the stewards and they **went/were going** and **opened/were opening** the door to see what **went/was going** on.

    A: And what **happened/had been happening**?

    B: The pilot **got/had got** in!

    A: You're joking!

    B: No, **they'd locked/they'd been locking** him out. Seems quite funny now, but it **didn't/wasn't doing** at the time.

▌Grammar link

for more on narrative
tenses see page 120

3   In the extract in 2 how many examples can you find of the:

    past simple? ☐   past perfect simple? ☐

    past continuous? ☐   past perfect continuous? ☐

Telling anecdotes   4   According to publisher David Weinberger, 'We live stories; we breathe stories; most of our best conversations are about stories.' How useful is it in business to be able to tell a good story? Do you agree that the best ones are usually true?

5 Listed below are the typical stages in a story or anecdote. Add the expressions in the box to the correct place in the list. They were all in the conversations in 1.

> And the strange thing was …   I ended up …
> And then, to top it all, …   Did I ever tell you about the time I was …?
> Way back in (*1985*) it was.   But that was nothing compared to …
> Anyway, to cut a long story short, …   This was around the time of …
> Seems quite funny now, but it didn't at the time.

Opener   I'll never forget the time I was …

_____

Context   It's quite a few years ago now, but I can still remember it.

_____

_____

Emphasis   You're not going to believe this, but …   You should have heard/seen …!

_____

_____

_____

Close   Anyway, in the end …

_____

_____

_____

Lexis link

for more on the language of storytelling see page 120

6 Tick which one of the closes could also come straight after an opener.

Active listening

7 Match the following to make ten things you might say while listening to someone telling a story. They were all in the conversations in 1.

a	You're	god!		**f**	I'm not	terrifying!
b	I don't	earth for?		**g**	I see	read about this.
c	Oh, my	happened?		**h**	Sounds	be serious!
d	So, what	joking!		**i**	Oh, yes, I	what you mean.
e	What on	believe it!		**j**	You can't	surprised.

Fluency

8 Tell the story of your worst (or best) travel experience to the rest of the class.

The business lunch

Discussion

1 What's the most expensive meal you've ever had? Was it worth the money? Who was paying? Was it on expenses? Tell a partner about it.

2 Read the information below. Does it shock or amuse you?

Out to lunch

In 1997 a London banker made the headlines when he was sacked for taking a five-hour lunch break – from 11.30am to 4.30pm!

He won back his job after an industrial tribunal ruled that he had been unfairly dismissed. The court decided that five hours is not an excessive amount of time to conduct business over a meal.

Do you agree with the court ruling?

This one's on me

The world record for the most expensive business lunch ever is held by six Barclay's Bank employees, who in July 2001 ate at the Pétrus restaurant in London.

The three bottles of vintage claret alone which they consumed during the meal set them back a staggering £33,410 (charged to expenses, of course), bringing the total bill to just under £44,000!

How could so huge a bill be justified?

3 🔲 **14.2** You are in a noisy restaurant with a group of colleagues and have to keep going outside to answer your mobile. Each time you come back in, the topic of conversation has changed. Listen and see how quickly you can guess what it is.

a _____   d _____

b _____   e _____

c _____   f _____

4 Listen again and note down key words and phrases that helped you decide. Compare with a partner and then check in the recording on page 155.

Fluency 5 Work in groups. Use the chart below to practise chatting over lunch with business contacts. Start off by talking about what you've just ordered and then keep changing the subject as indicated until your meal arrives – it seems to be taking a long time! Try not to interrupt each other too abruptly, but keep the conversation moving.

> By the way, …   Incidentally, …   That reminds me …
> Before I forget, …   On the subject of …   Talking of …
> To change the subject for a moment …

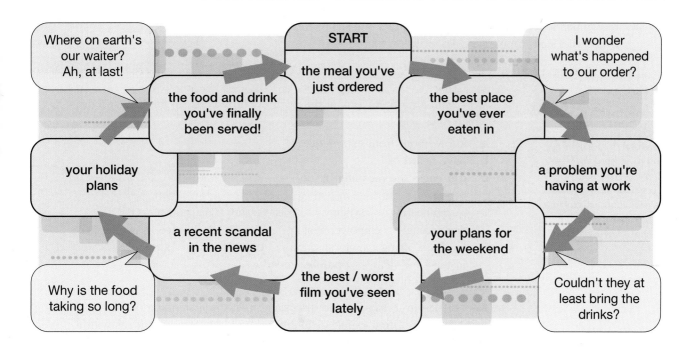

15 Big ideas

Why don't we just stop re-engineering and delayering and restructuring and decentralising and instead start thinking? *Henry Mintzberg, Canadian management thinker*

1 Read the article on business books and think about the questions on the right. Then discuss them with a partner.

A LICENCE TO
PRINT MONEY

Business and professional development books are the most lucrative area of publishing after fiction. At the last count, Amazon.com stocked 32,000 different titles – from meticulously researched case studies by Harvard academics to popular bestsellers like *The One Minute Manager* and *Who*
5 *Moved My Cheese*? Attention-grabbing titles assure us that *Everything is Negotiable* if we can just get used to *Thriving on Chaos* and learn how to *Awaken the Giant Within.*

The big names like Tom Peters, Charles Handy and Peter Drucker sit alongside less well-known but equally hyped volumes by psychologists,
10 hypnotherapists, sports stars, out-of-work actors and retired naval officers. At almost every airport bookshop you'll find at least three metres of business literature drawn from the combined wisdom of management consultants, self-made millionaires, samurai warriors, Italian Renaissance courtiers and even Winnie the Pooh.

15 But by far the bestselling business books of all time are the *Dilbert* series by disenchanted MBA-holder Scott Adams, who spent 17 years working in 'cubicle hell' at Pacific Bell before his cartoons about office life won him 150 million fans in 65 different countries. Says Adams, 'I feel that being a micro-celebrity is the best of both worlds. I get enough
20 recognition to feel good, but I can go to stores and still be treated rudely by the sales staff.'

1 Do you ever buy books on business or management?

2 Have you ever read one from cover to cover?

3 Would any of the titles mentioned appeal to you?

4 What do you think 'hyped' means?

5 What's the silliest business book you've ever seen?

6 What do you think 'cubicle hell' means?

7 Are you a Dilbert fan? If so, try to convert someone who isn't.

Buzzwords

2 Work with a partner. Look at the business buzzwords in the box and discuss which ones you

a know about from experience
b have heard of
c can guess the meaning of.

buzzword /ˈbʌzˌwɜːd/
noun [C] a word that has become very popular, especially a word relating to a particular activity or subject: *The buzzword of the moment is 'accountability'.*

from Macmillan English Dictionary

re-engineering	synergy	Total Quality Management (TQM)
downsizing	empowerment	emotional intelligence	marketspace
the glass ceiling	glocalisation	co-opetition	outsourcing
Just-in-Time (JIT)	portfolio career		

3 🔊 **15.1** Listen to two people discussing their understanding of the buzzwords in 2. There are three extracts. Take notes and compare your ideas with a partner.

How to become a management guru

Fluency The film director Frank Capra said, 'Don't follow trends. Start trends.' Work with a partner to start a trend and turn yourselves into instant management gurus!

Step 1 Read business journalist Stuart Crainer's advice on how to become a guru.

The Ultimate Book of Business Quotations by Stuart Crainer

'gurus once inhabited remote corners of the Indian subcontinent within easy reach of a plentiful supply of mind-enhancing stimulants and a Rolls-Royce dealership. Today's gurus are rather less colourful. Indeed, they are usually management consultants or business school academics. The route to guru status is to come up with a catchphrase (English purists need not apply), write a book (or employ a ghost writer), market it until it reaches the bestseller lists (this may involve buying a lot of copies), and then travel the world giving seminars which repeat the contents of the book. Along the way you have to strenuously deny you are a guru – it demeans the quality of your research and intellectual purity. If you are lucky, you can mine the lucrative world of management guru-dom for two years before your ideas are displaced.

Step 2 Come up with a memorable catchphrase or catchword – something that sums up your new idea. Like many gurus, you may find it helpful to invent a completely new word by combining two others, for example,
co-operation + competition = coopetition; global + local = glocal.

Step 3 Think of a good title for the bestseller you're going to co-author. Here are some ideas to get you started:

> The 3/5/7 Secrets of …   Instant …   How to …   Beyond …
> Stop *-ing* and Start *-ing*   The Age of …   The Art of …   Rethinking …
> Reinventing …   101/1001 Ways to …   The Idiot's Guide to …
> The Rise and Fall of …   … for the 21st Century   The Ultimate …   Managing …
> Everything You Ever Wanted to Know about … (but were Afraid to Ask)

Alternatively, go for a more creative title but make sure you explain what it means in the subtitle. For example, *The Rhinoceros and the Butterfly*: Hard and Soft Negotiation Tactics

Step 4 Work out the basic concept behind your idea. Don't worry about details: concentrate on the big picture. Quote somebody famous. Make up any statistics you need.

Step 5 When you're ready, present your brilliant idea to the class. Decide who are the 'Management Gurus of the Year'.

Business leaders

1 It's the biggest question in management literature: what's the secret of leadership? Look at the following real and fictitious leaders from the past and present. They all have one vital thing in common. What is it?

Julius Caesar	Mahatma Gandhi	Winston Churchill	Mao Tse-Tung
Bill Gates	John F. Kennedy	Saddam Hussein	the Buddha
Jeff Bezos	Alexander the Great	Margaret Thatcher	Ghengis Khan
Carly Fiorina	Cpt. James T. Kirk	Socrates Akio Morita	Joan of Arc
Vaclav Havel	Osama bin Laden	Queen Elizabeth I	Darth Vader
Richard Branson	Montezuma	Martin Luther King	The Lion King

2 ▭ 15.2 Listen and compare your ideas in 1 with the answer.

3 Is there a particular leader you admire? Tell a partner about them.

4 Work in three groups to read the profiles of six of the world's greatest business leaders. Group 1 read profiles **a** and **b**, Group 2 profiles **c** and **d**, and Group 3 profiles **e** and **f**. Complete each profile using the verbs in the boxes.

a   Jeff Bezos, Amazon

Since 1994 the founder of Amazon.com has seen his company grow from an office in a garage to become the number one virtual bookstore. A stream of acquisitions has permitted expansion into CDs and video, clothing, toys and medicines. In spite of the dot.com crash of 2001, Amazon has maintained its position as the world's largest retailer on the Internet.

The Bezos strategy

stay	diversify	establish	buck	pay

1 _____ a clear technological lead
2 _____ lean and efficient
3 _____ into new businesses
4 _____ close attention to logistics
5 _____ the e-commerce trend

b   Michael Dell, Dell Corporation

Dell is the founder and CEO of the Dell Corporation, the direct-sale computer business that has taken the PC world by storm. By bypassing retail stores and offering customers tailor-made systems at low prices, Dell has become the biggest in the business, and with its successful entry into the vast Chinese market, the company looks virtually unstoppable.

The Dell strategy

think	stick	cut	collaborate	put

1 _____ out the middleman
2 _____ customers before product
3 _____ with suppliers
4 _____ to what you're good at
5 _____ global

c   Ricardo Semler, Semco S/A

The president of the Brazilian marine and food-processing machinery manufacturer Semco, environmental activist and author of the bestselling *Maverick!* has created the world's most unusual workplace. At Semco it's the workers who choose and evaluate their bosses. Everyone has access to financial records and 30% of employees set their own salaries!

The Semler strategy

turn	ignore	eliminate	reward	involve

1 _____ employees in decisions
2 _____ hierarchies
3 _____ conventional wisdom
4 _____ the company upside down
5 _____ talent

d   Richard Branson, Virgin

Though head of the huge Virgin empire, Branson prefers to play the underdog. By competing with the likes of British Airways and Coca-Cola, he has earned a reputation for stealing business off complacent market leaders – and doing it in style. A skilled self-publicist, there seems to be almost nothing he wouldn't do to promote the vibrant Virgin brand.

The Branson strategy

generate	have	take	dare	stretch

1 _____ on the market leaders
2 _____ publicity
3 _____ your brand
4 _____ fun
5 _____ to be different

e Carly Fiorina, Hewlett-Packard

Fiorina has a reputation as one of the 'toughest cookies' in a tough business. After dropping out of law school, she had a number of dead-end jobs before rising meteorically to head one of Silicon Valley's heavyweights. Her no-nonsense style has antagonised some, but she silenced her critics by pushing through a highly successful merger with PC giant Compaq.

f Jorma Ollila, Nokia

Nokia has a long history going back to 1865. In those days it had diverse business interests in mining, rubber, paper and cable manufacture. Today, under the guiding hand of Ollila, it has overtaken Motorola and Ericsson to become the world's top mobile phone company – tightly focused and highly innovative in a notoriously cut-throat market.

The Fiorina strategy

take ride lead shake grow

1 _____ from the front
2 _____ things up
3 _____ by acquisition
4 _____ the flak
5 _____ out the recession

The Ollila strategy

seize sell innovate focus stay

1 _____ on your core business
2 _____ off non-core operations
3 _____ opportunities
4 _____ one step ahead
5 _____ or die

Fluency **5** Your CEO has left the company in mysterious circumstances and the six business leaders in 4 have all applied for the job! Who would you rather work for? And who would be best for the company? Team up with people from the other groups and hold an unofficial meeting to discuss the matter.

16 Teleconferencing

Teleconferencing is so rational, it will never succeed. *John Naisbitt, Megatrends*

1 Is business travel a perk or a pain? With today's sophisticated telecommunications, how much of it is really necessary?

2 Read the article below. Whose view do you share: George Mackintosh's or the airlines'?

Jet lag hater's
guide to business travel

George Mackintosh is not the airlines' best customer. In fact, he is working to keep other business people away from the executive lounge.

Mr Mackintosh runs Geoconference, which he
5 describes as Europe's fastest-growing teleconferencing company. His clients are the same corporate folk the airlines want to go jetting across the globe to meetings with colleagues and customers. Mr Mackintosh is
10 trying to persuade them that they can be more productive by staying behind their desks.

Geoconference sells, leases and manages tele- and videoconferencing facilities for multinational firms. Instead of spending valuable
15 time and money travelling to meetings, its sales pitch goes, you can have the same discussions from your own office using a video phone. Hundreds of people can take part at a time, talking to colleagues in dozens of countries.

20 Today Geoconference boasts an impressive list of blue chip clients. IBM, NatWest, Merrill Lynch and Allied Domecq use the company's technology.

But for all the business's early success, Mr
25 Mackintosh admits it has one inescapable weakness. 'Videoconferencing is never going to eliminate the need for at least one face-to-face meeting,' he said. 'If you are doing business with someone for the first time, I don't dispute the fact
30 that you need to meet them, look them in the eye and shake their hand. After that it is likely you are going to be speaking to them on the phone or by e-mail. Videoconferencing allows you to have a more personalised relationship.'
35 The airlines, no doubt, would disagree.

Adapted from The Guardian

Discussion

3 Which of the following would you consider doing by phone rather than face to face? Discuss your reasons with a partner. Would a video facility make a difference?

- a project meeting
- a job interview
- a negotiation
- a crisis meeting
- a sales presentation

Glossary
jet lag tiredness caused by international travel
sales pitch what you say to persuade people to buy
blue chip financially very solid

Trouble at the plant

1 ■ 16.1 Peter Devlin is CEO of the European division of Oriflamme, a manufacturer of candles and home fragrance products. Currently on a business trip to Vancouver with his marketing director Monica Brookes, Peter was woken at 2am by an unexpected phone call from his plant manager in Hamburg. Listen and answer the questions.

   a What has happened at the Hamburg plant?

   _____

   b Why didn't Max have any alternative?

   _____

   c What happened last time there was a similar disaster?

   _____

   d What does Peter suggest doing now?

   _____

Phrasal verbs

2 Complete the following sentences from 1 with the correct preposition. Use the synonyms in brackets to help you.

   a We're going to have to shut _____ the Hamburg plant immediately. (close)

   b Otherwise, the whole thing could go _____! (explode)

   c We'll have container lorries backed _____ from Hamburg to Lübeck. (queueing)

Idioms

3 You also heard the following idiomatic expressions in 1. Can you remember the missing words? The first two letters are given. Use the definitions in brackets to help you.

   a Who on ea_____ can that be? (I have no idea who this is.)

   b All he_____'s broken loose here. (Everything's in chaos here.)

   c Everything grinds to a ha_____. (Everything comes to a complete stop.)

   d There's not a mo_____ to lose. (We must act immediately.)

   e I'm sorry to get you up at this unearthly ho_____. (I don't like to disturb you so late/early.)

4 Work with a partner. List the implications of a crisis like the one above.

5 Now match the following. Did you include them in your list in 4?

   a a backlog of   bottleneck
   b a production   hazard
   c a safety   productivity
   d a fall in   orders

   e a damaged   manhours
   f adverse   reputation
   g lost   deliveries
   h delayed   publicity

> **Lexis link**
>
> for more on the vocabulary of personnel & production see page 123

Discussion

6 Work with a partner to discuss what immediate action Oriflamme should take to avoid the implications in 5.

7 🔊 16.2 Listen to the emergency teleconference and answer the questions.

Extract 1   **a** Who hasn't been able to join the teleconference? _____

b Where are Peter and Monica? _____

c How long will it take to fix the problem at the plant? _____

Extract 2   **a** What state is the plant in? _____

b Why can't the orders be met completely? _____

c Describe Monica's response to Peter's suggestion that they buy product from their competitors to sell on to their customers 'to cover the shortfall'.

enthusiastic ☐   positive ☐   lukewarm ☐   cool ☐   negative ☐   hostile ☐

Extract 3   **a** Why may Handelsmann be prepared to help?

_____

b Is there still a safety hazard at the plant?

_____

c What arrangement does Peter make with Otto?

_____

8 The minutes below were taken by Françoise Fleurie directly after the teleconference. Complete them using the verbs in the boxes.

Points 1 and 2:
~~confirmed~~   keep   estimated   assure   informed   ensure   authorised

Grammar link

for more on reporting see page 122

Points 3 and 4:
mentioned   pointed   follow   opposed   get   agreed   reach   proposed   smooth   OK'd

Hamburg Plant Shutdown: Minutes of the Teleconference   **Date:**
Participants: Peter Devlin, Monica Brookes, Max Schiller, Otto Mendel, Françoise Fleurie   Apologies: N/A
Next teleconference: 12pm ET

Point	Details	Action
1 Situation report	PD _confirmed_ that a total shutdown of the H'burg plant has been officially _____. OM _____ us that the site had been evacuated in order to conduct safety checks, but was later able to _____ us that the situation has now been brought under control.	OM to _____ PD up to date on any changes in the situation
2 Repairs estimate	MS _____ that repairs will probably take three days to carry out. The main reason given for the delay was the amount of time needed to obtain a replacement heat exchanger (48hrs).	MS to oversee and _____ completion of repairs within three days
3 Production plan	PD _____ rewriting the production plan to give priority to key customers, but OM _____ out that we hold insufficient reserve stocks to fully meet current orders. It was generally _____ that our European plants are too overstretched to transfer goods to H'burg.	OM to _____ a compromise re main customers' orders and _____ back to PD
4 Traded goods	PD's suggestion that traded goods be bought in from another supplier was initially _____ by MB on the grounds that it would damage Oriflamme's reputation. FF _____ the possibility of Handelsmann being able to help us out. This was provisionally _____ by PD.	FF to _____ up the Handelsmann offer and _____ things over with key customers

Reporting **9** Complete the puzzle using the extracts from the teleconference in 7 to help you.

a	OK, so we're just	_ _ _ **t**	_ _ _ for Otto.
b	Let's go	_ _ **e**	_ _ and get the meeting started.
c	Max, could you first of all just	_ _ **l**	_ us in on what's going on?
d	Well, Pete, it's difficult to say at the	_ _ _ **e**	_ _.
e	I'll see what I	**c**	_ _ do.
f	I'm already	_ **o**	_ _ _ _ _ on that.
g	Monica, is there any	_ _ _ **n**	_ in us buying in traded goods?
h	Pete, you know how I	**f**	_ _ _ about buying from the competition.
i	Just for the time	_ **e**	_ _ _.
j	What	_ _ _ : **r**	_ _ _ _ _ _ do we have?
k	Can I	_ _ _ **e**	in on that?
l	I've already	_ _ _ **n**	on to Handelsmann.
m	OK, get back to them and see if we	**c**	_ _ hurry things up a bit.
n	And get somebody in after-sales to	_ **i**	_ _ round all our biggest customers.
o	OK, I'll see to it	**n**	_ _.
p	Otto, keep me posted if there's any	_ _ _ _ **g**	_ in the situation.

Desert island blues

The RJK Group is one of the world's leading advertising agencies with an impressive list of blue-chip clients. At the moment RJK (UK)'s top creatives are on location on the remote island of Oamu-Oamu in the South Pacific, filming a commercial for *Vivacity*, the new shower gel range from French cosmetics and toiletries giant Éternelle. But after eight days on the island, the film shoot is turning into a disaster.

Step 1 Work in groups of three. You are about to take part in a teleconference to decide what to do about the situation. First check your latest e-mail and make a note of any points you want to bring up.

Speaker A CEO of RJK (UK): You are currently attending an international conference in Milan. Read e-mails 1 and 2.

Speaker B Creative Director, RJK (UK): You are currently in the middle of a pitch for the €15m Heineken account. Read e-mails 3 and 4.

Speaker C Account Director, RJK (UK): You are currently on two weeks' holiday in Mauritius. Read e-mails 5 and 6.

Step 2 Hold the teleconference using the agenda below. The CEO should chair the meeting. Report what you have learned from your e-mail and try to commit to a definite course of action on which you all agree. The final decision, however, is the CEO's.

Agenda: Éternelle Account – *Vivacity* Shoot

1 Situation report: Clarification of the situation on location
2 Financial considerations: Éternelle account – budgetary constraints
3 Action plan:
 • Change of location? If so, where?
 • Switch to studio filming? Implications?
 • Change of actress? Contractual problems?
 • How to present change of plan to client?
 • Any other suggestions?

1

I'm becoming increasingly concerned about the costs we're running up on the Éternelle account. I think we're in serious danger of exceeding our budget.

As you know, the Éternelle marketing people were extremely unhappy when we came in €250,000 over budget last time, and it was for this reason that they insisted at the planning stage on a ceiling of €2.5m for the *Vivacity* campaign.

I've been looking at the figures and we're well past the €2m mark already. The main problem is this two-day film shoot on Oamu-Oamu which has already cost us €1m. The Hollywood actress the client insisted on using is costing us €100,000 a day! What on earth is going on there?

I estimate that with post-production costs, we could run €500,000–€700,000 over budget on this one.

We desperately need to talk.

Gavin Hartnell, Chief Financial Officer, RJK (UK)

2

I'm hearing rumours of a budget overrun on the *Vivacity* campaign. Please tell me I'm imagining things!

Had lunch with Éternelle's new head of marketing, Thierry DuPont, and he sounded pretty annoyed with what he called our 'endless production hold-ups'. He even said they may be forced to postpone the *Vivacity* launch.

I'm sure I don't need to remind you that Éternelle is by far this company's biggest European client (worth €10m annually) and that the loss of their account would have a drastic effect on both Group turnover and our reputation in the industry.

Your creative director must be in contact with our team on Oamu-Oamu. Are they still having weather problems or what?

I'm counting on you to sort this one out. Don't let me down.

Nathan T. Auerbach, RJK Group President

3

Well, we've had eight days of incessant rain, two cameras damaged in transit and now the electricity generator's broken down. Whose idea was it to use a real desert island for the shoot?

Flying Sandra in and out from Fiji every day is proving totally impractical. Didn't I say using a big Hollywood star was asking for trouble? She came down with some kind of tropical fever two days ago and hasn't come out of her hotel room since. So far we've only got about 15% of the commercial in the can.

To keep costs down the crew are staying on Oamu-Oamu until we're finished. Today is the first fine day, but there's still no sign of Sandra, so we're just getting some footage of the island.

I strongly suggest we either fly out a replacement or seriously consider filming the whole thing in a studio in Britain.

Ridley Hurst, Film Unit Director

4

No doubt you've already heard from Ridley. The good news is that Sandra's PA tells me she may be well enough for filming tomorrow. My suggestion is that we forget Oamu-Oamu and find a nice secluded spot here in Fiji. I'm sure that would suit Sandra much better if she's still not feeling too good. I've sent some of the team out scouting the beaches for possible locations.

The bad news is that the animal handler's gone missing. You remember that we wanted to use real animals on this shoot instead of adding them digitally later? Well, now I'm left here with 36 African parrots and a rather lethal-looking python.

Ridley seems to think we'd be better off doing the whole thing in a studio, but I think it would be a shame to pack up and leave now we're all here. Might be rather hard to explain the unnecessary expense to the client, too. Are we insured for this?

Amelia DeVine, Senior Account Manager, RJK (UK)

5

Sorry to bother you on holiday, but we're having major problems with the *Vivacity* shoot. As you've no doubt heard through the grapevine, we're running six days over schedule owing to bad weather, logistical problems and a leading lady with a fever ...

I've been asked to look into alternatives and have come up with the following, which I thought I'd better copy you in on:

1 If we fly the film crew home to do the commercial in a studio, with set building, studio hire and post-production, we could be looking at an extra €750,000. Plus we'd be unlikely to finish on schedule.

2 Finding an A-list actress to replace Sandra at such short notice would be extremely difficult, although there is provision for her replacement, if unable to perform, in the terms of our contract. I did speak to someone at a lookalike agency who said he had 'Sandra's twin' and could let us have her for €5,000 a day.

Jason Roberts, Account Manager, RJK (UK)

6

I must say I am very disappointed with the number of delays on the *Vivacity* project. These problems with the film shoot are just the latest in a series of expensive mistakes. I trust the extra costs will not be coming out of our agreed budget.

Your Group President Nathan Auerbach tried to persuade me over lunch that everything was going well, but now I'm told we may have lost our actress for the commercial. I should emphasise that in France the use of celebrities to endorse products is a proven and powerful advertising technique. Sandra's appearance in the *Vivacity* commercial was part of the original brief to your agency and any replacement would have to be approved by my marketing department.

I might add that, as RJK's Account Director with overall responsibility for our account, I'm surprised to see you've found time to take a vacation in the middle of this crisis.

Thierry DuPont, Director of Marketing, Éternelle (Europe)

17 Negotiating deals

Don't ever slam a door. You might want to go back in. *Don Herold, US negotiator*

Fluency

1

a Are you a good negotiator? Work in groups of three to try out your negotiating skills. Speaker A see page 137. Speaker B see page 139. The third person in the group should observe and take notes on the kind of language the other two use.

b Speakers A and B, did you reach an agreement or did you get into an argument? What was the main problem you faced?

c Try the negotiation again, but this time read the extra information on page 131 first. The observer should again take notes.

d Was the negotiation easier this time? Did you manage to reach a compromise? Find out from the observer if the language used was different in the two negotiations.

2 🎞 **17.1** Listen to a management trainer giving feedback to some trainees who have just finished the negotiation in 1. Do you agree with the analysis?

Compound adjectives

3 Complete the collocations by matching the compound adjectives. Then match each adjective to its definition. You heard all the phrases in 2.

a	a single-	sum game	one which is very direct
b	a long-	win situation	one from which both sides feel they've gained
c	a win-	issue negotiation	one that lasts
d	a one-	term relationship	one where one side wins what the other side loses
e	a zero-	on conflict	one that happens only once
f	a head-	off deal	one where only one topic is being discussed

4 You also heard the following expressions in 2. Can you remember the missing words? The first few letters are given. The definitions in brackets may help you.

a There's little room for man_____. (It's difficult to change your position.)

b win at all cos_____ (do whatever you have to do to win)

c It simply wasn't worth the hass_____. (It was too much trouble.)

d The negotiation ended in dead_____. (Neither side was prepared to move.)

e resort to emotional black_____ (make people feel guilty to get what you want)

f reach some kind of comp_____ (an agreement that partially satisfies both sides)

> **Lexis link**
>
> for more on the language of negotiations see page 124

Negotiating style

High-pressure tactics   **1**   Listed below are the ten most common high-pressure tactics negotiators use. Match each to its description. The first one has been done for you.

Tactics	Description
1 The shock opener	**a** Make it look as though you are ready to leave the negotiating table if your demands are not met, that you are not prepared to move an inch further.
2 The vinegar and honey technique	**b** Point out at the start that, though you are prepared to negotiate A, B and C; X, Y and Z are definitely not negotiable.
3 The strictly off-limits ploy	**c** Having obtained a concession from your opponent, inform them that you need your boss's approval before you can do what they ask in return.
4 The take-it-or-leave-it challenge	**d** Make unreasonable demands early on in the negotiation. When you later 'see reason' and modify your demands, they'll be all the more welcome.
5 The I'll-have-to-check-with-head-office ploy	**e** Make a ridiculous initial demand (or offer), but keep a straight face as you make it. This works particularly well on inexperienced opponents.
6 The sorry-about-my-English ploy	**f** Don't make all your demands right at the start. Make a small demand and get agreement on it before you make the next, and the next …
7 The good cop, bad cop approach	**g** Pretend not to understand any proposal you don't like the sound of. You'll make your opponent uncomfortable by forcing them to repeat it.
8 The once-in-a-lifetime offer	**h** Pressurise your opponent by suggesting that the offer you're making is only for a limited period and if they don't act quickly, they'll miss it.
9 The salami technique	**i** After the deal has been done, make one modest extra demand in the hope that your opponent will not want to jeopardise the agreement for one small detail.
10 The last-minute demand	**j** One of your team is friendly and flexible, the other unpleasant and unreasonable. Your opponent will want to please Mr/Ms Nice to avoid Mr/Ms Nasty.

1	2	3	4	5	6	7	8	9	10
e									

Discussion   **2**   How might you respond to each of the tactics in 1? Can you see any risks in using them yourself?

3   🔊 **17.2** Listen to extracts from two different negotiations. Which tactics in 1 are they trying to use? How successful are they?

Extract 1 ☐ ☐

Extract 2 ☐ ☐

The language of bargaining

4 Reconstruct the following sentences from the negotiation extracts in 3 by putting the words in **bold** in the correct order. Then listen again and check your answers.

a OK, so, do **take agreement we're in on I it** volume?

_____

b Wouldn't it be a **idea before talk to good we prices go** any further?

_____

c But in **happy principle taking about you're** forty cases, right?

_____

d Look, **price back getting to a for** moment.

_____

e Can you give us some **what idea of of kind figure were you** thinking of?

_____

f There **seems slight a been have to** misunderstanding.

_____

g With **prices respect simply are your not** competitive.

_____

h I'm afraid that **absolute really bottom our is** line.

_____

i Let's set the price **side moment the issue to one for**, shall we?

_____

j I'll throw **free service 12 parts and months' as in** well.

_____

k Now, I **can't fairer that say than**, now can I?

_____

l What we'd really like to **movement see is more on bit a** price.

_____

m A 6% discount **quite is had not what in we** mind.

_____

n We were **closer hoping something for bit a** to 10%.

_____

o I don't think **stretch far could I as as** that.

_____

p Surely **sort we something out can** here.

_____

q Would **meet willing be you to** us halfway?

_____

r We might **position be a increase to in** our order.

_____

s We'd need to **bit on flexibility see a more** terms of payment.

_____

t I suppose **manoeuvre room there be may some for** there.

_____

5   Look back at the expressions in 4 and answer the following questions.

    a   Find two phrases which mean 'bad news coming'.

    _____

    b   Explain the use of the word _seems_ in **f**. _____

    c   If you change sentences **e** and **n** into the present tense, does this make them sound more or less negotiable? _____

    d   Do the question tags in **i** and **k** make it easier or more difficult to disagree?

    _____

    e   Does the negative question form in **b** make the suggestion
more persuasive? ☐   more diplomatic? ☐   both? ☐

    f   Why do you think the speakers use words like _slight, some, a bit_ and _quite?_

    _____

Grammar link

for more on the grammar
of diplomacy &
persuasion see page 124

    g   What is the overall effect of changing _wouldn't_ to _isn't_ in **b**, _can_ to _will_ in **e**, _could_ to _can_ in **o**, _would_ to _are_ in **q**, _might_ to _are_ in **r** and _may_ to _is_ in **t**?

    _____

Showing disapproval

6   The following expressions from the negotiations in 3 show strong disapproval, but think twice before using them yourself as they may cause offence. Complete them using the pairs of words in the box.

lot + that   joke + something   other + time   way + earth

    a   Is this meant to be some kind of _____ or _____ ?

    b   There's no _____ on _____ I'm paying you €4.

    c   Oh, come on! You'll have to do a _____ better than _____ .

    d   Frankly, I think we're wasting each _____ 's _____ here.

Negotiating strategy

7   🔊 **17.3** Listen to five experienced negotiators talking about strategy and answer the questions.

Speaker 1   What does T.I.E. stand for? _____

Speaker 2   How can a friendly attitude be counter-productive?

    _____

Speaker 3   Why is silence more powerful than talking?

    _____

Speaker 4   How do you avoid pointless debates?

    _____

    What are the two most useful phrases in a negotiation?

    _____

Speaker 5   What did the Huthwaite Research Group discover?

    _____

    The speaker mentions three things it's better to phrase as questions. What are they? _____

Idioms

8   Discuss the meaning of the following idioms with a partner. They were all in 7.

    a   Give them an inch and they'll take a mile.

    _____

    b   Play your cards close to your chest.

    _____

    c   Don't take 'no' for an answer. _____

Negotiating a recording contract

Discussion **1** What kind of music are you into? Compare your tastes with a partner.

Pop trivia **2** Work with a partner to answer the following questions. If you've no idea, just have a guess! Then check your answers in the article.

    a Who are the world's wealthiest rock band?
    b Who are the world's five most bankable solo performers?
    c What are the two bestselling albums of all time?
    d What are the two bestselling singles of all time?
    e Which pop song has been recorded in over 2,000 versions?

Inside the music business

The world's biggest band When Mick, Keith, Charlie and Ronnie come on stage at the Giants Stadium in New York to 40,000 adoring fans, they have the satisfaction of knowing that the Rolling
5 Stones are easily the world's wealthiest rock band. Having generated more than $1.5 billion in gross revenues since 1989, two thirds of that earned on tour, they have made more money than even fellow megastars U2, Bruce Springsteen and Sting.

10 **Financial acumen** Now firmly established rock legends, the Stones are also a rock-solid business. It was their chief financial advisor, London banker Prince Rupert zu Loewenstein, who was first to see that, whilst concerts make the most money, music rights
15 provide the steadiest income stream. And though the Stones may never have produced a real blockbuster on the scale of Fleetwood Mac's *Rumours* or Pink Floyd's *Dark Side of the Moon*, Jagger and Richards have made over 40 albums and written more than
20 200 songs. Each time they get airplay, they collect 50 per cent of the royalties. According to *Fortune* magazine, that amounts to $56 million in the past decade. Microsoft alone paid them $4 million to use *Start Me Up* in the Windows 95 commercial.

25 **Big business** The music business has come a long way since the Stones started out in the 60s. In those days record labels like Motown, Island and Elektra all had their own distinctive sound, and you could have a string of top ten hits but still barely be able to afford
30 the bus fare home from your latest sell-out gig. These days just five major music companies – UMG, Sony, Warner, EMI and BMG – control 75 to 80 per cent of all commercially released recordings and the sums of money involved are huge.

35 **Bankability** Today's most profitable solo performers are Michael Jackson, Madonna, Elton John, Celine Dion and Garth Brooks. The back catalogues of Sinatra and Elvis also bring in millions. In fact, dead Elvis started out-earning live Elvis in 1988. Unbelievably, the world's
40 bestselling single of all time remains Bing Crosby's *White Christmas*, closely followed by the version of *Candle in the Wind* Elton John sang at the funeral of Princess Diana, and the most recorded pop song ever is The Beatles' *Yesterday*, which exists in over 2,000
45 different versions. But the real money has always been in albums, not singles. The two top-sellers are Michael Jackson's *Thriller* and Alanis Morissette's *Jagged Little Pill*. Both have sold around 30 million units worldwide.

Rights and rip-offs With this kind of money at
50 stake, it's not surprising that the relationship between artist and record company can be an uneasy one, with young up-and-coming bands often too dazzled by the prospect of stardom to look closely at the small print in their contracts. Even established performers like
55 Prince and George Michael have had well-publicised clashes with their management. Courtney Love went so far as to file a lawsuit against Geffen Records to be released from her contract. And Mariah Carey found herself in the opposite situation, reputedly being paid
60 off to the tune of £19.5 million when Virgin Records decided it didn't want to record her after all.

The future of music But soon it may be the record companies themselves who start losing out. Piracy already costs the industry $4.3 billion a year, and with
65 the arrival of MP3, only sound quality stands in the way of all music being burned onto CD on personal computers. Some 'Indie' music labels like Bombco produce albums
70 exclusively on the Internet and artists as high-profile as David Bowie have experimented with website launches of their latest recordings. Of course, the major
75 music companies have fought back by creating downloadable music services of their own, but with more direct access to the consumer, bands may yet be able to
80 fulfil their dream of being immortalised without first having to sell their soul.

Bing Crosby ▶

3   Find words and phrases in the article which mean:

    a   money earned before tax and costs (paragraph 1) _____

    b   the most regular source of money (paragraph 2) _____

    c   highly successful album, book or film (paragraph 2) _____

    d   money paid to artists each time their work is sold or performed (paragraph 2)

        _____

    e   a series of bestselling records (paragraph 3) _____

    f   a musical performance to which all the tickets are sold (paragraph 3)

        _____

    g   earning more than (paragraph 4) _____

    h   likely to become popular soon (paragraph 5) _____

    i   excited at the chance of becoming stars (paragraph 5) _____

    j   the details in a contract – often limiting your rights (paragraph 5)

        _____

    k   angry disagreements (paragraph 5) _____

    l   well-known (paragraph 6) _____

    m   becoming famous (paragraph 6) _____

    n   do anything to win fame (paragraph 6) _____

4   🔲 17.4 A major record label is considering signing a new band. Listen to an extract from a meeting between their A&R people (talent scouts) and senior management.

    a   Why does Kate think they have to sign the band quickly?

        _____

    b   What are the band's strengths?

        _____

    c   Why isn't Ronnie as impressed as Kate?

        _____

    d   Why does Ronnie sound more enthusiastic at the end of the meeting?

        _____

Fluency   5   Work in two teams to negotiate a recording contract between the record company and the up-and-coming rock band you heard about in 4.

    Team A you are representatives from the band *The Penitents* and their managers. The high-profile record company *Starburst* is interested in signing your band. See page 137 for your negotiating objectives.

    Team B you are executives from the record company *Starburst* and their lawyers. You are interested in signing the promising new band *The Penitents*. See page 139 for your negotiating objectives.

18 Shaping the future

The best way to predict the future is to invent it. *Alan Kay, director of research at Apple*

Discussion **1** Read the following and discuss the likelihood of the predictions using the expressions in the box.

> It's already happened.
> According to this, it should've already happened, but it hasn't so far.
> I suppose it's inevitable.   It's bound to happen sooner or later.
> It might just happen.   It's pretty unlikely in the foreseeable future.
> I can't see it happening in my lifetime.   It could never happen.
> There's no way it could happen.   It's pure science fiction.

BTexact Technologies

BTEXACT
TECHNOLOGIES 2001

The future is hard to predict but one thing is certain – in the distant future the world will be a very different place. The technology timeline is produced to give BT researchers and managers a view of what the operating environment may be like at any future date, so that our products and services can be better targeted to the needs of the customer. Not all these technologies will be successful in the marketplace. Some won't ever be implemented at all, but as the rest come on stream, our lives will improve in many ways.

Innovation	Date expected
• Designer babies	2005
• Cars with automatic steering	2008
• 25% of TV celebrities computer-generated	2010
• Insect-like robots used in warfare	2010
• Academic study unnecessary in the age of smart machines	2013
• First manned mission to Mars	2015
• Space hotel for 300 guests	2015
• Electronic pets outnumber organic pets	2020
• Fully functioning artificial eyes	2024
• Holographic TV	2025
• Virtual reality used extensively in retirement homes	2025
• Emotion control devices	2025
• Robots physically and mentally superior to humans	2030
• First Bionic Olympics	2030
• Direct human-to-computer brainlink	2030
• Moonbase the size of a small village	2040
• Time travel invented	2075
• Faster-than-light travel	2100

2 Which of these technologies would

  a be the most beneficial to society?   **c** be the most controversial?

  b have the most marketing potential?

3 All the adjectives in the box can be used to talk about the future. Add them to the timeline below.

distant	near	foreseeable	immediate	not-too-distant

sooner ◄—————————————————————————————► later

In the _____ _____ _____ _____ _____ future.

4 Complete the sentences with one word from the boxes. Then finish at least five with some predictions of your own concerning business, politics, the environment, leisure or life in general.

way	indications	era	possibility	possibilities	future

  a I think one industry that definitely has a bright _____ is …

  b Recent developments in … open up all kinds of exciting _____

  c All the _____ are that …

  d I think we're about to enter an _____ of …

  e As far as I can see, … is still a very long _____ off.

  f As far as … is concerned, we can't exclude the _____ that …

future	outlook	brink	store	prospects	horizon

  g I think the long-term _____ for … are limited.

  h I think the part of the world facing the bleakest _____ is …

  i I believe we may be on the _____ of …

  j The _____ for anyone involved in the … business is uncertain.

  k There seems to be political change on the _____ in …

  l It's impossible to tell what lies in _____ for …

5 Read out the predictions you made in 4 to the rest of the class. Be prepared to support your views.

The futurists

Discussion 1 What are the latest trends and developments in your line of business?

2 The business magazine *Fast Company* regularly features a column called *Futurist.* Work in two groups to read the predictions of six futurists they have interviewed. Group A read summaries 1–3. Group B read summaries 4–6. Choose a title for each summary, perhaps using words and phrases from the text.

1 _____

Christopher Dewdney is a fellow of the McLuhan Programme in Culture and Technology at the University of Toronto. According
5 to him, 'None of us is naturally human anymore.' At the moment we are in transition between the human and post-human – a condition he calls 'transhuman'. 'The goal of transhumanism,' explains Dewdney, 'is to surpass our current biological limitations, whether they be lifespan, physical beauty or the capabilities of our
10 brain.' Ironically, just as humans are beginning to play with their DNA structure and become more 'artificial', machines are becoming more 'lifelike'. At some point in the future 'we won't be able to differentiate between the two'. But, more significantly, the world may end up being divided into those who can afford to be genetically enhanced and those who can't, leading to 'a new class of beings
15 who will actually look and act like a different human species' – one that might even threaten conventional human beings.

2 _____

Ian Angell is Professor of Information Systems at the London School of Economics. Describing himself as 'an anarchic capitalist', he firmly believes that 'business should be running the world'. His disturbing vision of the future is one where an elite of brilliant business people and technologists will be allowed to run their own enterprises with a
5 minimum of government intervention. Indeed, the wealth-creating skills of these 'new barbarians', as Angell calls them, will be in such demand that countries will actually compete with each other to attract them as residents. But whilst these corporate free agents will be living in largely unregulated tax havens, billions of the less fortunate will be left behind living in crumbling, inefficient and crime-ridden megacities. 'Every
10 major technological shift creates winners and losers,' says Angell. 'Europe's a disaster because of a sentimental attachment to the welfare state, which is a vestige of the Industrial Age.'

3 _____

Gary Wright is a corporate demographer for the consumer products giant Procter & Gamble. Although world population, currently around six billion, is set to hit 12.5 billion by the end of the century, in the developed world it's not population growth but an ageing population that will have the most far-reaching consequences. By 2010 43%
5 of American adults will be over 50. As Wright points out, that's 97 million people. And as more and more take early retirement, fewer and fewer working people will be left to support them. Most of today's successful businesses grew up in a period of population explosion and rapid economic progress. But will business continue to flourish in the 'no-growth' or 'slow-growth' environment of the future? 'To an extent, immigration will
10 offset population declines,' says Wright, and, indeed, in many parts of the developing world the majority of people are under 35. But this could have serious cultural and political implications.

4

Michele Bowman is the senior vice-president at Global Foresight Associates in Boston.
In her opinion, in the networked world of the future, where you live will have very little
effect on where you work, and citizenship will be far less important than 'cybership'. As
Bowman points out, 'Electronic immigrants, also known as cross-border telecommuters,
5 are nothing new.' In fact, with cheaper international telecommunications, many western
companies already employ people in the developing world as 'back office staff' dealing
with such things as customer relations. In 2002 there was a public outcry in the UK
when British Telecom proposed routing domestic telephone directory enquiries via
India and Pakistan. Bowman claims that: 'As the global economy becomes more
10 integrated and interdependent, the ranks of these workers will grow' – and not only in
routine jobs. Electronic immigrants may 'soon infiltrate high-end technical fields such as
engineering and IT'.

5

Peter Cochrane is head of research for British Telecom Laboratories. His specialism is
the speed of business. Here's one of Cochrane's startling statistics: 'A generation ago,
the average person had a 100,000-hour working life – 40 hours a week, 50 weeks a year,
for 50 years. Today we can do everything that person did in 10,000 hours. In the next
5 generation, people will be able to do it in 1,000 hours.' In other words, what our
children will be able to achieve in just six months took our parents their entire working
lives. Cochrane says 'We're addicted to speed' and we'll increasingly be willing to pay
large sums of money to save our most precious commodity – time. This may mean
actually prolonging our lives through anti-ageing medical advances or simply packing
10 more into the lives we've got by multitasking at work and by combining several leisure
activities at once in what Cochrane calls 'parallel time'. One thing's for certain: genuine
free time will cease to exist.

6

John Naisbitt is one of the world's leading futurists and the author of a series of
bestsellers on the subject. In his latest blockbuster *High-Tech High-Touch*, Naisbitt
makes the observation that even as we rush to embrace technology that makes our lives
easier, we're also starting to reject technology that makes us feel less alive, less human.
5 Neither a technophobe nor a technophile, Naisbitt sees a great future for this middle
way he calls 'high-tech high-touch'. High-tech is wanting the heart transplant, the brain
scan, the gene therapy. High-touch is wanting more time with the family doctor. High-
tech is chatting on the Internet to someone on the other side of the world. High-touch is
chatting with your neigbour on the other side of the garden fence. High-tech is the
10 dashed-off e-mail. High-touch is the beautifully handwritten letter on headed notepaper.
For business the message is clear: give the technology you're trying to sell the personal
touch, or fail.

3   Team up with people from the other group. Explain your choice of titles,
summarise what you read and discuss possible implications and opportunities for:

- society as a whole
- the world of business
- you personally
- your company

4   ▣ **18.1** Listen to six business people's opinions on the issues in 3 and compare
your views.

Back to the future

When Elvis Presley died in 1977, there were 37 Elvis impersonators in the world.
Today there are 48,000. If the current trend continues, one out of every three
people in the world will be an Elvis impersonator by 2010.

Mark Gibbs, *Navigating the Internet*

1 Business or pleasure?

Tense review

Practice 1 Read the e-mail and underline the best grammatical choice in each case.

From: Charles Wellcome
To: Deborah Newton, Stephen Clark, Willem Maas, Tatiana Korbutt
Cc:
Subject: this year's client hospitality event

Dear all

As you (1) **know/are knowing**, the annual client hospitality event (2) **is fast approaching/will fast approach** and, as yet, we (3) **did not make/have not made** a final decision on where to hold it this year. One or two of you (4) **already came forward/have already come forward** with suggestions, which (5) **are currently considered/are currently being considered**, but, as we (6) **will have to/are having to** make the necessary arrangements quite soon, I'd like everybody's input on this asap. I (7) **thought/have thought** now (8) **was/has been** as good a time as any to start the ball rolling.

What I particularly (9) **want/am wanting** to avoid is a repetition of the fiasco we (10) **had/have had** last year at the show jumping event. Apart from the fact that very few of our clients (11) **have/are having** even the remotest interest in the sport, the atrocious weather (12) **meant/was meaning** that we (13) **walked/were walking** backwards and forwards through the mud between the showring and the hospitality tent all day. The whole thing (14) **was/has been** a complete disaster. People (15) **still complained/were still complaining** about it six months later!

This year we (16) **have planned/had planned** to do something more cultural like go to the opera or even a musical, but (17) **I've wondered/I've been wondering** if this is a good idea. A musical event (18) **doesn't seem/isn't seeming** to be the best place to network. We can hardly ask the singers to keep the noise down while we all (19) **have/will have** a good chat!

I (20) **do think/am thinking**, however, that an indoor event (21) **makes/is making** most sense, so can I ask you to (22) **think/be thinking** along those lines over the next few days? (23) **I've scheduled/I'd scheduled** a meeting for next Friday to discuss the matter further. So, (24) **I'm speaking/I'll speak** to you all then.

Charles

Practice 2 Try to complete the tense quiz in under five minutes.

1 *He **leaves** at five* means
   a today   **b** every day   **c** either

2 *We're **having** a meeting* means
   a now   **b** soon   **c** either

3 *Profits **went up**.* Are profits up now?
   a yes   **b** no   **c** maybe

4 *Profits **have gone up**.* Are profits up now?
   a yes   **b** no   **c** maybe

5 *He's **gone**.* Is he here?
   a yes   **b** no   **c** maybe

6 *I've just **been**.* Am I back?
   a yes   **b** no   **c** maybe

7 *When I arrived he **was** just **leaving**.* Was he there when I arrived?
   a yes   **b** no   **c** we don't know

8 *When I arrived he'd just **left**.* Was he there when I arrived?
   a yes   **b** no   **c** we don't know

9 *I've **tried** to phone her.* Am I still trying?
   a probably   **b** probably not   **c** we don't know

10 *I've **been trying** to contact her all morning.* Am I still trying?
   a probably   **b** probably not   **c** we don't know

Summary

You use the **Present Simple** to talk about permanent facts (*I'm Spanish*), routines (*I get home at seven each evening*) and scheduled future (*The bus gets in at one*).

You use the **Present Continuous** to talk about current, perhaps temporary, activities and situations (*I'm staying at the Hilton*) or future arrangements (*I'm flying to Rome in the morning*).

You use the **Present Perfect** to talk about things that started in the past and continue up to the present (*It's rained for a fortnight*), personal experiences no matter when they happened (*I've only ever snowboarded once*) and things which have an immediate consequence (*I've lost my car keys*). Words like *already, yet* and *since* are often in the same sentence as a present perfect verb.

You use the **Present Perfect Continuous** to talk about temporary situations that started in the past and may or may not be completed (*I've been working here since January 2002*).

You use the **Past Simple** to talk about finished past actions or states (*I studied engineering at Oxford*). Phrases like *last week, a year ago*, etc. make the time reference clear.

You use the **Past Continuous** to talk about an action in progress in the past (*The company was losing money*). The Past Continuous gives the background to more important events which are in the Past Simple.

You use the **Past Perfect** to emphasise that one event happened before another in the past (*By the time I left college, I'd already decided I didn't want to be a lawyer*).

Some 'state' verbs like *think, know, understand* and *seem* are not generally used in the continuous form unless the meaning is different: *I think = I believe; I'm thinking = I'm considering something*.

will is a modal verb and, amongst its other uses, one of many ways of talking about the future (*I'll see you later*).

Lexis: Conversation

A bore is a fellow talking who can change the subject back to his topic of conversation faster than you can change it back to yours. *Laurence J. Peter, creator of the 'Peter Principle'*

1 Match the sentence starters on the left to the nouns on the right to make complete statements.

a	It was a very posh	bestseller.
b	It was the trip of a	restaurant.
c	It was a very close	news!
d	That's terrific	acquaintance.
e	It's your typical Hollywood	hotel.
f	The economy's in a	blockbuster.
g	She's really just an	match.
h	I've just read his latest	lifetime!
i	It's a top-class	sell-out.
j	I hear their latest tour was a	mess.

2 Find words and phrases in 1 which mean:

  a a game in which the score is almost level

  _____ _____

  b expensive and high-quality _____ or

  _____

  c successful film or book _____

  d someone you know a little _____

  e a very bad state _____

  f a play or concert to which all the tickets are

  sold _____

3 Put the conversation in the correct order.

☐1 We were just talking about this new sports centre they're building in town. Do you play any sport at all, Kim?

☐ Not yet, no. Why, are you doing something?

☐ Against Real Madrid? No, I missed it. I had to go to a birthday party.

☐ No problem. Oh, before I forget. I've got two tickets to see them in Manchester if you're interested.

☐ No, me neither. Talking of football, did you see the match last night?

☐ Oh, right. Thanks for telling me. Incidentally, have you still got my *Rolling Stones* CD?

☐ Me? Well, not really. I used to play a bit of football.

☐ No, nothing special. By the way, sorry to talk business, but did you remember to send that estimate to Clive?

☐ Pity. It was a great game. On the subject of parties, have you made any plans for New Year's Eve yet?

☐ Did you? Me too. I was never any good, though.

☐ Oops! Yeah, sorry. I meant to give it back to you. I'll bring in it tomorrow. Thanks for lending it to me.

☐ Yeah, I sent it yesterday. Oh, that reminds me. Clive said to tell you he won't be able to make Thursday's meeting. He said he'd call you.

☐13 Are you kidding? Of course I'm interested! I've never seen them live.

4 Find six expressions in 3 to guide the conversation or change the subject.

  a I_____, ...

  b T_____ of ...

  c B__ the w___, ...

  d B_____ I f_____, ...

  e T____ r_____ me, ...

  f O__ t____ s_____ of ...

2 Exchanging information

Conditionals

Practice Put a cross next to the ending (1 – 4) which isn't grammatically possible and then correct it. The first one has been done for you.

a As long as we're well prepared, …
1 we've got nothing to worry about ✓
2 we shouldn't have any problems. ✓
3 we couldn't go wrong. ✗
4 we'll be fine. ✓

Correction
we can't go wrong.

b I'll send them an e-mail …
1 if you'll tell me what I should say.
2 if you think it's worth it.
3 unless you'd rather do it.
4 provided I hadn't lost their address.

Correction

c If you're going out, …
1 get me a newspaper, will you?
2 you're going to miss the meeting.
3 you'd better take an umbrella.
4 I come with you.

Correction

d Do that …
1 and you'll regret it.
2 if it'll help.
3 if you'll get the opportunity.
4 – we'll lose business.

Correction

e I'd stay and help you …
1 if I knew anything about computers.
2 if I'm not going out this evening.
3 if I hadn't promised Jo I'd meet her.
4 if you asked me nicely.

Correction

f I'd be grateful …
1 if you could sort this out for me.
2 if you'd keep this to yourself.
3 if you don't tell anyone about this.
4 if you remembered that in future.

Correction

g If he actually said that to her, …
1 she'd kill him.
2 I'd have been very surprised.
3 it was very stupid of him.
4 he must have been mad.

Correction

h I wouldn't have asked you …
1 if I didn't think you could do it.
2 unless I trusted you.
3 if I'd known this would happen.
4 if you didn't say you wanted to do it.

Correction

i If it hadn't been for him, …
1 I'd still be working at Burger King.
2 I'd have got that job.
3 we might never have found out.
4 I hadn't had a chance.

Correction

Summary

You can use any tense in either half (clause) of a conditional sentence.

As well as *if, unless, as long as* and *providing/provided* (*that*), you can also use *and* as a conjunction in a conditional (*Do that **and** we'll get complaints*) or no conjunction at all (*Do that – we'll get complaints*).

Conditional clauses can come either first or second in the sentence. However, with *and* or no conjunction, conditional clauses come first.

You can put *will* or *would* in the conditional clause (*If you'll wait here, I'll go and get her for you; I'd be grateful if you'd give this matter your serious attention*), but this is unusual.

The Past Simple in a conditional can refer to the past (*Even if I **did meet** her, I'm afraid I don't remember her*), to a future possibility (*If I **resigned** tomorrow, I could get another job within the week*) or to an unreal situation (*If I **spoke** Italian, I'd phone her myself, but I don't*).

Conditionals with the Past Perfect can refer to the effects of the past on the more recent past (*If you'd **made** a backup, we wouldn't have lost the whole document*) or on the present (*If I'd **got** that job, I could be earning a fortune now*).

Lexis: Meetings

If a problem causes many meetings, the meetings eventually become more important than the problem.
Arthur Bloch, Murphy's Law

Metaphor: discussion is a journey

A lot of the language of discussion refers to journeys. Read the conversation and underline the references to movement and travel. There are 20.

Ian returns to the boardroom to find the meeting in chaos …

Ian Sorry about that. Had to take a phonecall from Bangkok. So, are we any nearer a decision?

Erik Not yet, but we're getting there. I think we're more or less on the right track, anyway.

Sonia Are we? I'd say we've got a long way to go yet. We just seem to be going round in circles.

Erik Well, we were making good progress before we got sidetracked, Sonia. Now, returning to the question of logistics …

Ella Sorry, but could I just go back to what I was saying earlier about freight charges?

Sonia Hang on, hang on. Aren't we getting ahead of ourselves here? We haven't got as far as discussing transportation yet, Ella …

Erik We don't seem to be getting very far at all!

Ian The conversation seems to have drifted a little while I was away … I can't quite see where all this is heading.

Erik We've certainly wandered away from the main topic. Now, logistics …

Sonia I was just coming to that. In my opinion, this whole plan is totally impractical.

Ian I don't think I like the direction this discussion is going in. OK, look, we've covered a lot of ground this morning, but I think that's about as far as we can go at the moment.

Erik Now, just a minute! We haven't come this far to break off now, surely …

Idiomatic expressions

1 In the fixed expressions below, delete the word you wouldn't expect to hear.

a So, what do you **reckon/guess**?

b I'd go **around/along** with that.

c I wouldn't go quite as **far/much** as that.

d Where do you **stand/sit** on this?

e Well, that goes without **saying/speaking**.

f I don't mind **either/each** way.

g I'm afraid it's not **so/as** simple as that.

h Any **responses/reactions**?

i The way I **view/see** it is this.

j I **wouldn't/couldn't** say that.

k **Yes and no/No and yes**.

l I **can't/couldn't** say, to be honest.

m I'd like us to **share/spare** our views on this.

n Oh, come **on/off** it!

o Well, I haven't **given/taken** it much thought.

p I'm **for/with** you there.

q To my **meaning/mind**, it's like this.

r To **a point/an extent** you're right.

2 Categorise the expressions in 1 according to their purpose.

a asking for an opinion
☐ ☐ ☐ ☐

b giving an opinion
☐ ☐ ☐

c giving no opinion
☐ ☐ ☐

d agreeing
☐ ☐

e disagreeing
☐ ☐ ☐

f half-agreeing
☐ ☐ ☐

---

3 The following are all things you might do in a meeting. Match the words in columns one and two to make an idiom. Then match the idiom to its meaning in column three.

sit on	the shots	take the blame
pass	the music	refuse to make a decision
call	the fence	do as you're told
face	the can	put the blame on someone else
carry	the line	be in charge
toe	the buck	accept criticism for something you've done wrong

In general, avoid using idioms with other non-native speakers, but expect native speakers to use them quite a lot.

4 Voice and visuals

Modal verbs

Practice 1 In each of the sentences below, delete the modal verbs that are incorrect.

a We ... now, but we can if we want.
(mustn't pay/don't have to pay/haven't got to pay)

b I ... my laptop, so I left it at the office.
(needn't take/didn't need to take/needn't have taken)

c We ..., if we'd known he wasn't coming in today.
(didn't need to wait/mustn't wait/needn't have waited)

d When I was a student, I ... for hours on end.
('d study/would have studied/used to study)

e I ... quite left-wing, but I've become more conservative.
(used to be/would be/must have been)

f She ... by now – it's after twelve.
(should have left/'ll have left/won't have left)

g I took my driving test three times before I ... pass.
(could/was able to/managed to)

Practice 2 Complete the conversation using the modal verbs in the box.

can't	can't	'll	'll	must	might
shouldn't		wouldn't		won't	would have
must have		could have		could have	
needn't have					

A Ivan, (1) _____ Alexis be here by now? It's gone four!

B Yeah, she (2) _____ got held up somewhere.

A But (3) _____ she have phoned?

B Well, you (4) _____ thought so.

A I mean, we're only having this meeting for her benefit. If she doesn't come soon, we (5) _____ bothered.

B Quite, though I (6) _____ think what (7) _____ held her up. I (8) _____ ring her and see what's going on. That's funny, I (9) _____ find her number. I (10) _____ sworn I put it in my diary. It (11) _____ be in here somewhere!

A Well, if you ask me, she (12) _____ just be coming now, anyway.

B Hang on. That (13) _____ just be her now. I (14) _____ go and check.

Summary

have to, have got to and *must* mean there's an obligation to do something.

don't have to and *haven't got to* mean there's no obligation to do something.

mustn't means there's an obligation *not* to do something.

I needn't have done means I did something but it wasn't necessary; *I didn't need to do* means it wasn't necessary so I didn't do it.

would do means *used to do* for repeated past actions.

She should have left means *I expect she's left* or *She's supposed to have left* or *It would have been a good idea if she'd left.*

You use *was able to* (not *could*) to talk about a specific past achievement.

That must be him is the opposite of *That can't be him.*

will is the most versatile modal verb and can be used for offers, spontaneous decisions, assumptions, predictions and to express willingness or determination.

Lexis: Presentations

Wise men talk because they have something to say; fools, because they have to say something. *Plato*

Types of presentation

1 Match the following to make nine different types of business presentation.

a	conference	pitch
b	sales	speech
c	pep	talk
d	press	conference
e	after-dinner	lecture
f	academic	speech
g	project	speech
h	welcome	demonstration
i	product	update

2 Which of the above would you give to:

a a group of journalists? ☐

b guests at a colleague's leaving party? ☐

c demotivated employees? ☐

d your immediate boss? ☐

e new recruits? ☐

f prospective customers or clients? ☐ ☐

Commenting on statistics

1 Put the following verbs and verb phrases in order from the best news to the worst.

> nearly doubled   almost halved
> quadrupled   plateau'd
> increased tenfold   more than tripled

Sales have

     a _____

     b _____

     c _____

     d _____

     e _____

     f _____

Which of the above means the same as *a fourfold increase*? ☐

2 Pair up the adjectives with ones which have a similar meaning and put them in order from the biggest to the smallest.

> slight   huge   significant   modest
> massive   moderate   considerable
> reasonable

   a   a _____ / _____

        b _____ / _____

        c _____ / _____   **increase**

        d _____ / _____

3 Describe the following success rates using suitable adjectives from the box.

> phenomenal   disastrous   disappointing
> encouraging   miserable   spectacular
> unimpressive   promising

       a _____ / _____ 95%

a(n)   b _____ / _____ 65%   **success**

       c _____ / _____ 25%   **rate**

       d _____ / _____ 3%

Metaphor: trends and developments

1 Complete the joke by matching each noun or noun phrase on the left to a verb or verb phrase on the right. Use a dictionary to check the literal and metaphorical meaning of the verbs, if necessary.

And on the stock market today …

mountaineering equipment   totally collapsed
military hardware   were up and down
lifts   went up sharply
kitchen knives   peaked
but the housing market   boomed

After a nervous start …

rubber   quickly recovered
medical supplies   shot up
the automotive industry   bounced back
rifles   picked up after lunch
and vacuum cleaners also   rallied

In some of the fiercest trading seen in the City …

swimwear   hit rock bottom
mining equipment   slumped
ice skates   plunged
alcoholic beverages   completely dried up
and the market for raisins   slipped a little

By close of trade …

fireworks   remained unchanged
Prozac   fell dramatically
but paper products   were stationary
men's socks   reached an all-time high
and theatre curtains   skyrocketed

2 Mark the verbs and verb phrases in 1 according to the trend they describe: up (↑), down (↓), up and down (↕), down then up (↘↗) and no change (↔).

Technical hitches Complete the embarrassing situations below and match each with a possible joke you could use to save face.

> slides   feedback   transparency
> microphone   acoustics

a Your _____ is turned down too low.

b Your PowerPoint _____ won't display and the projector lead has the wrong plug.

c The room you're speaking in has terrible _____.

d The PA system is producing deafening _____.

e You put your _____ onto the overhead upside down.

'I was going to use PowerPoint, but we don't seem to have any power, so what's the point?' ☐

'The last time I heard a noise like that was at a heavy metal concert.' ☐

'That was for any Australians in the audience. Now, here it is again for people from the northern hemisphere.' ☐

'OK, if it's still no good after we increase the volume, I think it may be your ears that need adjusting.' ☐

'Can you hear me at the front?' ☐

5 Problems on the phone

Complex question formation

Practice 1 Polite question forms

Rewrite the requests and offers to make them sound friendlier and more polite using the words in brackets to help you. Make any necessary changes to grammar.

a Can you turn the air conditioning up a bit? (think/could)

Do you think you could turn the air conditioning up a bit?

b Can you help me? (wonder/could)

_____

_____

c Don't mention this to anyone else. (could/ask you)

_____

_____

d Can you do some overtime next week? (think/could/ask)

_____

_____

e Do you want me to put in a good word for you? (would/like me)

_____

_____

f Can you stop whistling while I'm trying to concentrate? (would/mind not)

_____

_____

g Is it OK to leave early today? (do/mind/if)

_____

_____

h Do you want me to give you a few days to think about it? (would/help/give)

_____

_____

i Can I ask you a personal question? (Would/mind/I)

_____

_____

j When is Mr Alvarez coming back? (happen/know)

_____

_____

k Can you lend me €50 until Friday? (don't suppose/could you?)

_____

_____

_____

Summary

Being polite takes longer!

Modal verbs (*could, would*) soften a request that may be unwelcome.

'Type 1' conditionals (*Do you mind if I leave early?*) make requests more diplomatic.

'Type 2' conditionals (*Would you mind if I left early?*) make requests even more diplomatic.

Do you happen to know …? is useful when you're not sure the other person knows the answer to your question.

I don't suppose you could …, could you? is good way of asking people to do you a favour.

Practice 2 Question-and-answer sessions

A environmental consultant is fielding questions after his presentation. Complete the questions from the audience using the verbs in the box.

describing	telling	referred	dealt
came	pointed	mentioned	arrived
made	spoke	talking	quoted	be
explain	happen	discussing	elaborate
go	saying	believe	showing

a When you were _____ us about the number of species that become extinct each year, you _____ a figure of 27,000. Could you tell us how you _____ at that figure?

b Going back to what you were _____ about imposing a green tax on fossil fuels, do you honestly expect us to _____ that people would be prepared to pay such a tax? And, if so, would you _____ how it might be implemented?

c When you were _____ about natural resources, you _____ the claim that American farmers draw 20 billion gallons more water from the ground every single day than are replaced by rainfall. Could you just tell us where that figure _____ from?

d When you were _____ us the statistics for deforestation in Germany, you _____ in passing that 88% of conifer forests in Central and Eastern Europe are threatened by pollution. Could you _____ into a bit more detail on that?

e When you were _____ the recent impact of green issues on the world of business, you _____ to a survey carried out by *Greenpeace*. Do you _____ to have a copy of that survey with you?

f Going back to the question of clean air legislation – which I thought you _____ with very sensibly – you _____ out that setting a standard for industrial emissions is not the same thing as setting a health standard. Could you _____ a bit more specific?

g When you were _____ the question of toxic chemicals, you _____ about high levels of chemical waste in one American research facility. Would you care to _____ on that?

Summary

When you ask questions at the end of a presentation, it's a good idea to focus the presenter's attention on the context of the question before you ask it.

The **Past Continuous** gives the general context, and the **Past Simple** the more specific reference (*When you were **talking** about X, you **mentioned** Y. Could you say a bit more about that?*).

The use of *just* before a request makes it both more polite and harder to refuse (*Could you **just** expand on that a little?*).

The use of certain adjectives and adverbs can make your question sound more aggressive, even hostile (*What **real** evidence is there …? How can you be **so** sure …? Do you **honestly** expect us to believe …?*).

Lexis: Phone, fax and e-mail

Taking a mobile phone into the bedroom should be grounds for divorce. *Lord Deedes, journalist*

Complete the telephone conversation using the words in the box.

on	on	on	on	on	on	up	up	up	up
out	out	out	off	off	off	down	down	in	
around	as	under	back	by	for				

A design agency office is in chaos. The phone is ringing. Tina finally answers it.

A Hello? Tina Mallon.

B Tina. Thank goodness you're there!

A Hi, Geoff. What's (1) _____?

B Listen. I'm (2) _____ a bit of a mess here.

A Where are you?

B I'm just (3) _____ my way to see the people at FlexiPak and you'll never guess … I've left the file with the visuals in it back at the office!

A Oh dear … Well, can I fax them through to you at their office?

B No, I don't think they'd come (4) _____ properly.

A Geoff, I'm (5) _____ to my neck in it here. I can't access my e-mail because the server is (6) _____ this morning and I'm rushed (7) _____ my feet, running (8) _____ trying to sort things (9) _____ with IT and get those posters (10) _____ to Milan by midday.

B Look, Tina, this is urgent. Could you go over the road to the print shop, scan the visuals and ask them to e-mail them to me (11) _____ attachments? I'll give you FlexiPak's e-mail address.

A Geoff, I'm sorry, but I'm really snowed (12) _____ here.

B Tina, I wouldn't ask you if I wasn't desperate. I haven't got time to come (13) _____ and pick them (14) _____.

A Well, maybe it would be easier just to send them (15) _____ dispatch rider. Hang (16) _____. Let me take (17) _____ the details. Which visuals do you need exactly? Hello? Geoff?

B Tina?

A Geoff? You're breaking (18) _____. Are you (19) _____ your mobile? I can't hear you!

B Hello? Oh, what's going (20) _____ with this phone? I can't be (21) _____ of range. I must be running low (22) _____ batteries. No, it's charged. Tina, can you hear me? I'll have to ring (23) _____ and look (24) _____ a payphone or something. Tina?

Tina hangs up, smiling

A Now, maybe I can finally get (25) _____ with some work!

6 Leading meetings

Linking and contrasting ideas

Practice Read the meeting extracts below. For each of the words or phrases in **bold**, underline the word or phrase in brackets that is similar in meaning. Don't change any grammar or punctuation.

A Well, **in spite of** all these problems, I'd say we're still on target for a January launch.
(despite/even though)

B What, **even though** we've hardly completed phase one trials?
(in spite of the fact that/despite)

A Yes. **Although** obviously I'd have liked us to be further ahead by now, I'm confident we'll be ready in time.
(However/Whilst)

B Well, I admire your optimism, Sergio, but **nevertheless**, I think we should make some kind of contingency plan.
(all the same/however)

A I'm afraid that, **because of** the strong euro, exports are down again this quarter.
(consequently/owing to)

B And **as a result** our share price is falling.
(consequently/owing to)

A Quite. Now, **whereas** we've been able to sustain these losses so far, we clearly can't do so indefinitely.
(despite/although)

A Right, well, **as** nobody seems to be in favour of this proposal, I suggest we just scrap it!
(due to/seeing as)

B It's not that we're against it, Jakob, **although** it is an unusual idea.
(though/whereas)

C Yes, I'd like to support you on this one, Jakob, **but** I can't help feeling you're rushing things.
(whilst/and yet)

A Well, how much more time do you need? **In order to** put this before the board, I have to have your approval.
(To/So that)

A Now, I don't want to spend a lot of time on these new European guidelines. I do think we should go through them briefly, **however**.
(though/although)

B The guidelines do affect all of us, Renata.

A **Even so**, we have more important things to discuss.
(Whereas/Nevertheless)

A Well, everybody, **thanks to** all your hard work, the campaign has got off to a great start.
(as a result/as a result of)

B And **while** it's too early to say exactly how successful it will be, it's looking very good indeed.
(whilst/as)

A Yes. **So as to** give you a clearer idea, I've prepared copies of our sales projections for year one.
(so/in order to)

B The figures are broken down by country **so that** you can get the full picture.
(since/in order that)

A And, **since** we're celebrating, I brought along some champagne!
(seeing as/because of)

Summary

You can use the following words and phrases

- to make **contrasts and contradictions**:

while/whilst	though	although
even though	even so	and yet	however
nevertheless	all the same	despite
in spite of (the fact that)	whereas	but

- to express **purpose or intention**:

in order to/that	to	so as to	so (that)

- to link **cause and effect**:

because of	owing to	as a result (of)
consequently	as	since	seeing as
thanks to		

Lexis: Companies and capital

Crazy times call for crazy organizations.
Tom Peters, management guru

1 Group the following verbs according to meaning.

expand	streamline	start up	sell off
found	delayer	wind up	build up
establish	buy up	grow	liquidate
buy into	rationalise	acquire

set up _____ _____ _____

take over _____ _____ _____

restructure _____ _____ _____

develop _____ _____ _____

close down _____ _____ _____

2 A manager is comparing business in the past with business now. Complete what he says using the words in the boxes.

1–8
economy vision customer stakeholders value global flatter outsourced

9–16
flexibility effectiveness layers learning functional total empowered networked

'Well, the most important difference, obviously, is that nowadays we're all operating in a (1) _____ market, rather than simply a national one – the so-called borderless (2) _____. And the increased amount of competition means that this company, at any rate, has gone from being product-driven to much more (3) _____-oriented. And whereas we used to focus on price, now we focus on customer (4) _____. And where we used to set goals, we now have something called a corporate (5) _____. A lot of it is just a change in terminology but it certainly looks like we're doing something new!

'A company's chief responsibility used to be to its shareholders, but these days we prefer to talk about (6) _____ – not just the people with a financial stake in the company, but everyone who has an interest in the way it's run. A big change in the organisation of this company is that we now have a much (7) _____ structure, instead of the old hierarchy. Everything used to be kept in-house. Now a lot of work is (8) _____.

So, we're a (9) _____ company now, with fewer (10) _____ of management. For the most part, we work in cross-(11) _____ teams, which gives us much greater (12) _____. And we aim to have an (13) _____ rather than simply loyal workforce. That means we give training and development top priority. In fact, we like to think we're a (14) _____ company. For us, now, (15) _____ is a much more important concept than efficiency and we see product quality as just one part of a (16) _____ quality mindset.'

The financial pages

1 Match the heads (a–h) and tails (1–8) of the following headlines.

  a Disappointing pre-
  b Venture
  c $500m rights
  d Kagumi plan ¥200b stock
  e Fears of another rise in base
  f Contex reject hostile takeover
  g Government crackdown on offshore
  h Record fourth-

  1 rates hit housing market
  2 investments
  3 tax profits for Kovak
  4 bid from Avalon
  5 quarter earnings tipped to top €90m
  6 capital dries up
  7 market flotation
  8 issue to finance acquisition

a	b	c	d	e	f	g	h

2 Find words and phrases in 1 which mean:

  a attempted acquisition by predator company
    _____

  b exceed _____

  c rate of interest charged by banks _____

  d predicted _____

  e strict new laws or measures _____

  f profits for the period October to December
    _____

  g badly effect _____

  h money invested in a foreign country with lower tax _____

  i when a company goes public and issues shares
    _____

  j runs out _____

3 Divide the following into good (✓) and bad (✗) news.

deepening recession ☐   cash bonanza ☐
downturn in demand ☐   sales boom ☐
economic slowdown ☐   market meltdown ☐
windfall profits ☐   housing slump ☐
upswing in the economy ☐

8 Promoting your ideas

The passive

Practice 1 Make the following extracts from reports more formal by:

- using the passive
- replacing the words in **bold** with an adverb from the box
- deleting the subject.

thoroughly	unofficially	tentatively
provisionally	~~roughly~~	currently
generally	unanimously	formally

a Our site engineers estimate that construction will take **about** 18 months to complete.

It *is roughly estimated that construction will take 18 months to complete.*

b They've given us the go-ahead, **but it's not official yet**.

We've _____

_____

c We're considering several options **at the moment**.

Several _____

d **Almost everyone** felt that the project was taking too long.

It _____

_____

e **Everyone** agreed that the proposal required further discussion.

It _____

_____

f We have tested **every part** of the new software.

The _____

_____

g The company will announce the plant closure **at the official press conference** next week.

The _____

_____

h They've OK'd the training budget **at this stage, but they may change their minds**.

The _____

_____

i They suggested that we could import the raw materials, **but stressed that this was only a suggestion**.

It _____

_____

Practice 2 Make the accusations below less personal by removing all references to 'we' and 'you' and making any necessary grammatical changes.

a But we understood that you'd agreed to this.
But it *was understood that this had been agreed.*

b We assumed that you'd accept this.

It _____

_____

c We state quite clearly in the contract that you must make your payments on the first of the month.

It _____

_____

d We presumed that you would comply with current health and safety regulations.

It _____

_____

Practice 3 Rewrite the impersonal e-mail below using only active verbs and replacing some of the more formal words and phrases with friendlier-sounding alternatives from the box.

in this way	each other	get the chance
look forward	pencilled in	up to speed
seeing you there	exchange views	meet
various	from now on	

---

interdepartmental meeting

From: Robert Masters
To: All departmental managers
Cc:
Subject: interdepartmental meeting

It has been decided that an interdepartmental meeting will henceforth be held every month. Heads of department will thus be able to network and generally be brought up to date on recent developments in other departments. Furthermore, they will be given the opportunity to have their voice heard on a number of matters relating to overall corporate strategy.

The first meeting is scheduled for next Thursday. Your attendance would be appreciated.

Robert Masters

---

interdepartmental meeting

From: Robert Masters
To: All departmental managers
Cc:
Subject: interdepartmental meeting

Summary

You use the **passive** when you are more interested in actions, views and decisions than in the people who actually took them. The **passive** sounds more formal and objective than the **active**. For this reason it is frequently used in reports.

If the subject of the **active** sentence is *they, you, one, people, everyone* or *no one*, it is usually unnecessary to refer to it in the **passive** e.g. *No one can do it* becomes *It can't be done ~~by anybody~~.*

When using reporting verbs in the **passive**, you need to insert the word *it* e.g. *They said 'There was absolutely no corruption'* becomes ***It was strongly denied that there had been any corruption.***

The **active** generally sounds more personal than the **passive**. The danger is that in criticisms it can also sound more aggressive, and so in delicate negotiations the **passive** is often preferred to depersonalise potential conflict.

Lexis: Phrasal verbs

Turn on, tune in, drop out.
Timothy Leary, 60s counterculture guru

1 The five most common verbs used in phrasal verbs are: *get, come, go, take* and *put*. Complete each set of sentences using one of these verbs in the Past Simple and a particle from the box. Use the definitions in brackets to help you.

> on   on   on   into   into   out   out   through
> through   off   off   over   over   around
> down   across   for   in   under   up

a We _____ _____ too much work (accepted)

_____ a few details. (wrote)

_____ a bank loan. (obtained)

_____ the project. (got control of)

b They ____ _____ the recession. (survived)

_____ an accounting error. (discovered)

_____ a lot of money. (inherited)

_____ pressure to resign. (received)

c She _____ _____ to talk about training. (proceeded)

_____ the figures with us. (checked)

_____ the idea. (started to dislike)

_____ option B. (chose)

d We _____ _____ the problem in the end. (avoided)

_____ an argument. (became involved in)

_____ a ton of paperwork. (completed)

_____ well. (had a good relationship)

e They ____ _____ hours of work on it. (did)

_____ the meeting. (postponed)

_____ a press release. (issued)

_____ most of the cash. (provided)

2 Some phrasal verbs have three parts. Complete the sentences using the pairs of particles in the box.

> on about + on with   round to + on to
> in for + back to   out of + ahead with
> up against + round to   in for + down as
> along with + in with   up with + up for

a I'm afraid haven't got _____ doing that report yet, but I'll get _____ it as soon as I've finished these spreadsheets.

b I know there's no point going _____ it, but I really don't get _____ this new boss of ours.

c I'm not putting _____ this situation a moment longer – it's time I stood _____ myself!

d I know it's too late to back _____ it now, but I'm really sorry we went _____ this agreement.

e I'm afraid I can't go _____ this – it just doesn't fit _____ our plans.

f We seem to be coming _____ a lot of opposition from marketing at the moment, but hopefully they'll soon come _____ our way of thinking.

g I put _____ that promotion I was telling you about but they haven't got _____ me about it.

h I hear Jon's come _____ a lot of criticism from the board and may have to stand _____ chairman.

9 Relationship-building

Multi-verb sentences

Practice 1 Decide which of the verbs below precede the infinitive with *to*, the *-ing* form or both and tick the appropriate boxes. The first one has been done for you.

	to do	doing		to do	doing
agree	✓	☐	manage	☐	☐
admit	☐	☐	enjoy	☐	☐
suggest	☐	☐	hope	☐	☐
try	☐	☐	miss	☐	☐
put off	☐	☐	avoid	☐	☐
aim	☐	☐	expect	☐	☐
stop	☐	☐	promise	☐	☐
refuse	☐	☐	go on	☐	☐
carry on	☐	☐	fail	☐	☐
remember	☐	☐	dislike	☐	☐

Practice 2 Complete the conversation using the correct form of the verbs in brackets.

A Hi, James. Client meeting overran a bit, did it?

B Mm. And Lucy and I stopped _____ (have) a coffee on the way back.

A Oh, right.

B By the way, did you remember _____ (send) those invoices off?

A What invoices?

B Stuart! I distinctly remember _____ (ask) you to deal with the invoices. They should have gone last week.

A Well, I've been a bit busy trying _____ (fix) this wretched computer!

B OK, look, stop _____ (do) whatever you're doing and deal with them now, would you? And what's wrong with the computer?

A No idea. It keeps crashing.

B Well, have you tried _____ (ask) Callum about it?

A Of course I have. I've been trying _____ (get) through to him all morning. But he's like you, isn't he? He's never in!

Practice 3 Complete the conversation using an appropriate preposition and *-ing* form from the boxes below.

about	about	of	of	in	on	for

being	telling	changing	wanting	making
putting	having			

A Of course, Tim succeeded _____ _____ a complete fool of himself at the drinks party.

B Did he?

A Oh, yes. Well, he will insist _____ _____ those tasteless jokes, won't he? The president's wife was not amused.

B Well, he can forget _____ _____ in for that promotion, then, can't he?

A Hm, not much chance of that here, anyway. You know I complained _____ us _____ to work another weekend?

B Mm, I hear Angela went mad about it.

A Yeah, she practically accused me _____ _____ disloyal to the company! Can you believe it?

B Sounds like her.

A Did I tell you I was thinking _____ _____ jobs?

B No, but I can't say I blame you _____ _____ to get out of this place!

Practice 4 Match the three parts of each sentence below to complete the meeting extract.

A Look, it's high time   not   putting it off, Sam.
B OK, but I'd rather   of   made a decision.
A Well, there's no point   we   rushing this?
B Bill, what's the use   in   make it today.

C OK, OK. I think   I'm   better move on.
B Ricardo, it's   we'd   doing, Sam.
C That's the last thing   we   end this meeting.
B Otherwise, we might   no good   avoiding the issue.
C OK, look. I suggest   as well   take a short break.

Summary

Some verbs can precede both the infinitive and the *-ing* form, but the meaning usually changes (*I **like to** work out twice a week* = I think it's a good idea; *I **like working** out* = I enjoy it).

Some verbs normally followed by the *-ing* form change when there's an indirect object (*I suggest **stopping** now → I suggest we **stop** now*).

When a verb is followed by a preposition other than *to*, the *-ing* form is usually used (*They apologised **for** not **getting** back to us sooner*).

Modal verbs always precede the other verbs in a sentence and are followed by the infinitive without *to* (*You **must** be wishing you'd never come to work here!*).

Certain expressions always precede the *-ing* form: ***It's no good** complaining*; ***There's no point (in)** complaining*; ***What's the use of** complaining*?

A number of expressions take the past form: ***I'd rather** you **didn't***; ***It's time** we **went***.

A number of expressions of intention take the infinitive with *to*: ***I'm planning to** do it later*; ***I've been meaning to** have a word with you*.

Lexis: Social English

The real art of conversation is not only to say the right thing at the right place but to leave unsaid the wrong thing at the tempting moment. *Dorothy Nevill*

1 Complete the conversation extracts from a dinner party using the pairs of verbs in the boxes.

```
reckon + is      makes + think      's + be
see + doing      is + accept      looking + ask
think + happen      got + joking
tells + going      mean + talking
```

A So, what do you (1) _____ is going to _____ with this Ukrainian contract then?

B Good question. You know, something (2) _____ me we're not _____ to get it.

A Oh, really? What (3) _____ you _____ that? It (4) _____ not like you to _____ so pessimistic.

B Well, for one thing, we've gone in way too high. My guess (5) _____ they'll _____ a lower tender.

A Mm. By the way, have some more meat – there's plenty of it. You know, I don't (6) _____ price _____ really the issue.

B No?

A No. I (7) _____, we're _____ long-term here. This is a seven-year project, maybe longer.

B So?

A So, reliability is what they'll be (8) _____ for, if you _____ me. They'll pay more for that.

B You've (9) _____ to be _____. This is one of the most price-sensitive markets in Eastern Europe. The way I (10) _____ it, we'll be _____ well just to get part of the contract. They'll probably get a local firm in to do the main work.

A Hm, well, that's bad news ...

```
knew + coming      might + known
hear + going      stop + get      's + help
shouldn't + saying      suppose + heard
can't + say      had + would      is + getting
```

A I (11) _____ you've _____ the news about Alex?

B About her leaving to join HP? Well, we (12) _____ that was _____, didn't we?

A I suppose so. The word (13) _____ that Eduardo's _____ her job now. You know, I (14) _____ a feeling he _____.

B Mm. I (15) _____ really _____ I'm surprised. He's had his eye on it for a while. And, anyway, if you get engaged to the executive vice-president's daughter, it (16) _____ bound to _____ your career prospects, isn't it?

A He's what? I (17) _____ have _____! He'll (18) _____ at nothing to _____ a promotion.

B Well, you didn't (19) _____ this from me, right, but there's a rumour _____ around that ... well, maybe I (20) _____ be _____ this, but ...

A No, no, go on! I'll go and open another bottle of wine ...

2 Underline eight new expressions in 1 that you could use yourself.

10 Taking decisions

Articles

Practice Complete the text with *a*, *an*, *the* or zero article (/), as necessary.

> They say 'All's fair in __ love and __ war.'
> And when it comes to getting __ good deal,
> __ same is true of __ business. For __
> example, in 1803, __ half of what is now __
> USA was actually bought from __ French for
> three cents __ acre! How were they able to
> get such __ bargain? At __ time, __ Emperor
> Napoleon was preparing to go to __ war with
> __ Britain and was desperate to sell.

Summary

The **indefinite** article is used:

- before a singular countable noun when it is unspecified and mentioned for the first time e.g. *I need **a** holiday.*

- before singular countable nouns in exclamations e.g. *What **a** day!; It was such **a** nuisance!*

- before the names of professions e.g. *She's **an** engineer.*

- before a singular countable noun where a plural could be used to mean the same thing e.g. *There's no such thing as **a** free lunch = There's no such thing as free lunches.*

- to mean *per* when talking about prices, speed, rates etc e.g. *€3 **a** kilo; three times **a** day.*

The **definite** article is used:

- before a noun that has been mentioned before e.g. *I used to have two BMWs and a Lotus, but I had to sell **the** Lotus.*

- before a noun that is later specified in the same sentence e.g. ***The** guy I met in Rio runs his own business.*

- when it is clear from the context what we are referring to e.g. *I'll drop you off at **the** hotel.*

- when the thing referred to is unique e.g. ***the** human race.*

- before an adjective referring to a group e.g. ***the** Dutch.*

The **zero** article is used:

- before mass or abstract nouns e.g. *Greed is good.*

- before the names of most countries. Exceptions include: *the USA, the UK* and *the Netherlands.*

- in certain fixed expressions e.g. *go to war.*

Lexis: Marketing and legal English

Contracts are made to be broken, but a handshake is the law of God. *JR Ewing, character in TV series 'Dallas'*

The marketplace

1 Complete the adjectives by writing in the missing vowels. The adjectives range from positive to negative.

	b_ _m_ng	thr_v_ng	☺
	h_ _lthy	b_ _y_nt	
The market is	v_l_t_l_	_npr_d_ct_bl_	
	w_ _k	sl_gg_sh	
	fl_t	d_pr_ss_d	☹

2 Complete the sentence using some of the adjectives in 1 and information that is true for you.

The market for _____ in _____
is _____, whereas the _____
market is _____.

3 Complete the collocations by writing a noun from the box before each set of three nouns below.

> brand   market   distribution
> marketing   advertising

	mix drive strategy		campaign expenditure agencies
	forces research share		awareness loyalty stretching
	network channels costs		

4 Which terms in 3 are the following examples of?

a Omnicom   Publicis   Doyle Dane Bernbach   Dentsu

_____

b competition   the state of the economy   political stability

_____

c 'the four Ps': product, place, price, promotion

_____

d wholesalers   retailers   sales reps

_____

e Virgin cola   Camel watches   Ferrari sunglasses

_____

5 Listed below are some of the terms commonly used in marketing departments, but the second word in each collocation has been switched with another. Can you switch them back? The first two have been done for you.

market **outlet** ◄	subliminal **relations**
competitive **brand**	price **marketing**
retail **challenger** ◄	niche **analysis**
mass **sensitivity**	public **advertising**
price **market**	consumer **market**
leading **advantage**	permission **war**

6 Which of the terms in 5 refer to:

a the number two player in a market after the market leader? _____

b the importance the customer gives to prices?

_____

c a small number of customers requiring a particular type of product or service?

_____

d the shop or store through which products are sold to the consumer? _____

e a method of persuading consumers to buy by invisible, psychological means? _____

_____

f getting customers' permission before sending information to them? _____

7 The verbs and verb phrases in the box all form strong collocations with *the market*. Put them into the most likely chronological order. One of them has been done for you.

break back into enter be squeezed out of
dominate compete in target

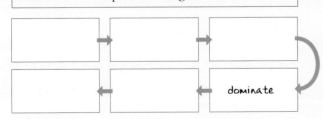

The verbs and verb phrases in the box all form strong collocations with *the competition*. Put them into the most likely chronological order. One of them has been done for you.

take on come up against destroy
succumb to outclass fight back against

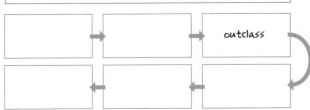

Business law

1 Divide the following into ten things that might lead to a court case.

taxevasionunfairdismissalcriminalnegligenceracial
discriminationbaddebtinsidertradinginsurancefraud
sexualharrassmentfalseaccountingembezzlement

Which of the above mean:

a sacking someone without good reason?

_____

b buying shares using privileged information?

_____

c stealing money that you're responsible for in your job? _____

2 Use the words in the box to make three things that might lead to legal problems.

contract	interests	breach	funds
misuse	conflict		

a _____ of _____
b _____ of _____
c _____ of _____

Which of the above mean:

• to spend company money in an unauthorised way? ☐
• not to abide by a written agreement? ☐
• a situation in which someone cannot make fair decisions because they may be affected by the results? ☐

3 Complete the following using the verbs in the box.

be	take	pay	bring	start
declare	file	settle	appeal	

a _____ someone to court
b _____ legal proceedings against someone
c _____ a lawsuit against someone
d _____ out of court
e _____ found liable for damages
f _____ compensation/a fine
g _____ bankruptcy
h _____ against a verdict
i _____ an action against someone

Which of the above means to reach an agreement without asking the court to decide? ☐

12 E-mailing

Future forms

Practice 1 Present tenses for the future

Match the verbs in **bold** to their main function below.

Our train **leaves** (1) at six. So our taxi**'s coming** (2) at quarter to.

I'm not working (3) this Saturday! It**'s** (4) my wedding anniversary for goodness' sake!

an arrangement ☐   an indisputable fact ☐
a refusal ☐   a schedule or timetable ☐

Practice 2 *will*

1 Match the remarks on the left to the way they were later reported.

  a I**'ll** help you.   He promised to be there.

  b You**'ll** regret it.   He suddenly had an idea.

  c I**'ll** be there.   He offered to help me.

  d I**'ll** try it this way.   He refused to do it.

  e I **won't** do it!   He warned me about it.

2 All the sentences below refer to the future. Complete them using *'ll* (or *will*), as necessary. Use (/) if neither *'ll* (or *will*) is necessary.

  a If I ___ see her, I ___ tell her.

  b I ___ say goodbye before I ___ go.

  c We ___ start the meeting as soon as they ___ get here.

  d I expect they ___ want a coffee when they ___ arrive.

  e The people who ___ get here early ___ get the best seats.

Practice 3 *will be doing*

1 In each pair of sentences below tick the one you are more likely to hear.

  a We**'ll land** at Heathrow in about fifteen minutes.

  b We**'ll be landing** at Heathrow in about fifteen minutes.

  c **Will** you **go** past the chemist's this morning?

  d **Will** you **be going** past the chemist's this morning?

  e Give me five minutes and I**'ll call** you back.

  f Give me five minutes and I**'ll be calling** you back.

  g By the way, I **won't attend** the meeting.

  h By the way, I **won't be attending** the meeting.

2 Match the sentences a–d to what was said next.

  a I don't think I'll go. ☐

  b I don't think I'll be going. ☐

  c Will you go to the post office this afternoon? ☐

  d Will you be going to the post office this afternoon? ☐

  1 At least that's what they've told me.

  2 If you're not too busy, that is.

  3 And if so, could you post this for me?

  4 I certainly don't want to.

Practice 4 Lexical future

In English there are a lot of *be (+ word) to* expressions to talk about future intentions and expectations.

  a We're to

  b We're due to

  c We're about to

  d We're hoping to

  e We're aiming to   meet them to discuss the matter.

  f We're planning to

  g We're intending to

  h We're going to

Which of the sentences above refer to:

1 something which will happen very soon? ☐

2 something which has been formally arranged? ☐

3 something which other people are expecting? ☐

4 something which has already been decided? ☐

5 something we'd like to happen, but it may not? ☐ ☐ ☐ ☐

Practice 5 Future in the past

Put the sentences into the past and match them to what was said next.

a We're going to fly Lufthansa.

_____ ☐

b We're meeting at three.

_____ ☐

c I'm just about to leave.

_____ ☐

d I think we'll have problems.

_____ ☐

1 Can it wait till the morning?

2 But something's come up.

3 But there's been a change of plan.

4 But I never expected this!

Practice 6 Past in the future

Tick the sentences which refer to the future.

a They won't have heard the news yet.

b I'll have missed my chance by then.

c You'll have seen our advertisements, I suppose.

d Another month and I'll have been working here for ten years.

Summary

The **Present Continuous** and *be to* are frequently used to talk about fixed arrangements.

The **Present Simple** is often used either to talk about schedules and timetables or to refer to the future after words like *if, when, as soon as, before,* etc.

There's a range of expressions including *be going to* and *be hoping to* which are used to talk about plans and intentions.

Both *will* and *going to* can be used to make predictions: *will* for opinions and *going to* for more informed predictions.

'll is frequently used to make offers, promises and take initiatives.

will be doing is used to talk about something which will be in progress or which is part of a routine.

will have done and *will have been doing* are used to talk about something which will already be completed at a future time. The continuous form usually emphasises the activity rather than its completion.

Lexis: Prepositional phrases

Preposition: something you should never end a sentence with. *Jill Etherington, journalist*

1 In each box write the preposition that precedes the words and phrases below.

	present first least
	first glance the very most
	any rate the latest
	the same time best

	the whole average the contrary
	second thoughts reflection
	the one hand the other hand
	no account

	practice other words theory
	no circumstances general short
	particular effect some respects
	any case

	a result a general rule
	a matter of fact a last resort

	to now to a point

	the top of my head

2 Complete the meeting extracts using some of the phrases in 1.

A Well, I haven't had time to study them in detail but, at _____ _____, I'd say these figures were quite encouraging.

B Yes, on _____ _____, they're pretty much in line with what we were expecting. In fact, in _____ _____, they're even better.

A Have you been in touch with New York yet?

B As _____ _____ _____ _____, I have.

A And are they in favour of this new initiative?

B One or two of them aren't, but in _____, yes.

A Well, that's something at _____ _____.

A I'm going to authorise this budget increase, but on _____ _____ is this project to go over budget again.

B Yes, OK.

A By the way, how much are the admin costs on this?

B I couldn't tell you off _____ _____ _____ _____ _____, but it shouldn't be more than 30% of the budget at _____ _____ _____.

A 30%! On _____ _____, I think we'd better look at this whole budget again.

A This idea of yours is fine in _____, but in _____, I don't think it'll work.

B But you were all for it when we spoke about it last time!

A On _____ _____, I was as sceptical then as I am now. In _____ _____, even if I supported you, this strategy would only save us a few thousand pounds at _____.

3 Underline the other seven prepositional phrases in 2.

13 Making an impact

Rhetorical techniques

Practice 1 Repetition

Decide which word in each statement could most effectively be repeated after a short pause and underline it. Read the statements aloud to check. The first one has been done for you.

a This is <u>very</u> important.
   ('This is very ... very important.')
b This is a much better option.
c It's now or never.
d There'll always be a market for quality.
e It is here in Europe that the best opportunities lie.
f And today we start to turn this company around.

Rewrite **a** so that you can repeat the word *important*.

_____

_____

Practice 2 Sound repetition

Replace one word in each sentence with a word from the box that starts with the same sound as other words in the sentence.

team	~~better~~	simpler	promotion
willing	past	dynamism	

better
a It's bigger. It's ~~superior~~. And it's British.
b I'm not interested in our history or in our present, but in our prospects for the future.
c We'll reach our targets together as a group.
d We need the right product at the right price with the right advertising.
e We have the drive, energy and determination to succeed.
f Are we prepared to work towards that goal?
g The new system is both more secure and significantly easier to install.

What sound is being repeated in each of the sentences above?

a _ **b** _ **c** _ **d** _ **e** _ **f** _ **g** _

What do sentences **a**, **b**, **d** and **e** all have in common?

_____

_____

Practice 3 Contrasts and opposites

Complete the sentences using the idea of contrast to help you.

a It's not a question of time; it's a qu<u>estion</u> of mo<u>ney</u>.
b If *we* don't seize this opportunity, some_____
   el_____ w_____.

c Tackling a few minor problems now will save us a whole l_____ of ma_____ pr_____ la_____.
d Some people are saying we can't afford to advertise, but I s_____ we c_____ aff_____ n_____ to.
e I'm not saying we're certain to succeed: what I a_____ s_____ is we'll ne_____ kn_____ unt_____ we tr_____.
f Three years ago this company was going nowhere; to_____ it's num_____ o_____ in the ind_____.

Practice 4 Rhetorical questions

Rephrase the statements as negative questions and change the second person plural to the first person.

a This is what you need to be doing.

_____

b You should be learning from your mistakes.

_____

c Deep down, you all know this to be true.

_____

Practice 5 Rhetorical questions + repetition

Complete the following using one word in both gaps.

problem	answer	point	result
chances	advantages		

a So much for the disadvantages, but what about the _____? Well, the _____ are obvious.
b We're losing control of the company. So what's the _____? Clearly, the _____ is to centralise.
c What are our _____ of success? Well, frankly, our _____ are slim.
d So what's the _____ of offering an unprofitable service? The _____ is it makes us look good.
e So what's the basic _____ with this system? The basic _____ is it's far too complicated!
f Three years of R&D and what's the net _____? The net _____ is a product that doesn't work!

Practice 6 Inversion

Rephrase the statements below making any necessary changes in word order.

a This company is not only leaner, it's also greener.

Not only _____

_____

b We mustn't under any circumstances panic.

Under no circumstances _____

_____

c We've done better in Mexico than anywhere.

Nowhere _____

_____

d We'll only be ready to launch after exhaustive tests.

Only after _____

_____

Summary

In adverb + adjective phrases it is more effective to repeat the adverb (Practice 1).

If you want to repeat an adjective, it is more effective to use an adverb before repeating it (Practice 1).

It is more effective to repeat consonants than vowels (Practice 2).

Lists of three are especially memorable (Practice 2).

In a contrast it is more effective to make your main point second (Practice 3).

Asking questions (particularly negative questions) is a more effective way of getting audiences to think than making statements (Practice 4).

Talking about 'us' is a more effective way of building rapport than talking about 'you' (Practice 4).

Rhetorical questions sound more convincing when you answer them using some of the same words (Practice 5).

You can give weight and formality to what you say by sometimes reversing your word order (Practice 6).

Lexis: Metaphor

If this thing starts to snowball, it will catch fire right across the country. *Canadian politician Robert Thompson*

1 Business English is full of metaphor (describing one thing in terms of another). Match the following expressions. Then match them to their metaphorical reference.

takeover	recovery	**war**
ballpark	debate	**fire**
heated	flow	**health**
economic	figure	**water**
cash	battle	**sport**

2 Complete the sentences using the words in the boxes.

growing	coming	pooling	pouring
sowing	trickling		

Money is liquid

a They're _____ millions of dollars into R&D.

b A small amount of cash has started _____ in.

c We should be _____ our resources – together we'd have sufficient capital to fund new research.

Ideas are plants

d After years of work, our plans are finally _____ to fruition.

e There's _____ support for the project – most of the people we spoke to think it's a good idea.

f They're _____ the seeds of doubt in the mind of the customer and, as a result, we're losing sales.

victory	attack	goalposts	guns
stakes	fight	odds	idea

Argument is war

g They shot down my _____ before I'd even had a chance to explain it.

h We came under _____ from the marketing team.

i He didn't put up much of a _____. In fact, he just seemed to give in completely.

j She stuck to her _____ and refused to move an inch.

Competition is sport

k We've scored a significant _____ in the home market.

l The _____ are high – we're risking the future of this company.

m The _____ are against us, but there's still a chance we can succeed.

n We don't know what our objectives are supposed to be because they keep moving the _____.

14 Out and about

Narrative tenses

Practice Read the story about Pepsi A.M. and underline the best grammatical choices.

The Story of Pepsi A.M.

In the late 1980s Pepsi (1) **thought/was thinking** it (2) **identified/had identified** a lucrative gap in the highly competitive soft drinks market: breakfast cola.

Although it (3) **wasn't conducting/hadn't conducted** very thorough market research, it (4) **seemed/was seeming** that a lot of young consumers (5) **switched/were switching** from coffee to cola for breakfast. Pepsi's R&D department promptly (6) **went away/were going away** and (7) **came up with/had come up with** Pepsi A.M., a breakfast cola 'with all the sugar and twice the caffeine'!

But what the company (8) **wasn't realising/hadn't realised** was that the Pepsi drinkers (9) **were/were being** perfectly happy with the normal brand. Pepsi A.M., on the other hand, (10) **sounded/was sounding** like something you would only drink in the morning. Six months after its launch it obviously (11) **didn't sell/wasn't selling**.

Marketing experts (12) **were/had been** quick to point out the company's mistake. What (13) **had it thought of?/had it been thinking of?** At a cost of millions, it (14) **had developed/had been developing** a product nobody actually (15) **needed!/was needing!**

Pepsi A.M. (16) **was/had been** immediately withdrawn.

Summary

You use the **Past Simple** to talk about the main events in a story or to give factual information about the past.

You use the **Past Continuous** to talk about the things happening at the same time as these main events. Events in the **Past Continuous** are often interrupted by those in the **Past Simple**.

You use the **Past Perfect Simple** and the **Past Perfect Continuous** to look back from the time of the story to an earlier time, but the **Past Perfect Continuous** usually emphasises the activity rather than its completion. For this reason, it is not normally used with 'state' verbs like *be, know, seem, understand, mean* and *like*.

Lexis: Storytelling

Storytelling is in the genes.
Gerry Spence, American lawyer

Descriptive power

1   When describing things in a story or anecdote, try to avoid overusing *(not) very + neutral adjective*. Replace the dull descriptions in **bold** with more interesting alternatives from the box.

---

totally pointless   absolutely fabulous
quite inedible   absolutely hilarious
drop-dead gorgeous   absolutely filthy
utterly astonished   absolutely delighted
utterly furious   really fascinating
utterly miserable   absolutely ancient

---

a   The meeting was ~~not very useful~~.
    totally pointless

b   It was a **very interesting** book.

    _____

c   They were **very happy** about the idea.

    _____

d   The food was **not very good**.

    _____

e   The weather was **very bad**.

    _____

f   Their boss was **very good-looking**.

    _____

g   Her apartment was **very nice**.

    _____

h   I was **very surprised**.

    _____

i   The whole thing was **very funny**.

    _____

j   The PCs they were using were **very old**.

    _____

k   He looked **very angry**.

    _____

l   The hotel was **not very clean**.

    _____

2 If you do use neutral adjectives, try using a more interesting adverb to describe them. Match the following pairs of adverbs to a suitable adjective from the box.

| expensive | beautiful | disappointing | funny |
| dangerous | enjoyable | quiet | difficult |

hysterically/hilariously _____

stunningly/breathtakingly _____

outrageously/prohibitively _____

immensely/thoroughly _____

bitterly/terribly _____

deathly/blissfully _____

highly/downright _____

exceedingly/fiendishly _____

The art of exaggeration

Complete the conversation below using the words and phrases in the boxes.

1–7
~~you'll never guess~~   like something out of
is literally   you should have seen
and that's putting it mildly   I'm telling you
me tell you

8–13
I'm not exaggerating   let's just   talk about
you'll never believe   believe me
out of this world

(in the bar)

A Did I tell you about my trip to Sweden?

B No, I don't think so. On business, were you?

A Yeah, but (1) *you'll never guess* the hotel the Swedes had booked us into.

B Somewhere posh, was it?

A No, not exactly. It's called *The Ice Hotel.* Have you heard of it?

B No, I don't think so.

A Well, (2) _____ this place. (3) _____, it was (4) _____ a James Bond movie! Right in the middle of nowhere. And completely built out of snow and ice!

B What? You mean the walls were made of ice!

A Walls, ceilings, doors, tables, beds, chandeliers, the lot! The whole thing (5) _____ made of ice!

B But, hang on. That's not possible, is it? I mean, it would just melt!

A It does. They have to rebuild it from top to bottom every summer.

B You're joking.

A No, it's true. But in the winter it's minus nine or something.

B So how come you didn't freeze to death?

A We nearly did. Let (6) _____, it was like an igloo in there. (7) _____ But (8) _____ say we'd had plenty to warm us up in the bar before we went to bed!

B It's got a bar?

A Of course it has. (9) _____, you need a few vodkas in you if you're going to stay in a place like that!

B I can imagine.

A And they even make their cocktail glasses out of ice so you don't need any in your drink.

B Now, you're having me on.

A No, it's true. (10) _____ All the glasses are made of ice.

B Amazing! But it doesn't sound like the sort of place I'd want to stay in.

A Actually, it wasn't that bad once you got used to it. And it was great at night, lying in bed under a reindeer skin, looking up at the Aurora Borealis lighting up the midnight sky. (11) _____ spectacular; it was (12) _____! And, (13) _____ who we bumped into in the bar one night.

B Who?

A Naomi Campbell and Kate Moss!

B Oh, come on! You mean the models?

A Yeah, apparently, it's a really trendy place, this *Ice Hotel.* It's where all the cool people go.

B Yeah, very funny! So you'd recommend it then?

A Yeah, I would, but make sure you take a bottle of something strong with you, if you know what I mean. Anyway, are you about ready for another?

B Oh, yeah, thanks.

A Whisky and soda, wasn't it?

B Yes, please. No ice …

Reporting

Practice 1 Look at some silly things politicians have said and report each, making grammatical changes where necessary e.g. *have(n't)* → *had(n't)*, *did(n't)* → *had(n't) done*, *I* → *he*, *this* → *that*, etc.

a   We have managed to distribute poverty equally.
Vietnamese Foreign Minister, Nguyen Co Thach

Mr Thach announced that _____

_____

b   I have opinions of my own, strong opinions, but I don't always agree with them.
US President George Bush Sr

President Bush affirmed that _____

_____

c   I will not tolerate intolerance.   *US Senator Bob Dole*

Senator Dole insisted that _____

_____

d   It isn't pollution that is harming the environment – it's the impurities in our air and water that are doing it.   *US Vice President Dan Quayle*

Vice-president Quayle pointed out that _____

_____

_____

e   I haven't committed a crime – what I did is fail to comply with the law.
New York City mayor, David Dinkins

Mayor Dinkins denied that _____

_____

_____

f   I can't believe that we are going to let a majority of the people decide what is best for this state.
US Representative John Travis

Mr Travis said that _____

_____

_____

Practice 2 Read the meeting extracts and write a summary of each using the words in brackets to help you.

Jon   First of all, I'd like to hear your views on this.
(Jon/open/meeting/invite/comments/group)

Jon opened the meeting by inviting comments from the group.

Anna   I don't think this training programme is necessary.
Niels   Neither do I.
(Anna/question/need/training programme. Niels/be/same opinion)

_____

_____

Anna   And what about the training budget for this?
Jon   I haven't made up my mind about that yet.
(Anna/raise/issue/training budget. Jon/reply/ not come/decision)

_____

_____

Niels   So the board's OK about this?
Jon   Absolutely.
(Jon/confirm/project/give/go-ahead)

_____

_____

Jon   How about bringing in consultants?
Anna   I don't think that's a good idea.
(Jon/wonder/if/be/good idea/bring in consultants. Anna/be/against)

_____

_____

Niels   Anna and I think the situation should be reviewed.
(both Anna/Niels/recommend/review/situation)

_____

_____

Niels   Well, I'm very much against these spending cuts.
Jon   But they won't affect your department, Niels.
Anna   Jon's right. These cuts won't affect us.
(there/be/some initial opposition/spending cuts)

_____

_____

Anna   So, you see, Niels, the new system will actually be an improvement.
Niels   Hm, well, on reflection, I suppose you're right.
Jon   So do I take it we're now in agreement on this?
(issue/finally/resolve)

_____

Jon   I think this is an excellent proposal.
Anna   So do I.
Niels   Me too.
(there/be/unanimous agreement/proposal)

_____

Summary

In reports

- it is more important to communicate the basic message than to repeat the exact words that were spoken

- we tend to use the passive when what was said is more important than who said it
  e.g. *It was suggested that …*

- long conversations are often summed up in a simple noun phrase e.g. *There was some disagreement …*

Lexis: Personnel and production

The most critical resource wears shoes and walks out the door around five o'clock every day.
Jonas Ridderstråle and Kjell Nordström, Stockholm School of Economics

Organisational behaviour Combine one word from the box on the left with one word from the box on the right to complete each sentence below.

human	prospects
incentive	burnout
promotion	benefits
appraisal	management
fringe	theory
track	scheme
leadership	record
executive	qualities
sickness	interview
selection	procedure
motivation	record
change	satisfaction
job	resources

a These days people talk about _____ rather than personnel.

b Stress and overwork are both common causes of _____.

c Rates of pay, recognition and opportunities for personal growth contribute to overall _____.

d Demotivated employees tend to have a fairly poor _____ and are prone to absenteeism.

e An _____ is one way of monitoring employee performance and personal development.

f _____ include health insurance, a company car and contributory pension plan.

g For hardworking and ambitious young managers there are excellent _____.

h To get into Harvard Business School you have to go through a rigorous _____.

i Essential _____ include decisiveness and the ability to get the most out of employees.

j The successful applicant must have an MBA and an excellent _____ in marketing.

k Many companies operate an _____ – commissions, bonuses, and so on.

l According to one _____, giving people more autonomy is better than a higher salary.

m In a global market in which nothing stays the same, _____ has a crucial role to play.

Operations management

1 Listed below are some of the terms commonly used in production departments, but the second word in each collocation has been switched with another. Can you switch them back? The first two have been done for you.

raw **goods**	zero **regulations**
supply **shift**	quality **production**
assembly **control**	safety **defects**
stock **line**	carrying **time**
finished **materials**	lead **costs**
night **chain**	batch **circle**

2 Which of the collocations in 1 refer to:

a unprocessed materials? _____

b the cost of storing and insuring stock?

_____

c the time between planning something and putting it into action? _____

d manufacturing an article in groups rather than singly? _____

e where the factory workers put the products together? _____

f factory workers who start work at the end of the working day? _____

g a group of workers and managers who meet to discuss quality? _____

h a series of suppliers selling on raw materials and finished components to manufacturers?

_____

17 Negotiating deals

Diplomacy and persuasion

Practice Look at the negotiation extracts. Make the direct remarks more diplomatic and persuasive using the words in brackets to help you.

Negotiation 1

A This is still too expensive.
(afraid/would still/a little out of/price range)

I'm afraid that would still be a little out of our price range.

B Well, how much do you want to pay?
(what sort/figure/did/in mind)

_____

_____

A $12 per unit.
(were thinking/somewhere/the region of/$12 per unit)

_____

_____

B I can't go as low as that.
(be honest/not/a position/quite/low/this stage)

_____

_____

Negotiation 2

A You said we'd get 90 days' free credit.
(were promised/90 days' free credit)

_____

_____

B Yes, but you said you'd be placing a larger order.
(respect/was understood/rather larger)

_____

_____

A Look, this is getting us nowhere. We want free credit.
(doesn't seem/getting/very far//afraid/must insist/free credit)

_____

_____

B Well, I can't offer you that unless you increase your order.
(unfortunately/unable/offer/you're prepared/slightly)

_____

_____

Negotiation 3

A We need a commitment from you today.
(had/hoping/some kind)

_____

_____

B Impossible! We're still unhappy about these service charges.
(this point/might/a bit difficult//not entirely/service charges)

_____

_____

A But you said you were OK about those!
(was assumed)

_____

_____

B Not at all. Look, I think we should go over these figures again.
(afraid//shouldn't we/figures/again)

_____

_____

Summary

Modal verbs (_would/might/could_, etc) are often used to soften the verb.

Modifiers are common (e.g. _a little difficult_).

Continuous forms keep your options open (e.g. _We were wondering; We had been hoping_).

Introductory softeners (e.g. _I'm afraid_) warn that bad news is coming!

Negative adjectives like _expensive_ are often avoided.

seem is common (e.g. _We don't seem to agree._)

There's a lot of approximation (e.g. _sort of_).

Qualifying phrases are common (e.g. _at the moment_).

Alternatives are preferred to _can't_ and _won't_.

The passive sounds less like an accusation (not _You promised us …_, but _We were promised …_).

Suggestions are often phrased as negative questions (e.g. _Wouldn't it be better to …?_).

Lexis: Negotiations

A negotiator should observe everything. You must be part Sherlock Holmes, part Sigmund Freud.
Victor Kiam, CEO of Remington

Sounding out your opponent Complete the questions using the prepositions in the box.

for	about	of	with	at	towards

What sort of …

a figure were you thinking _____?

b terms would you be happy _____?

c discount were you hoping _____?

d delivery time are we talking _____?

e time-scale are we looking _____?

f deadline are we working _____?

Discussing terms

1 These are all key points you may want to discuss in a negotiation. Write in the missing vowels.

pr_c_
d_sc__nt
cr_d_t
v_l_m_
tr_nsp_rt_t__n
p_ck_g_ng
d_c_m_nt_t__n
g__r_nt__

c_ns_gnm_nts
m__nt_n_nc_
d_l_v_ry t_m_
p_ym_nt t_rms
sp_r_ p_rts
_xch_ng_ r_t_
_ft_r-s_l_s s_rv_c_
p_n_lty cl__s_s

2 Complete the negotiator's proposal using the words and phrases in 1. Which one is not needed?

_____

'Well, on a repeat order of this (1) _____ – 20,000 units – we'd be able to offer you what I think you'll agree is a very generous

(2) _____ of 17%. I think you'd also find our (3) _____ _____ extremely favourable – 120 days' (4) _____, of course – and we'd cover any fluctuations in the (5) _____ _____ between the dollar and the euro.

'We'd also be prepared to include in our quoted (6) _____ all (7) _____ costs. That is to say, we'd handle the shipping charges, insurance and all the necessary (8) _____ to save you doing the paperwork yourself. We would have to use the same carrier for each delivery, however, which means the (9) _____ _____ would be 14 days. I hope that's acceptable to you.

'Now, all our products come with a three-year (10) _____ which includes full (11) _____ and (12) _____ _____. There's also a free 24-hour customer helpline, so your customers would be getting excellent (13) _____ _____.

'I think we could also be fairly flexible on (14) _____ if you decided to increase or reduce your order from time to time.

'So, that just leaves the question of (15) _____. We normally use styrofoam containers …'

Negotiating procedure

Complete the phases of a negotiation using the nouns in the box. Two of them have been done for you.

~~strategy~~	deadlock	interests	champagne	breakthrough	~~procedure~~	concessions
options	table	atmosphere	phase	position	details	proposals	time-out

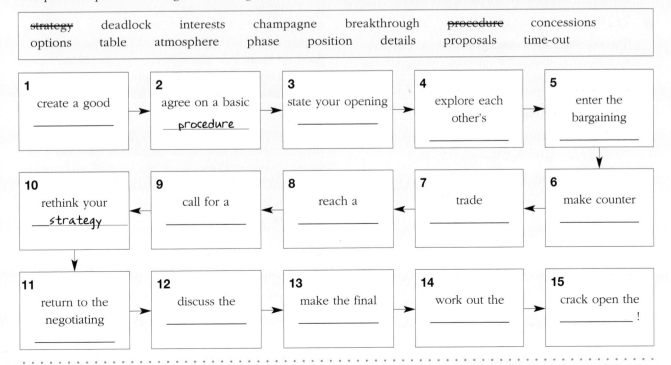

1 create a good _____

2 agree on a basic _procedure_

3 state your opening _____

4 explore each other's _____

5 enter the bargaining _____

6 make counter _____

7 trade _____

8 reach a _____

9 call for a _____

10 rethink your _strategy_

11 return to the negotiating _____

12 discuss the _____

13 make the final _____

14 work out the _____

15 crack open the _____!

2 Exchanging information

Fluency (p11, ex5)

Speaker A

1 Read out the following report to your partner. There are seven discrepancies in it (marked in **bold**). Can your partner spot them? If not, keep reading. Apologise for or justify any discrepancies your partner points out. If you lose your place in the text, ask your partner: 'Where was I?'

Report:

World trade fair

Our exhibition stand at the World Trade Fair in Munich was very successful again this year, attracting visitors from all over **Munich**. Although this was **our first appearance** at the Fair, our people did a great job and handed out **nearly three** brochures.

We met a group of Austrian business people at the **Frankfurt** Hilton, where we were staying, and arranged a formal meeting with them by the **pool**. They were very interested in our products and said they would e-mail us as soon as they got back to **Australia**.

Apparently, next year the Fair is being held outside Europe for the first time – **Paris** here we come!

2 Now listen to your partner reading out a report. There are also seven discrepancies in it. Can *you* spot them? Remain polite no matter how confused your partner seems!

> **Useful language:**
>
> Sorry, I thought you said …
>
> Hold on, didn't you just say …?
>
> Wait a minute. You just said …, didn't you?

1 Business or pleasure?

The hot buttons game (p9, ex6)

Speaker A

You're at a cocktail party with Speaker B, a very important client. You've been having a great time so far, but they don't seem to be having much fun. You don't know them very well socially, so try to find out what they're interested in – their 'hot buttons'. There's a list of conversation starters and topics on page 9. Keep changing the topic until you hit one of their hot buttons – they must be interested in something! And try to remain cheerful and positive no matter how dull and unfriendly they may seem!

The hot buttons game (p9, ex7)

Speaker A

You've just enjoyed the best annual dinner your company has ever laid on. Maybe it's because you've taken full advantage of all the delicious wines on offer, but you seem to be very talkative tonight. Look at the list of topics on page 9 and choose a favourite – your 'hot button'. Try to engage the person sitting next to you, Speaker B, in a conversation on this topic, which you're sure they must be as interested in as you. If other topics come up, just deal with them quickly and try to get back to what you really want to talk about.

2 Exchanging information

Breaking the bad news (p15, ex2)

Read your new board's proposals opposite. Agree in your group which one(s) you are going to submit at the interdepartmental meeting. Most of the news is not good, so break it as gently as you can. Put forward each proposal one step at a time. Pause between each step for questions and reactions from the other people at the meeting.

Invite discussion of each proposal and take notes on any comments or alternative suggestions for your follow-up report. Even though you yourself may not be in favour of the proposal(s) you put forward, you should at least initially show loyalty to your new bosses by sounding positive.

Proposal 1: Positive discrimination
- Board alarmed at low number of women in management positions
- Men currently outnumber women 13:1
- Plan to introduce policy of positive discrimination
- For 18-month trial period only women appointed to management positions
- No applications for promotion from male employees accepted
- Possible 'strategic demotion' of men to create more opportunities for women

Proposal 2: Work environment
- A lot of staff (35%) complaining about feeling tired and stressed
- Board thinks one of main causes may be poor work environment
- Feng shui expert called in – recommendations include radical changes to office layout
- Reception area to be turned into a water-garden to create positive 'chi' (energy)
- Internal walls to be removed to improve 'channels of communication'
- Desks ideally to be moved during the year to remain 'in harmony with the seasons'

Proposal 3: Rightsizing
- Board feels that company is overstaffed – streamlining obviously necessary
- Up to a third of current staff may have to go
- Action must be taken quickly to prevent bad work atmosphere
- No time to evaluate performance of all members of staff
- Board suggesting a LIFO (last-in-first-out) procedure
- People with the company for less than a year laid off first

Proposal 4: Travel budget
- Board deeply concerned about cost of business travel (nearly $3m last year)
- Insist on 60% cut in travel budget
- Propose three main courses of action (see below)
- All flights from now on to be economy class (no exceptions)
- Motels and two-star hotels to be used in preference to four-star
- Meal allowance to be reduced to $20 a day (no alcoholic drinks)

Proposal 5: Language training
- Board keen to market products more internationally
- English now language of international business but many staff (65%) already speak it
- In board's view, Chinese is business language of the future
- Mandarin, however, is one of world's most difficult languages
- Therefore, compulsory Chinese lessons (in employees' own time) to start immediately
- All new staff to be encouraged to accept two-year transfer to new subsidiary in Beijing

Proposal 6: Company cars
- Complaints from junior managers that sales reps get free company cars and they don't
- Board therefore rethinking whole policy on company vehicles
- Overall increase in vehicle budget not an option
- Currently reps drive Ford diesel estate cars (unnecessarily large)
- Proposal – all staff at assistant manager level and above to be issued with a company scooter
- More environmentally friendly (in line with new 'green initiative') and quicker in city traffic

Proposal 7: Customer relationship management
- Board extremely dissatisfied with amount of customer complaints
- Complaints both about products themselves and general quality of service
- In future, board would like to see staff take more personal responsibility for their work
- Rewards for fault-free production and excellent service clearly not motivating staff
- New proposal is that a system of penalties be introduced
- All product faults to be paid for by staff and bad service to result in immediate dismissal

Proposal 8: Team spirit
- Board strongly believes not enough team spirit
- Problem particularly noticeable at the production plant
- Obviously takes time to build a team, but certain things could be introduced right away
- Has been suggested a company song could be sung every morning
- The idea has proved very popular at big companies like IBM, General Electric and Mitsubishi
- Second idea is that all staff (including managers) wear a uniform in company colours – orange and green

1 Business or pleasure?

The hot buttons game (p9, ex6)

Speaker B

You're at a cocktail party with Speaker A, one of your many suppliers. You generally hate this kind of event and so far you've had a miserable evening. Look at the list of topics on page 9 and choose just two you are prepared to have a conversation about – your 'hot buttons'. If Speaker A tries to engage you in conversation on any topic apart from your hot buttons, say very little. Do nothing to change the topic, but show enthusiasm if one of your hot button topics comes up.

The hot buttons game (p9, ex7)

Speaker B

You've been at your company's annual dinner for the last five hours and are utterly exhausted. The person sitting next you seems to want to talk non-stop about the same boring topic. As they're an important client, you can't just ignore them or tell them to shut up. So, be polite, but keep trying to steer the conversation towards something more interesting. Use the list of conversation starters and topics on page 9.

2 Exchanging information

Fluency (p11, ex5)

Speaker B

1 Listen to your partner reading out a report. There are seven discrepancies in it. Can you spot them? Remain polite no matter how confused your partner seems!

> **Useful language:**
>
> Sorry, I thought you said …
>
> Hold on, didn't you just say …?
>
> Wait a minute. You just said …, didn't you?

2 Read out the following report to your partner. There are also seven discrepancies in it (marked in **bold**). Can *they* spot them? If not, keep reading. Apologise for or justify any discrepancies your partner points out. If you lose your place in the text, ask your partner: 'Where was I?'

Report: Korean negotiations

We held our first meeting with the Koreans two months ago at their headquarters in **Osaka**. Since then we've had **twelve weeks** of tough negotiations. There were some cultural difficulties at first. Of course, we've never done business in the **Middle East** before.

They were very positive about our products, although they weren't happy with **the design, performance, price and maintenance costs**. Initially, they were demanding a discount on orders of over 10,000 units of 17%, but we finally managed to beat them down to **18**.

We haven't heard anything from them so far, but the e-mail they sent **this morning** looks promising – an initial order of **a dozen units**.

3 Material world

Quiz answers (page 16, ex1)

1 b	2 b	3 b	4 b	5 c	6 a	7 a
8 c	9 d	10 b	11 d	12 c		

Billionaire fact file

- 298 of the world's 450 billionaires are American and so are 2.5 million of the 7.2 million millionaires.

- Real estate in Eaton Square is currently worth £10,775 per m² and the average price of a flat there is £1.5m.

- Famous residents of Santa Barbara's 'Millionaires' Row' include Kevin Costner, Michael Douglas and John Travolta.

- Hiring a jumbo jet for an hour and spending a night in the Bridge Suite both work out at exactly $25,000, but a Harvard MBA would set you back nearly three times that in tuition fees.

- To get your private helicopter pilot's licence you'd need to spend around $15,000 on flying lessons.

- The Chopard watch would cost you a staggering $25m, but the Grachvogel dress a mere £1m.

- The fire-damaged Hendrix guitar went at auction for $300,000.

- British investor Joseph Lewis once paid €2.2m for a round of golf with Tiger Woods.

- The Royal Family of Qatar have a yacht as expensive as Ellison's, but theirs is not for sale!

- The Aston Martin DB5 is the car featured in the James Bond Movie *Goldfinger*.

- The record-breaking Van Gogh was the *Portrait of Doctor Gachet*, sold at Christie's in 1990.

4 Voice and visuals

Giving feedback (p22, ex4)

Speaker B: Presenter

You work for a major management consultancy and have just given a presentation to an important Taiwanese client. The presentation didn't go very well and unfortunately your boss was in the audience.

You are meeting your boss now, and are not expecting very good feedback. Make it clear that the disaster wasn't entirely your fault. Defend yourself using the following information, and assure your boss that this will never happen again.

- You've been asking your boss for a new laptop for ages – the one you've got just can't handle PowerPoint properly.
- You've been on the road for four weeks and are completely exhausted – this is your tenth major presentation. To make matters worse, the laundry ruined your best suit and left you with virtually nothing to wear.
- You've no excuse for the poor handouts. It was obviously a printer problem and you forgot to check them.
- Nobody told you your Taiwanese audience hardly spoke any English – by the time you realised you were halfway through your talk.
- Some of your jokes may not have translated very well, but you were just trying to break the ice.
- You're sure the video you were going to use was stolen from your hotel bedroom.
- No one checked the microphone: the amplifier was turned down much too low.

> **Useful language:**
>
> How was I supposed to know …?
>
> It's not my fault. You should have …
>
> Somebody should have …
>
> It might have helped if …
>
> Look, I'm not trying to make excuses, but …
>
> I can hardly be blamed for …*ing*, can I?
>
> Rest assured, it won't happen again.

5 Problems on the phone

Fluency (p27, ex5)

Speaker B

If you don't know Speaker A well, swap lists of the following with them before you start your telephone conversation:

- your partner's name, job and main interest
- your children's names, ages and main interests
- when and where you went on your last holiday
- your own main interest
- your favourite sport (spectator or player?)
- the name of a close colleague
- a problem you've been having at work recently

You are the sales director of Möbelkunst, a designer furniture manufacturer in Berlin. Your stylish products are getting rave reviews in the press, but business in Germany has not been good lately. Fortunately, you have recently won some very big overseas orders – one of them with Mi Casa, a large chain of furniture stores in Mexico. The only problem is Speaker A, Mi Casa's director of purchasing, who seems to like phoning you rather too often for no particular reason.

It's 5pm on Friday afternoon. You would normally be getting ready to go home soon, but today there's been a crisis to deal with – your factory in Potsdam has just turned out 1,000 leather sofas in bright pink (rather than dark red) by mistake. You're still trying to sort a solution out with your plant manager. The last thing you need now is any interruptions.

9 Relationship-building

Questionnaire analysis (pp46-47, ex5)

How you network in specific situations will, of course, be influenced by many factors, but, in general, the most effective strategy will be: **1a**, **2c**, **3b**, **4b**, **5c** and **6c**.
1c, **2b**, **5b** and **6a** could be risky.
3a and **4c** might be unfair to other people.
1b, **3c**, **4a** and **5a** may show a certain lack of assertiveness.

11 Branded planet

Discussion (p60, ex3)

Answers

a fact   **b** hoax   **c** fact   **d** fact   **e** hoax   **f** fact
g fact   **h** hoax

4 Voice and visuals

Quiz answers (p20, ex2)

1 12 $\frac{1}{2}$ seconds
2 55% is visual; 38% is vocal; 7% is verbal
3 Mel Gibson; Julia Roberts
4 400,000; 400%; 85%
5 b is false

4 Voice and visuals

Giving feedback (p22, ex4)

Speaker A: Boss

You are a senior partner in a major management consultancy. You have just attended a presentation by one of your best consultants to an important Taiwanese client. Unfortunately, the presentation was an absolute disaster from start to finish.

You forced a smile during the presentation but are now going to tell Speaker B exactly what you thought of their performance. Base your criticisms on the following information. Try to end on a positive note by making some suggestions for future presentations.

- Speaker B was wearing a T-shirt and jeans. The Taiwanese must have felt deeply insulted.
- You could hardly hear a word Speaker B said.
- They made no attempt to modify their English for a foreign audience.
- The PowerPoint slides were not working properly – it all looked very unprofessional.
- The handouts were virtually illegible. There was no excuse for this: there was plenty of time to prepare.
- You have no idea what happened to the video you were expecting to see.
- You nearly died when they cracked a joke about China. The Taiwanese left the room in silence, clearly not amused.

> **Useful language:**
>
> Why did/didn't you …?
>
> You should(n't) have …
>
> Couldn't you at least have …?
>
> Don't you think it would have been a good idea to …?
>
> Well, anyway, in future I suggest you …
>
> And next time – if there is a next time – just make sure you …

5 Problems on the phone

Fluency (p27, ex5)

Speaker A

If you don't know Speaker B well, swap lists of the following with them before you start your telephone conversation:

- your partner's name, job and main interest
- your children's names, ages and main interests
- when and where you went on your last holiday
- your own main interest
- your favourite sport (spectator or player?)
- the name of a close colleague
- a problem you've been having at work recently

You are director of the purchasing department for Mi Casa, a large chain of furniture stores in Mexico. You like to get in touch with your suppliers from time to time – not necessarily to do business, just to maintain the relationship. It's 10am on Friday morning, most of your week's work is done and the weekend is fast approaching. Phone Speaker B, the sales director of Möbelkunst, a designer furniture manufacturer in Berlin, for a little chat.

Keep the conversation going by asking lots of questions (using Speaker B's list as a starting point). You don't really want to do any business today, but Möbelkunst's stylish chairs, tables and lamps have been very popular with your customers. If the terms were right, you might want to increase your order – even double it – for a trial period.

6 Leading meetings

In the chair (p34, ex1)

Speaker A

Meeting 1: Genetic profiling (chair)

You have been asked by head office to chair a meeting on the possible introduction of genetic testing for job applicants at all levels. Your company already insists on a medical when people apply for a job, as well as psychometric tests and checks on possible criminal records. Now they think a genetic profile would help to reduce the risk of employing or promoting people with potentially serious diseases and mental health problems. The test would probably be voluntary – this hasn't been fully discussed with the legal department yet – but refusal to undergo it may affect a candidate's chance of employment or promotion.

You have read that vulnerability to stress, alcoholism and strokes – the three main causes of people being off work for prolonged periods – are all to some extent genetically inherited, but the idea of genetic testing does seem quite drastic and is bound to provoke a certain amount of hostility.

Leader's brief: Open the meeting, inform those present of HQ's proposal, make sure everyone gets a chance to speak and no one dominates. Try to avoid digressions and keep the meeting short. Give your own opinion only after everyone else has spoken and try to reach a decision on what recommendations to make to HQ.

Meeting 2: Employee surveillance (in favour)

You have heard a rumour that head office is planning to introduce a system of checking up on employees using PC monitoring software and closed circuit television (CCTV). You are about to attend a meeting to discuss the subject. At the moment you are firmly in favour of the idea, but listen to what the other participants have to say before finally making up your mind. You are sure that huge amounts of company time and money are being wasted by employees accessing gaming and adult websites during working hours. You've even heard some of the male staff joking about it. An article you read in *Business Week* claims that employees who play computer games whilst at work cost US firms $100 billion a year – or 2% of GDP. You also remember the famous case of Chevron, who, by failing to monitor computer use, ended up being sued by four female employees who had suffered sexual harassment through the internal e-mail system. The company finally had to pay out $2.2 million in compensation.

Hidden agenda: You've heard that a junior manager in your department, who seems to have his sights set on your job, spends hours in private chatrooms on company time. In order to catch such people, you think the computer surveillance should be covert.

Meeting 3: Alternative management training (against)

You have heard a rumour that head office is planning to introduce a series of alternative management training courses for all levels of staff. You are about to attend a meeting to discuss the subject. At the moment you are not keen on the idea, but listen to what the other participants have to say before finally making up your mind. Frankly, you don't believe that 'fads' like this represent very good value for money. A friend of yours works for a firm that sent him and his colleagues to a Benedictine monastery to learn about 'Morality in the Workplace'. Predictably, it was thought to be a complete waste of time. You've also heard about weird courses offered by drama groups, orchestras, circuses, the army and even the prison service where executives spent a week in jail to build team spirit.

Hidden agenda: You have a close friend who is in charge of in-company training at a prestigious business school in the United States. If your company booked a course, you personally might get some kind of 'thank you'.

17 Negotiating deals

Fluency (p90, ex1c)

Extra information for second negotiation

You and the other speaker are ex-neighbours and very good friends. Your kids even used to play together. You both moved to different areas of the city about six months ago and meant to keep in touch, but, what with work and settling into new homes, you just haven't had the time.

6 Leading meetings

In the chair (p34, ex1)

Speaker B

Meeting 1: Genetic profiling (against)

You have heard a rumour that head office is planning to introduce genetic testing for future job applicants. You are about to attend a meeting to discuss the subject. At the moment you are strongly against the idea, but listen to what the other participants have to say before finally making up your mind. One thing you are fairly sure of is that genetic screening without consent would be illegal under civil law. You certainly consider it unethical. Also, since some of the conditions screened for (such as sickle cell disease) affect mostly black people, and others (such as breast and ovarian cancer) solely women, you are concerned that the tests could easily lead to racial and sexual discrimination.

Hidden agenda: There is a genetically inherited disease that runs in your family. Although you do not have the condition yourself, you are worried that it might show up in a genetic test and that you might be discriminated against if you applied for promotion.

Meeting 2: Employee surveillance (chair)

You have been asked by head office to chair a meeting on the possible introduction of surveillance and electronic security equipment to check up on employees of the company. In your business confidentiality is essential as many of your workers are dealing with highly classified information. Of course, a lot of your company files are encrypted, but leaks still happen. HQ is also concerned about the amount of time employees appear to be spending making personal phone calls and sending private e-mails. Details of what system to install have not yet been fully discussed, but suggestions include Internet monitoring software, random phone tapping and closed circuit television (CCTV) throughout the building.

You yourself are a little alarmed at the number of unnecessary e-mails sent back and forth over the company intranet and have overheard staff making international phone calls that were clearly not business. Monitoring Internet access and phone use is common practice in many companies these days and you don't see why anyone would object unless they had something to hide. CCTV seems a bit radical, however.

Leader's brief: Open the meeting, inform those present of HQ's proposal, make sure everyone gets a chance to speak and no one dominates. Try to avoid digressions and keep the meeting short. Give your own opinion only after everyone else has spoken and try to reach a decision on what recommendations to make to HQ.

Meeting 3: Alternative management training (in favour)

You have heard a rumour that head office is planning to introduce a series of alternative management training courses for all levels of staff. You are about to attend a meeting to discuss the subject. At the moment you are fairly enthusiastic about the idea, but listen to what the other participants have to say before finally making up your mind. You already have an MBA, but have never found what you learnt at business school much use in the real world of business. On the other hand, an ex-colleague of yours went on a course to learn about negotiating technique from an Olympic gold medal-winning judo player and says it was the best business training she's ever had.

Hidden agenda: You have a favourite cousin who runs a company that teaches business people creativity through song, poetry and drama workshops, stand-up comedy and exotic sports like Zen archery and rodeo riding. He's not doing too well at the moment and could do with more clients.

8 Promoting your ideas

Answers (p41, ex1)

USA – Extract 3

Germany – Extract 1

Japan – Extract 4

UK – Extract 5

France – Extract 6

Kuwait – Extract 2

5 Problems on the phone

Fluency (p29, ex7)

Speaker B

At the end of each conversation, give Speaker A a score out of ten for **a** helpfulness and **b** assertiveness.

1 Speaker A will phone you with a problem. You are very busy at the moment (you decide what you're doing) but try to give them some advice. If you can't, suggest someone they could phone who might be able to help.

2 You are Speaker A's boss. It's 6pm and you still have a mountain of papers on your desk to go through before the morning (you decide what sort of papers they are). Phone Speaker A and ask them if they'd mind staying on for an hour or so to help you out. Be diplomatic but don't take no for an answer – unless they can suggest someone else.

3 Speaker A has just been promoted and you are now their boss. But a colleague from an overseas division of your company (you decide who) is going to spend the next three months working on an international project in your division and they need to be provided with a suitable office. Speaker A's office would be ideal (you decide why). Phone them and try to get their agreement without causing any bad feeling.

4 You have been working on an important report for nine months. Because of a lot of unforeseen difficulties and complications (you decide what) you are a month behind schedule and now need six, rather than two, more weeks to finish it. On completion of the report you are due to present your findings to senior management and you think they will be impressed. Much to your annoyance, however, you think your boss, Speaker A, is going to try to speed things up by bringing in someone else to help you finish the job and take half the credit for all your hard work.

9 Relationship-building

Fluency (p47, ex6)

Speaker B

You are
- the chief purchasing manager for MacGregor Sports Goods, based in St Andrews, Scotland
- responsible for 37 stores in Scotland, selling sports equipment but specialising in golf and fishing supplies
- at an international conference in Dublin, which has been quite enjoyable so far – apart from the lashing rain!
- staying at the Fitzwilliam Hotel until tomorrow afternoon – you're flying back to Scotland at 6pm

You have
- a lot of experience in the golf business, having previously run a golfing holiday company in Edinburgh
- a relative who is a famous sports personality (you decide who)
- met Speaker A before at the Golf World Expo in Marbella, Spain, but you're not sure what they do

You think
- Speaker A is based in the USA – California, perhaps?

You want
- to reintroduce yourself to Speaker A and find out what they do

---

Useful language:

Hello. I don't know if you remember me, but …

What do you do, by the way?

Well, in that case, perhaps …

---

9 Relationship-building

A dinner invitation (p51, ex1)

Host: Ulterior motive

You're considering promoting your guest to a more senior post (you decide what) at your company's subsidiary in Melbourne. You are very impressed with your guest's work record and general management ability, but you haven't made up your mind yet about the promotion. So, drop a few hints during the evening and see what the reaction is. Don't be too specific at this stage and be ready to change the subject if things don't go according to plan!

6 Leading meetings

In the chair (p34, ex1)

Speaker C

Meeting 1: Genetic profiling (in favour)

You have heard a rumour that head office is planning to introduce genetic testing for future job applicants. You are about to attend a meeting to discuss the subject. At the moment you are basically in favour of the idea, but listen to what the other participants have to say before finally making up your mind. You know that 350 million working days are lost each year in the EU alone through illness – stress being the cause of 41 million of those. UK companies lose £13 billion annually because of employees going off sick. If people with potential social problems (such as alcoholism or drug abuse) could be screened out at the job application stage, it would make for a healthier workforce and could save the firm millions.

Hidden agenda: Your department has been particularly affected by people taking sick leave. At the moment you are trying to cope without three of your key managers – one of them, you suspect, has a drink problem.

Meeting 2: Employee surveillance (against)

You have heard a rumour that head office is planning to introduce a system of checking up on employees using PC monitoring software and closed circuit television (CCTV). You are about to attend a meeting to discuss the subject. At the moment you are very much against the idea, but listen to what the other participants have to say before finally making up your mind. You firmly believe that a good work atmosphere is built on trust and that such security measures should only be taken when there is strong evidence to suggest that company facilities are being abused. Moreover, you suspect that phone taps, video cameras and PC monitoring may just be the thin end of the wedge. You've heard in some companies workers have also been videotaped in toilets and locker rooms and investigators have even been hired to follow them home. What next? Electronic tagging devices? Implants?

Hidden agenda: You often surf the Internet on your office PC during coffee and lunch breaks (never during working hours, however) and regularly log on to chatroom channels. You see this as valuable networking and not an abuse of company Internet access. Still, if Internet monitoring was introduced, you'd prefer the company to announce the fact and not investigate past use.

Meeting 3: Alternative management training (chair)

You have been asked by head office to chair a meeting on the possible introduction of a series of alternative management training courses. In the past, your firm has sent junior members of staff on practical office skills courses and middle and senior management on executive courses at several top business schools. But the feedback has sometimes been rather negative. As people at all levels in your company require a high degree of creativity, HQ is proposing to hire the services of a number of 'arts and business' companies to help employees 'think outside the box'.

Suggestions so far include: working with a renowned artist to produce a 5m x 30m company mural to be displayed at HQ; putting on a variety show with the help of professional actors with all members of staff taking part in song, dance and comedy routines; choreographing a modern ballet to dramatise the challenges facing the company; and music lessons from professional musicians leading to an end-of-year company jazz session. Many big-name companies have found similar training to be highly enjoyable and successful – why not your company too?

Leader's brief: Open the meeting, inform those present of HQ's proposal, make sure everyone gets a chance to speak and no one dominates. Try to avoid digressions and keep the meeting short. Give your own opinion only after everyone else has spoken and try to reach a decision on what recommendations to make to HQ.

11 Branded planet

The name game (p61, ex1)

(the author's suggestions)
Your choice of name will principally depend on:
- the sound of the name (and if there are different ways of pronouncing it, could that be a problem?)
- the appearance of the letters (some letters have proven customer appeal: Zs and Xs, for example)
- linguistic and cultural associations (does the word look or sound like another word in your language or the target market's language?)

For an English-speaking market, the following names would be effective:
1 Zyex – visually attractive combination of letters; sounds quite masculine and 'techie'
2 Ios – short and simple; sounds pure, classical and feminine (Eos was the Ancient Greek goddess of the dawn)
3 Areon – suggests lightness, speed and mobility
4 Zantis – has exotic associations (By**zanti**um, Atl**antis**) but, if said quickly, sounds quite like 'scientist'

5 Problems on the phone

Fluency (p29, ex7)

Speaker A

At the end of each conversation, give Speaker B a score out of ten for **a** helpfulness and **b** assertiveness.

1 You are having problems with your computer – it either won't do something you want it to or it's just done something you definitely didn't want it to (you decide which). Phone Speaker B and see if they can give you any advice. If not, ask them who you should phone instead.

2 Speaker B, your boss, will phone you with a problem. It's 6pm and you are just on your way out of the office when the phone rings. You've arranged to go out with a few colleagues this evening (you decide when and where). This is the fifth time this month your boss has held you up right at the end of the day.

3 You have just been promoted and Speaker B is now your boss. You particularly like your great new office (you decide why), which is exactly what you need to do your new job (you decide why). Someone told you today that a colleague from an overseas division of your company may be coming to work at your division for a few months and you are waiting for your boss to phone and give you the details.

4 Speaker B is usually a star member of your team, but at the moment they are a month behind with an important report and you are under pressure from head office get it completed on schedule (within the next two weeks). You think the best idea is to bring someone else in (you decide who) to help get the report finished in time and team present the final results to senior management with Speaker B. Phone and make your suggestion as tactfully but forcefully as you can.

9 Relationship-building

Fluency (p47, ex6)

Speaker A

You are
- the sales director for Fairways, a golfing equipment manufacturer based in Florida
- at an international conference in Dublin, which you are really enjoying so far – great place, excellent talks
- staying at the Fitzwilliam Hotel for the next two days – you have a meeting tomorrow at 10am
- currently looking for new agents and distributors in Northern Europe

You have
- just come back from a disappointing business trip to Scotland – you didn't find any suitable agents
- met Speaker B before, but can't remember where – a trade fair in Portugal?

You think
- Speaker B runs some kind of golfing holiday agency
- Speaker B is related to a famous sports personality – a tennis player, maybe?

You want
- to talk to Speaker B about running a joint promotion with their travel company

> **Useful language:**
>
> Haven't we met somewhere before?
>
> Aren't you … or am I mistaken?
>
> I thought you might be interested in …

9 Relationship-building

A dinner invitation (p51, ex1)

Guest: Ulterior motive

You've secretly applied for and been shortlisted for a better job (you decide what) at another company in San Francisco. You've been fairly happy in your current job and you don't want to upset your host, so break the news gently at some point during the evening and try to see if they'll write you a good reference. Be careful what you say and be ready to change the subject if things don't go according to plan!

13 Making an impact

Fluency (p73, ex4)

Group A: Bhutanese Preservation Party

1   The success of our current gradual development programme

Since 1993 life expectancy has increased from 49 (for women) and 46 (for men) to 66 (for both).

In the same period infant mortality has halved.

78% of the population now have access to safe drinking water.

Adult literacy has increased from 4% to 54%.

95% of people who leave Bhutan to work or study abroad return.

2   The risks of overdevelopment

Alaska, Bali, Mongolia and Tahiti once enjoyed a lifestyle like that in Bhutan and have suffered irreparably from too-rapid development.

The arrival in Bhutan of the Internet and cable and satellite television stations like MTV is causing envy and dissatisfaction among Bhutan's young people.

3   The natural environment

The Bhutanese forests are home to many species of flora and fauna, which have as much right to be here as we have – 60% of Bhutan should remain virgin forest and 26% as parkland.

Many of Bhutan's indigenous species are on the endangered list: the red panda, snow leopard and tiger (now the third most endangered animal on Earth).

The mountains are sacred and must be kept off-limits to tourists and climbers, who would disturb the spirits.

We welcome respectful tourists but their number must be restricted to the present quota of 7,000 a year.

4   Our religion

Our historic monasteries and temples are places of worship, not tourist attractions.

The teachings of the Buddha show that what matters is our long-term karma or spiritual development, not short-term gain and profit margins.

14 Out and about

Fluency (p76, ex11)

Speaker A

Hold short conversations with a fellow passenger, Speaker B, on three different international flights.

Use the information below to get you started, but invent any extra information you need to keep the conversation going for a minute or two.

1   Flight BA1311 from Dubai to London Heathrow, business class (9pm)

You are an engineer travelling back from Dubai, where you have been working for Royal Dutch Shell (Emirates) for the last five years, to take up a senior position at head office in London. Your three-year-old son is accompanying you on the flight, but your partner won't be joining you in the UK for another couple of weeks. You're not looking forward to the flight much because your son is quite a hyperactive child and you can never sleep on planes anyway. Try to start a conversation with the person sitting next you, Speaker B. They seem to be playing with their hand-held computer at the moment.

2   Flight AF6001 from Paris to Rio de Janeiro, economy class (3am)

You are a product manager for Pfizer Pharmaceuticals on your way from a project meeting in Paris to another meeting in Rio. You have an appointment with a group of Brazilian research chemists with whom you are collaborating on a new kind of miracle travel sickness pill, which, if all goes well, could be on the market in six months. So far your journey has been a nightmare. Your original flight was cancelled due to bad weather and the only seat you could get was in economy class on the red-eye leaving at two-thirty in the morning. To top it all, it looks like it's going to be a bumpy flight. You can't sleep, so you might as well try and read your book, a crime novel you picked up in the airport called *The Pentangle* by A. J. Bell. Seems quite good.

3   Flight LH1706 from Los Angeles to Munich, first class (2pm)

You are a film producer for Touchstone Pictures flying from a meeting with Oscar-winning actor Al Pacino in Los Angeles to a casting meeting in Munich. You are looking for a German- and English-speaking actor to play the part of an environmental activist in your latest film and would prefer to choose an unknown rather than a big box-office star. You've just enjoyed your second glass of complimentary champagne, when you notice that the passenger sitting next you looks perfect for the part! You can't believe your eyes, but remind yourself they are probably a business executive with no acting ability whatsoever. At the moment they are watching the in-flight movie on their headphones, but try to find an excuse to get talking to them.

17 Negotiating deals

Fluency (p90, ex1a)

Speaker A

It's 6pm on Christmas Eve and you're still at the office. You've been so busy lately, you've hardly had a moment to spend with your family. You even had to miss your young son's first match for the school football team last week to attend an important meeting. Apparently, you were the only parent not there.

Fortunately, you have a chance to put things right. You know there's something kids are all going mad for this Christmas – the Z-Cube Gaming System. At $189, it's a little more than you were planning to spend, but it would be great to see the look on your son's face when he opens it. After phoning seven stores without success, you finally find one that has three left. You try to reserve one, but the shop assistant says 'Sorry, only my boss can do that and she's not here. But if you hurry, you should be OK. We're open till 6.30.'

You fly out of the office and into a taxi. You get to the store just before it closes. To your horror, you see there's only one Z-Cube left. It has a big label on the box saying 'LAST ONE'. But as you head for it, you see another person with the same idea (Speaker B) coming in the other direction. You both reach the box at the same time and grab opposite ends …

17 Negotiating deals

Fluency (p95, ex5)

Team A: The Penitents (band and management)

Obviously, you are delighted that a record company as high-profile as *Starburst* is interested in signing your band. If the deal goes through, you stand to make a lot of money. You are aware, however, that relatively unknown artists are vulnerable to exploitation by the big labels and should take this into account in your dealings with them.

Read your negotiating objectives opposite and then work with your team to plan your overall strategy. In particular, make sure you know which of your objectives are:

1 tradeables (things you'll concede to get what you really want in return)
2 ideals (things you'd really like to get, but not if it costs you the deal)
3 essentials (things you absolutely have to get or the deal's off)

1 **Band line-up**
The four members of the band – the lead singer and rhythm guitarist, lead guitarist, bass guitarist and drummer – all met at college in Dublin and have played together through good times and bad for five years. You've heard a rumour that *Starburst Records* may want to make changes to the line-up – perhaps sacking the drummer, who is also the band's female backing vocalist.

2 **Term**
You'd like a three-year commitment from *Starburst*. It can often take several albums before band members make a profit, so you'd like them to commission at least two albums during that time. If, after three years, the contract is terminated, you'd prefer to keep the rights to all the songs you have recorded – otherwise you would have to pay *Starburst* a fee to perform or re-record your old material.

3 **Royalties**
You think a 15% royalty on net receipts from album sales would be fair. If the band's current popularity does not last, you'd like to make as much as money as possible before the bubble bursts.

4 **Deductions**
You expect *Starburst* to cover all the costs of packaging and promotion, including any TV advertising. Accessing marketing power is one of the advantages of signing to a major label.

5 **Advances**
You are more interested in a good long-term relationship with *Starburst* than instant cash. Nevertheless, a $200,000 non-repayable advance would allow band members to cover living costs, purchase of equipment and stage costumes, etc.

6 **Territory**
You're happy for *Starburst* to have 'universal rights' to your material globally, provided the terms are right. Otherwise, you'd like to be able to approach other labels in the States and Asia.

7 **Touring**
Touring is an essential part of building a band, especially in the early stages of its development. But some of the band members have other jobs and family commitments. They wouldn't want to take on more than 20 weeks' touring (not consecutively) in the first year unless the financial rewards were high – say, 50% of ticket sales.

8 **Songwriting**
The lead singer, Rick Harlow, writes all the band's songs. He says he wants the usual 50:50 split with the music publisher on fees for airplay on radio and TV and other public performances.

13 Making an impact

Fluency (p73, ex4)

Group B: Progress Party of Bhutan

1   The need to speed up the rate of progress

22% of the population still have no access to clean drinking water.

40% of children are malnourished.

33% of them are unable to attend school.

Almost half the population remains illiterate.

2   Infrastructure and communications

The 'last paradise on earth' image is counter-productive – Bhutan is exactly the kind of country that could benefit most from the Internet economy for both commercial and educational purposes.

Until 1999 Bhutan was without TV and there was only one cinema. More needs to be spent on the Bhutan Broadcasting Service (BBS) and Sigma Cable Service.

Bhutan's Internet ISP DrukNet, though popular, is still too expensive (seven cents per minute), but the use of websites and e-mail has reduced international phone bills by 90% and should be promoted.

3   Bhutan's enormous potential as tourist resort

Many of the current improvements in Bhutan are the result of foreign investment, principally from India and Singapore. Why shouldn't other countries be encouraged to invest as well?

Bhutan's superb wildlife and fabulous mountain scenery would be ideal for ecological tourism and adventure holidays.

Limiting the number of tourist visas to just 7,000 a year and insisting that 86% of the land area remain undeveloped is missing a huge opportunity.

Druk Air, the world's smallest commercial carrier, consists of just two planes flying six or seven times a week.

4   The youth of Bhutan

45% of the population of Bhutan is under 15 years of age – it is time to respond to the needs of the younger generation instead of living in the past.

14 Out and about

Fluency (p76, ex11)

Speaker B

Hold short conversations with a fellow passenger, Speaker A, on three different international flights.

Use the information below to get you started, but invent any extra information you need to keep the conversation going for a minute or two.

1   Flight BA1311 from Dubai to London Heathrow, business class (9pm)

You are the partner in a small software company specialising in computer-assisted engineering applications for the oil industry, and are travelling back home from a series of meetings with potential clients in Dubai. It's been an exhausting trip and not as successful as you would have liked. Frankly, you'd just like to skip dinner and try and get some sleep. First, however, you think you'll order a martini while you update your client files on your PalmPilot. You are not pleased to see that the person sitting next to you, Speaker A, has a young child with them. There goes your relaxing flight.

2   Flight AF6001 from Paris to Rio de Janeiro, economy class (3am)

You are a financial speculator who specialises in medical, pharmaceutical and biotech stocks. You are coming back from a meeting in Paris to Rio where you live with your American partner, the crime novelist A. J. Bell. Due to the cancellation of your business class Varig flight, you've ended up in economy class on an early morning Air France flight instead. And you are already regretting this – there's barely room to move and, to make matters worse, the plane seems to be experiencing some turbulence. You've never been a great flyer and are starting to feel a bit sick. Perhaps talking to the person sitting next to you would take your mind off it. But they seem to be reading a book. Actually, the book looks quite familiar …

3   Flight LH1706 from Los Angeles to Munich, first class (2pm)

You are a highly paid German-English interpreter based in Munich and travelling back from LA, where you've been assisting at the American launch of the new BMW sports car. When you arrived for your business class flight this morning, you were delighted to find that it was overbooked and that you had been upgraded to first class. You've had quite an exciting, if stressful, week in LA and are now thoroughly enjoying the flight home. You've had an excellent lunch and have just tuned into the in-flight movie on your personal video screen. You've already seen the film, but don't mind seeing it again as it stars your favourite actor, Al Pacino. And anyway, the person sitting next to you looks like some big millionaire business type.

17 Negotiating deals

Fluency (p90, ex1a)

Speaker B

It's Christmas Eve and you and your family are placing the last few presents under the tree. Your partner turns to you and whispers how excited your young son is: 'Thank goodness you bought him that new gaming system back in November. Apparently, the stores have completely sold out, and it's all he's talked about for months. You remembered to get him the blue one, didn't you?'

You feel a sudden surge of panic. Oh, no ... the Z-Cube Gaming System! How could you have forgotten? You meant to get one months ago, but you've been so busy it completely slipped your mind. You mumble something to your partner about going out to get some better lights for the tree and spend the next three hours searching every store in town. But nobody has one. One shop offers to order it for you, but it will take at least a fortnight ...

In desperation, you try a tiny shop in a side street. It's just about to close as you walk in. To your relief, you see they have one Z-Cube left – and it's a blue one. You can't believe your luck. It has a big label on the box saying 'LAST ONE'. But as you head for it, you see another person with the same idea (Speaker A) coming in the other direction. You both reach the box at the same time and grab opposite ends ...

17 Negotiating deals

Fluency (p95, ex5)

Team B: Starburst Records (executives and lawyers)

You are very excited about this band's prospects. *The Penitents* are musically exceptionally strong with proven song-writing abilities. What's more, they have already generated a lot of media interest. However, the risks with a new signing are always high. Fashions change quickly in your business and you should bear this in mind in your dealings with the band's management.

Read your negotiating objectives opposite and then work with your team to plan your overall strategy. In particular, make sure you know which of your objectives are:

1 tradeables (things you'll concede to get what you really want in return)
2 ideals (things you'd really like to get, but not if it costs you the deal)
3 essentials (things you absolutely have to get or the deal's off)

1 **Band line-up**
Three of the four members of the band – the lead singer/rhythm guitarist, lead guitarist and bass guitarist are exceptionally talented, though the lead guitarist has a reputation for hitting members of the paparazzi and was recently involved in an unpleasant incident aboard an airliner that resulted in his being banned for life. The weak link is the drummer, who simply must be replaced.

2 **Term**
You are prepared to offer a one-album deal, but would like to retain an option on at least two subsequent albums, if the first is successful. You'd also like to keep the performing and recording rights to all the songs – otherwise, if you don't renew their contract and they later become successful with a different label, you won't be able to profit from their backlist of songs.

3 **Royalties**
You think a 10% royalty on net receipts from album sales would be fair. This might be renegotiable after the first three albums, but you'd like to offset the initial risk of taking on the band by maximising profits in the early stages.

4 **Deductions**
If sales of the first album are good (at least 200,000 units), you may want to run a TV campaign. In this case you would like to deduct the cost of 20% of this from the band's royalties.

5 **Advances**
Since advances are normally non-repayable, you'd prefer to offer a relatively modest one on the first album (say $80,000) and promise higher ones on later albums once the band is established.

6 **Territory**
As you'll be spending a substantial amount of time and money on promoting *The Penitents*, you require total 'universal rights' to sell their music globally.

7 **Touring**
With a band like *The Penitents* touring is a key part of building a fan-base. The band is particularly strong live and you would like to capitalise on that. You'd expect them to tour for at least eight months in their first year. Your preferred schedule would be: release two singles, record the first album and do the tour. You'd want 80% of the revenue from ticket sales but will pay for hotels, coach travel and food while on tour.

8 **Songwriting**
The standard songwriter-music publisher split on fees for airplay on radio and TV is 50:50. You're quite happy with this arrangement as long as you retain the rights (see item 1).

Recordings

1 Business or pleasure?

▣ 1.1

Conversation 1

A: Hi, mind if I join you?

B: Er, **not at all. Be my guest**.

A: Only if I have to sit through 'Rule Britannia' by the Band of the Royal Scots Dragoon Guards once more I think I'll scream.

B: And I thought you Americans were supposed to like all that traditional British stuff.

A: Yeah, well, you can have too much of a good thing. Thought I'd come out here and enjoy the view. I must say, though, it was an excellent dinner. Fabulous ship too.

B: Yes, isn't it? I'm James McRae, by the way. BP, engineering division.

A: Hello, James. I'm …

B: Helen Keating. Exxon Mobil.

A: Yes, how did you … oh … ? **Have we met somewhere before?**

B: We have indeed, but I obviously failed to make much of an impression.

A: Wait a minute. **It's not like me to forget a face**. I know – Riyadh. The Petrochemicals Conference. **I thought I recognised you**.

B: As matter of fact, we had dinner together.

A: **You're kidding!** Now, I think I would have remembered that.

B: Well, there were rather a lot of us in the group. At least forty. I don't think we actually spoke.

A: Aha. OK. Yes, **it's all coming back to me now. I seem to remember** spending most of the evening fighting off some creepy little guy called Alan.

B: Alan Sullivan. My boss.

A: Oops! I'm sorry. I didn't mean to …

B: No problem. He's not my favourite person either. Anyway, Helen, looks like we've got the best part of the Royal Yacht to ourselves this evening. How about another drink?

A: OK. Why not? I'll have another Armagnac. Oh, look, the fireworks are starting!

B: So they are. I'll be right back.

Conversation 2

A: **So, Mr Ishida, let me freshen your glass**.

B: Thank you. I'm fine.

A: Some more strawberries, then, perhaps?

B: Er, **not at the moment, thank you**.

A: I am sorry about this weather. Typical English summer, I'm afraid. The forecast did say we might have showers. But I'm sure it'll blow over in half an hour or so. **So, how are you enjoying the match?**

B: Ah, very entertaining, I'm sure …

A: Good. Splendid … **So, tell me, have you been to one of these big tournaments before?** The American Open perhaps?

B: Ah, no, I haven't.

A: Ah. But **I hear** you're quite a tennis fan, though.

B: Er, **not really**. In fact, I never watch tennis normally.

A: Oh, … I see. My marketing people must have made a mistake.

B: Maybe they meant table tennis. I used to play for my university in Tokyo – many years ago.

A: Table tennis! Ah, yes. **I understand** the Japanese are world table tennis champions, isn't that right?

B: **As a matter of fact**, that's the Chinese.

A: Ah, yes, of course … Erm, **so, do you still play?**

B: **Not any more**. Much too old for running around now.

A: Oh, **I'm sure that's not true**.

B: I assure you it is true, Mr Thompson. Bad heart, you see. Doctor's orders.

A: Oh, right. Sorry. Erm, … **I see** the Nikkei's looking strong. **That must be** good news for you.

B: **Not especially**. For Japan economic recovery is still a long way off.

A: Oh? **I read somewhere** that things were improving. **Or am I mistaken?**

B: Over-optimism, I'm afraid.

A: Ah, well, I suppose, er … Oh, look, the rain's stopped! Yes, the players are coming back on. Excellent. **So, shall we return to our seats?**

C: Quiet, please. Hewitt to serve. Hewitt leads by three games to two and by two sets to love.

▣ 1.2

Conversation 1

A: Alistair, we've been here nearly three hours! Can't we just make our excuses and go? You know how I hate these things.

B: Look, Fiona, I'm not enjoying myself any more than you are, but this is business. Besides, I need to speak to Julian about this Internet advertising idea of his.

A: Oh, all right. Where is Julian, anyway? We haven't seen him all evening …

C: Hello! You must be Julian's guests. I don't think we've met. I'm Dan Wilson, Creative Director at JJK Advertising. I work with Julian.

B: Ah, pleased to meet you, Mr Wilson. No, we've not met. **Julian's mentioned your name, of course**. Alistair Hamilton. And this is my wife, Fiona.

C: **A pleasure to meet you both at last.** And **please call me Dan.**

A: **We were just wondering** what this pile of dirty laundry was doing in the middle of an art gallery.

B: Fiona!

C: So, you're not a fan of contemporary art then, Fiona – **you don't mind me calling you Fiona, do you?** Actually, this, er, 'dirty laundry', as you call it, came second in this year's Turner Prize, believe it or not.

A: Doesn't surprise me in the least, but, er, still just looks like dirty laundry to me, I'm afraid.

C: Well, yes, but I don't think that's what the artist would call it.

A: What does he call it, then?

C: Erm, I'm not sure. I'll check the catalogue for you … Here we are – erm, exhibit 12, oh, 'Dirty Laundry'.

A: What did I tell you?

C: Yes, quite. Erm, Alistair, **I wonder if we could have a word?** Julian tells me you're not very happy with the new Internet campaign.

B: Er, yes. **Would you excuse us a moment, Fiona?** Dan and I need to talk.

A: Oh, don't mind me. There's the heap of broken glass in the room next door I'm just dying to see.

B: Er, right. Well, **I'll catch you later**, then … Now, look, Dan, the thing is …

Conversation 2

A: Ricardo! **Glad you could make it**.

B: Hello, Tom. **I wouldn't have missed it for the world**. It's not every day I get invited to something like this. I hear Schumacher's out, so it should be a good race.

A: Yes, it certainly evens things up a bit with Ferrari down to one car. **Talking of** races, how's the South African bid going? I heard it was just between you and Swedish Steel now.

B: Hm, yes, the negotiations are still going on, but we're hopeful. I don't think the Swedes can beat us on price.

A: Well, let me know how it goes. We'd be happy to organise the transportation if you need it. We'd do you a good deal.

B: Sure, I'll certainly keep you in mind if we win the contract.

A: Great … Ricardo, **there's someone I'd like you to meet**.

B: Oh, really?

A: Yes, but first let me get you something to drink. **Can't have you standing there with an empty glass**. What are you on? Champagne?

B: Just mineral water for now, thanks.

A: Oh, dear … Here you go.

B: Thanks. **So, who's this person you wanted me to meet?**

A: Ah, yes … Oh, here she is now. Élise, this is Ricardo Piquet. Ricardo, Élise de Cadenet. Élise is …

C: Hello, Ricardo. **Long time no see**. What is it, five years?

B: Hello, Élise. Must be five at least. **You haven't changed a bit**.

C: **Neither have you. Charming as ever**.

A: Ah, **I see you two know each other already**.

C: **Ricardo and I go back a long way**, Tom. A very long way.

B: Yes, actually, we first met in Monaco – at the Grand Prix, funnily enough … So, Élise, last I heard you were getting married again.

C: And divorced again. I'm between husbands at the moment. Far too busy setting up this new business in Biarritz.

A: Er, well, **I'll leave you two to chat. See you later**. Don't forget the race starts at three.

B: Yes, see you later, Tom. So, Élise, how about a drink?

C: Mm, sounds good. **I'll have whatever you're having**.

B: Er, waiter, two champagnes, please.

2 Exchanging information

▭ 2.1

A: Right. That brings us on to our main business this morning – the new Quasar Online Gaming System. As you already know, the news is not particularly good. In spite of a considerable investment in design and marketing, **I'm sorry to report that the project has not been a complete success**.

B: Not a complete success? **What you mean is, it's failed** – dismally!

A: Now let's not overreact, Alan. Certainly, it's failed to meet our original expectations. And, yes, **technically speaking, we have run into negative profit** …

B: Negative profit! What do you mean negative profit? **You mean we've made a loss** – an enormous loss if these figures are anything to go by!

C: Can we come back to the figures later, Alan, if that's OK? First, let's consider why sales are so disappointing. Now, in my view, it's not the product, but the market. **I think there's a general lack of consumer confidence**.

B: **In other words, sales are falling**. Look, I'm sorry, Hannah, but you're just looking for excuses. It's obvious that Quasar is simply not sophisticated enough for today's market.

A: Alan, we leave sophistication to companies like Sony and Nintendo and Sega. What we do is copy the technology and do it cheaper.

C: Alan, **you know we've always been a market-driven organisation** …

B: Market-driven? **What you really mean is we've never had an original idea**. I say we need to be developing an innovative new product line …

A: What, when the market's so massively oversupplied? I don't think so. **Now is not the time to expand, but to consolidate**.

B: **So what you're saying is let's do nothing**.

A: No, I'm saying let's consolidate.

B: I see. And what will this 'consolidation' mean in terms of our staff? Redundancies, I suppose.

C: Well, obviously, **there will have to be some restructuring of the department**.

B: **You mean people are going to lose their jobs**.

C: It's a possibility, yes. And **we may also have to consider outsourcing production to cut costs**.

B: **In other words, our assembly plant may be closed down too**. I can't believe I'm hearing this!

A: **Of course, we won't be able to finalise anything today**.

B: **You mean we'll have to hold another meeting!** Huh! If we've all still got a job by then, that is.

A: Yes, well, I'm glad you raised that point, Alan.

B: What do you mean?

▭ 2.2

a

A: Right, I'm allowing an hour and a half for this meeting. Kate is going to fill us in on how the appraisals went. That'll take about a quarter of an hour or so. So that only gives us 45 minutes to deal with everything else. We'd better get started.

B: Sorry, **I thought we had an hour and a half**.

A: What? Oh, yeah, sorry. We've got 75 minutes, haven't we? Still, there's a lot to get through.

b

A: Look, it's no good going on about pay rises. We pay nearly twice what most of our competitors do. And I really don't see how people can expect another salary increase this year, when they're already earning three times the average rate.

B: Hang on a second. **You said we pay twice as much, not three times**.

A: Hm? Oh, all right, twice as much, then. It's still a lot more than everybody else.

c

A: You know as well as I do that this project was supposed to take sixteen weeks. And this isn't the first time we've run over budget, is it? I mean a 20% overspend is pretty serious. And surely three months was sufficient time to complete the project.

B: Just a minute. **I thought you said sixteen weeks, not three months**.

A: OK, OK, that's four months, then. But you've taken nearly six.

d

A: Frankly, with the Asian economic situation the way it is and the euro getting stronger, we're not doing well in the Far East. Southern Europe is where we should be concentrating our efforts. As a matter of fact, Spain is now our second biggest market after China.

B: Hold on. **Didn't you just say we're not doing well in the Far East?**

A: Well, I meant apart from China, obviously! China's always been a huge market for tobacco products.

e

A: I'm sorry, but I don't want us bringing in people from outside the company to sort this problem out. There's a lot of highly confidential information on our intranet. And we should really be able to deal with this ourselves. There's a guy I play golf with who runs his own consultancy. He's offered to help us out.

B: Wait a moment. **You just said you didn't want to bring in people from outside the company**.

A: Erm, well, what I mean is I don't want just anybody. This guy's different. I've known him for years.

▭ 2.3

a

Twelve and a half billion dollars.

b

Five hundred and eighty thousand, seven hundred and fifty-three euros.

c

Two-thirds.

d

Eight thousand, four hundred and ninety-one dollars.

e

Four to one.

f

One point zero five square kilometres.

g

Two hundred and ninety-eight cubic metres.

h

Fifty-two to fifty-eight million yen.

i

Four hundred gigabytes.

j

Point zero zero one two per cent.

▭ 2.4

A: OK, everyone. It's bad news, I'm afraid. As you may have heard, the latest European sales figures are looking extremely disappointing.

B: **Are you saying they've fallen short of projections again?**

A: I'm afraid so. In fact, we may be 30% down. Now, this will be the third quarter in a row we've missed our targets and, frankly, unless things pick up considerably next quarter, we may have to rethink our whole pricing strategy.

C: **Are you suggesting we introduce price cuts?**

A: If we still can, Anna. Certainly if we'd done that a year ago, it might have stimulated demand. But do it now and we may end up running at a loss. As you know, we're barely breaking even on some of our product lines as it is.

D: **Surely you're not saying it's time to phase them out!**

A: No, no, of course not. At least, not yet. But what I am saying is that we need to keep production costs down somehow if we want to remain competitive.

B: **Does this mean we should be investing more in new technology?**

A: If only it was that simple, Erik. But right now we're not really in a position to invest in anything, even if we wanted to. No, I'm afraid the situation calls for more drastic action. It's clearly time for a major restructuring.

D: **Are you telling us there could be layoffs?**

A: I don't see how we can avoid it, James – unless, of course, we can get some of our people to accept reduced hours.

C: **You mean some kind of job-share scheme?**

A: Yes, either that or introduce a four-day week – providing the unions don't oppose it. Of course, it's not just a question of costs. It's also a question of product. The fact is, better products are coming onto the market all the time.

D: **So you're saying we should be spending more on R&D.**

A: As I've said, capital investment is no longer an option for us. Pour any more money into R&D and we'll simply slide further into debt. And then there are all the problems we've been having with our overseas distributors.

B: **Does this mean you're thinking of centralising distribution?**

A: Well, that's one option, yes. But even if we decided to do that, and it's a big if, it would take time to implement – time we simply don't have. As you know, our share price has fallen to an all-time low of just 85 cents. And I wouldn't be surprised if, by our next meeting, it's fallen even further. The fact is, we're selling old product at inflated prices in a volatile market through inefficient distributors.

D: **I hope you're not suggesting the situation is hopeless.**

A: Well, let's put it this way: we've cancelled the Christmas party!

2.5

a

A: Right. Basically, the position is this: the contract is ours if we want it.

B: But we're not in a position to take on another project right now, are we?

A: I know. Jan, what's your position on this?

b

A: Look, it's not just a question of software, Alessandro.

B: Of course not. It's also a question of hardware. The entire system needs upgrading.

A: But that's out of the question. We can't afford that kind of capital outlay.

c

A: Sales are down. One option would obviously be to cut our prices.

B: That's no longer an option for us. We're barely breaking even as it is.

A: Well, then we've no option but to rethink our whole marketing strategy.

d

A: Well, there's no easy answer to this, but how about voluntary redundancy?

B: I don't think that's the answer, but maybe we could reduce people's hours.

A: That might have been the answer if we didn't already have a strike on our hands!

e

A: Now, let's not make a problem out of this. What if we just pulled out of Sudan?

B: Well, I've no problem with that, but our partners won't be happy.

A: No, but that's not our problem, is it? The political situation is just too unstable.

f

A: I'll get straight to the point. We're getting too many customer complaints.

B: I agree with you. But the point is we don't have the staff to deal with them.

A: That's beside the point. We shouldn't be getting them in the first place!

g

A: I'm afraid the situation is serious. And if the press get hold of the story, …

B: Look, we'll deal with that situation if and when it arises. Let's not panic just yet.

A: You're right. What this situation calls for is calm and careful planning.

h

A: The fact is, we're simply not spending enough on R&D.

B: As a matter of fact, we've doubled our R&D budget this year.

C: That may be so, but the fact remains we're losing our technological lead.

3 Material world

3.1

A: Now, it's just coming up to 11 o'clock. Time for *Business Brief* with Malcolm McFadden. This week: the collapse of Barings.

B: The story of the collapse of Barings is not the biggest bank fraud of all time, but it is probably the most famous – not least because at the centre of the drama lies the colourful character of Nick Leeson.

Leeson was a typical working-class boy, a below-average student who failed his maths exams and left school with few qualifications. Nevertheless, he managed to land a job as a clerk at the royal bank Coutts in the City of London.

A succession of low-paid jobs at other banks eventually led in 1982 to his joining Barings, where he quickly made an impression and worked his way up from the very bottom to become its top currency trader at the Singapore office.

By 1993 Leeson was making his employers $10 million a year – 10% of Barings' total profits. His salary may have been a mere £50,000 but his bonuses were triple that. He and his devoted wife Lisa had a smart apartment in Singapore and spent their weekends partying or holidaying in exotic island resorts. Leeson worked hard and played hard, and fully enjoyed the high life.

But in 1994 the markets did a U-turn and Leeson seemed to lose his touch. The speculative losses built up. Amazingly, Barings had no idea of the scale of the problem, for Leeson had carefully hidden his mounting debts in an obscure account called Error Losses 88888. This enabled him to request further funds from the bank to çarry on trading, even though by the autumn his losses stood at $300 million.

By the time he was discovered that figure had risen to $1.3 billion. Two days before his 28th birthday Leeson went missing. On his desk he'd left a hurried note. It simply said: 'I'm sorry.'

To avoid imprisonment, Leeson and his wife briefly went on the run, first to Borneo and then to Frankfurt, where Leeson was arrested, extradited to Singapore and finally jailed for six and a half years in 1995. When the news of his arrest reached the world's futures markets, there were loud cheers of celebration.

Lisa Leeson stuck by her husband until the news of his infidelity on business trips to Japan finally broke their marriage. Divorced and now suffering from cancer, Leeson still managed to write his amazing autobiography *Rogue Trader* while in prison.

Barings, which for 233 years had built up an excellent reputation in financial circles, now faced the final humiliation – bankruptcy. Burdened with crippling debts, it was eventually bought by the Dutch ING Bank for the sum of one pound.

3.2

B: But the story for Leeson doesn't quite end there. After the terrible ordeal of surgery and chemotherapy, Leeson's health improved. Though he returned to the UK to find himself homeless and without a job, he went on to study at university, whilst occasionally giving speeches at conferences to make ends meet. His book *Rogue Trader* made him an estimated £50,000. And when it was made into a film starring Ewan McGregor, Leeson apparently received a great deal more. The man who could make $10 million a year with other people's money may not be finished yet.

But whatever Leeson's future, *Rogue Trader* will stand as a lasting record of the lengths the whizzkids and yuppies of the 80s and 90s were willing to go to in the so-called 'age of greed'. In it Leeson blamed the international banking system for his spectacular failure. 'We were all driven to make profits, profits and more profits,' he said, 'and I was the rising star.'

Speaker 1

Well, I don't have any problem investing in alcohol and tobacco products. Actually, I'm a smoker myself. Keep trying to give up but can't quite seem to manage it. Seems to me you can take this ethical investment idea a bit too far. I mean, who am I to say those businesses shouldn't be invested in? If they're good, profitable businesses, why not put your money into them? They're not doing anything illegal, are they? And anyway, if everybody stopped investing in cigarette companies, think of all the tobacco pickers and the cigarette factory workers who'd be out of a job. Gambling doesn't worry me too much either, not that I'm much of a gambler myself. I suppose I might be a bit worried about seeing my money going into manufacturing guns and missiles, though. But then again, someone's got to make them.

Speaker 2

What I want to know is: just what is an ethical investment these days? I mean, it's pretty hard to think of a company that doesn't do anybody or anything any harm in some way or another. Take books. To make books you have to cut down trees. Save the trees, books get more expensive, the poor can't afford them. Or how about shoes? To make leather shoes you have to kill animals. To make plastic shoes you have to pollute the environment. Or say you invest in a clothing company, then you've got to ask yourself who's making the clothes, where do they work and what are they getting paid for it? And what kind of clothes are they making? The latest fashions for the rich? Uniforms for the army? It's so complicated, you may as well just put your money where it's likely to do best and forget about the rights and wrongs of it.

Speaker 3

Whenever you make an important decision, you use your judgement and sense of right and wrong, don't you? So why should investment decisions be any different? As a matter of fact, a lot of 'green' investments have paid off very well in the last ten years, often outperforming less ethically sound stocks. I certainly wouldn't allow any of my hard-earned cash to go towards supporting companies that cause such misery, even though they're not actually illegal. And, anyway, who said cigarette companies were a good investment? What with all these court cases and the anti-smoking lobby, I don't think there's a great future there – at least, not in America. And arms? Well, in times of war I suppose that's a good business to be in, but the other day someone in the aviation industry actually told me that these days there's less money in making fighter aircraft than there is in making corporate jets. So, what does that tell you?

4 Voice and visuals

📼 4.1

Hello, this is Cheng Jing from Nanogen Taiwan. I just wanted to let you know that your presentation this morning was a tremendous success with everyone here. What a brilliant idea to do the whole thing in such a casual, low-budget and alternative way! Very clever. The board certainly got the message.

I hope we didn't seem unappreciative as an audience. Quite the contrary. You must understand that not all our vice-presidents have the benefit of my Harvard education. And some of them don't speak English very well. But they really liked your calm, quiet approach. So please pass on my congratulations to your excellent presenter.

Oh, by the way, the joke about Beijing was greatly enjoyed – even in translation. As you know, we Taiwanese always like a good laugh at the expense of our Chinese neighbours. So, see you at the next strategy meeting. Goodbye now.

📼 4.2

a
There's a whole market in Eastern Europe just there for the taking.

b
Quite frankly, the results we've been getting are absolutely incredible.

c
Now, I'm sure I don't need to tell you just how crucial this is.

d
Net profits are up ninety-seven per cent – yes, ninety-seven per cent.

e
Would you believe that so far we've not been able to sell a single unit?

f
Miss this deadline and we'll lose the biggest client this company's ever had.

📼 4.3

a
There's a whole <u>market</u> | in Eastern <u>Europe</u> | just <u>there</u> for the <u>taking</u>.

b
<u>Net profits</u> | are up <u>ninety-seven</u> per <u>cent</u> | – <u>yes</u>, | <u>ninety-</u> | <u>seven</u> | per <u>cent</u>.

📼 4.4

a
There's a whole <u>market</u> | in Eastern <u>Europe</u> | just <u>there</u> for the <u>taking</u>.

b
Quite <u>frankly</u>, | the <u>results</u> we've been <u>getting</u> | are <u>absolutely</u> | <u>incredible</u>.

c
Now, I'm <u>sure</u> I don't need to <u>tell</u> you | just how <u>crucial</u> | this <u>is</u>.

d
<u>Net profits</u> | are up <u>ninety-seven</u> per <u>cent</u> | – <u>yes</u>, | <u>ninety-</u> | <u>seven</u> | per <u>cent</u>.

e
Would you <u>believe</u> | that <u>so</u> far | we've <u>not</u> been <u>able</u> to <u>sell</u> | a <u>single</u> <u>unit</u>?

f
<u>Miss</u> | <u>this</u> | <u>deadline</u> | and we'll <u>lose</u> the <u>biggest client</u> | this <u>company's</u> <u>ever</u> <u>had</u>.

📼 4.5

A: Welcome back to CBN Business. To be or not to be? That is the question for an increasing number of companies putting their staff through drama courses, no less, in an attempt to turn them into better public speakers. Jon Heller meets a group of British managers making their theatrical debut.

B: 'Next time you are about to make a presentation, take a deep breath and imagine yourself walking on stage – about to give the performance of your life.' That's the advice of William Freeman of Cambridge Associates, one of a new breed of management trainers who believe that presenting is less about PowerPoint and more about acting the part.

At Prospero, a company with a similar aims, Tina Packer and Michael Lame have taken the idea one step further and put Shakespeare on the program. Who better to teach managers how to speak effectively and relate to an audience, they ask, than classically trained actors? Whether you're a platform speaker at the annual conference, a salesperson pitching a client or just chairing your weekly staff meeting, actors have powerful communication techniques you can learn from. Prospero is certainly in demand, regularly running courses at Columbia Business School, Harvard and MIT.

So what is it that makes someone a brilliant speaker? Richard Olivier, Royal Shakespeare Company director, creative management consultant and son of acting legend Sir Laurence Olivier, thinks it's 'self-belief'. According to Olivier, 'Much of leadership is acting. Not faking it, but taking on a role. Paradoxically, the acting makes it real.' But what do the trainees think? We questioned a few who'd taken a course in acting like leaders:

C: I thought my boss had gone quite mad at first. I mean, Shakespeare? No way, I thought! But, in fact, it's been really inspiring. And a lot of fun!

D: Frankly, I was terrified. Me, acting on stage? I don't think so. But I've learned a lot of stuff I never got on those boring presentation courses.

E: Well, the actors have been fun to work with. We've had a lot of laughs. I'm not sure how useful it all is, though – you know, in a business context. But, hey, it got us out of the office for a couple of days, so I'm not complaining.

F: Well, this really isn't my thing at all. I mean, public speaking just frightens the life out of me as it is, without getting up and acting in front of an audience. Frankly, it was hell. Never again!

G: Best course I've ever done – by far. Just totally brilliant. I never realised the true power of the voice and the confidence it gives you when you can make it work for you. I'd definitely recommend this kind of training.

B: So, there we have it. Time to shut down your laptop, brush up your Shakespeare and learn how to wow an audience with the professionals.

🔊 4.6

Take 1

I know what you're thinking || did he fire six shots || or only five? ||| Well | to tell you the truth | in all this excitement || I've kind of lost track myself ||| but being as this is a point four four Magnum || the most powerful handgun in the world || and would blow your head clean off ||| I guess you've got to ask yourself one question ||| do I feel lucky? ||| Well | do you | punk?

Take 2

What we're selling here || is freedom ||| We offer | through technology || what religion | and revolution | have promised || but never delivered ||| Freedom from the physical body || freedom from race and gender || from nationality | and personality | from place | and time || Communicating by cellular phone | and hand-held computer | PDA | and built-in fax-modem || we can relate to each other | as pure | consciousness

Take 3

The good news is | you're fired ||| The bad news is | you've got | all you've got | is one week | to get your jobs back ||| Have I got your attention now? || Good | Because we're adding a little something to this month's sales competition ||| First prize | as you know | is a Cadillac Eldorado || Second prize is a set of steak knives ||| Third prize is | you're fired || Do you get the picture? || Are you laughing now?

Take 4

I think | No | I am positive | that you are | the most unattractive man | I have ever met in my entire life ||| You know | in the short time we've been together | you have demonstrated | every loathsome characteristic | of the male personality || and even discovered a few new ones ||| You are physically repulsive | intellectually retarded | you're morally reprehensible | vulgar | insensitive | selfish | stupid || You have no taste | a

lousy sense of humour || and you smell ||| You're not even interesting enough to make me sick ||| Goodbye Darryl || and thank you for a lovely lunch

Take 5

I ||| am William Wallace ||| And I see | a whole army of my countrymen || here | in defiance | of tyranny ||| You have come to fight as free men || and free men you are || What will you do with that freedom? ||| Will you fight? ||| Aye | fight | and you may die || run | and you'll live ||| at least a while || And dying in your beds | many years from now || would you be willing | to trade | all the days | from this day to that | for one chance || just one chance || to come back here | and tell our enemies || that they may take our lives || but they'll never || take our freedom!

5 Problems on the phone

🔊 5.1

B: Hello?
A: Dan?
B: Speaking.
A: It's George. George Chatterton.
B: Ah, George … How are you?
A: Couldn't be better, mate, couldn't be better! Someone happened to mention they'd bumped into you the other day. So I just thought I'd give you a call. See how you're doing.
B: Oh, right. … yes … er, George …
A: So how's it going, mate? Just been promoted, so I hear.
B: Er, yes, that's right.
A: Glad to see they've finally started appreciating you.
B: Er, yes, thanks. So, George, **what can I do for you?**
A: Bit more money too, I imagine.
B: Hm? Oh, a bit, yeah. Well, George, **I expect you're calling about** that …
A: And how's that lovely wife of yours?
B: Suzanne? Oh, she's fine.
A: Splendid, splendid. And the kids?
B: They're fine too. Look, George, I *am* rather busy right now. I've just got back from holiday, actually, and you know what it's like. **Was there something you wanted to talk to me about?**
A: Of course, how silly of me! You've just been on that safari you were planning last time we spoke, haven't you?
B: Yes, and what with the new job and everything, there's a bit of catching up …
A: Kenya, wasn't it?
B: What?
A: The holiday – Kenya.
B: Yes. Listen. George …
A: You know, I've always wanted to go to Kenya …
B: Well, now, George, **I mustn't keep you.**
A: What's that?
B: **I'll let you get on.** I'm sure you've got things to do, busy guy like you. **It's been great talking to you**, though.

A: Yeah, likewise.
B: **We must get together soon.**
A: Yeah, yeah. As a matter of fact, I'm going to be in London for a few days next month.
B: Oh, god.
A: Sorry?
B: I said 'Oh, good.' Perhaps we can meet up for a beer.
A: Yeah, that'd be great.
B: But, erm, **I'll have to let you go now**, George. **Someone's just this minute stepped into the office.**
A: Oh, right, I see.
B: And it looks like **I've got an international call just come in on the other line** as well. Yes.
A: No worries. I'll call you back in half an hour, then. I haven't told you *my* good news yet. Wait till you hear it!
B: What? Er, no. Erm, George? George?

🔊 5.2

A: Hello. Thank you for calling the iDeals customer service line. All our customer service advisers are busy right now. Please hold and your enquiry will be dealt with shortly … This is the iDeals customer service line. Thank you for holding. All our customer service advisers are busy right now. Please hold and your enquiry will be dealt with shortly …
B: Oh, come on, come on!
C: Good morning. Lisa speaking. **How can I help you?**
B: Oh, hello. At last! I was just about to ring off.
C: I am sorry about that. The waiting system is a bit frustrating, isn't it? It's the only way we can offer our 24-hour service, you see.
B: Yeah, yeah. Look, it's about the computer I bought off you two weeks ago …
C: Yes? **What seems to be the problem?**
B: Well, I was transferring my files to it from my zip drive and it's lost the lot. Everything!
C: OK, now don't worry. I'm sure we can sort something out. First, can you give me a few details? The computer has lost all your data, you say?
B: Yes. But, you don't understand. It's wiped everything off the zip drive as well! My whole life, my whole life was in those files.
C: Oh, my goodness! Are you sure? Sounds like the problem's with your zip drive.
B: Of course I'm sure! And there's nothing wrong with my zip drive. I've had it years!
C: OK. **I can understand how upset you must be.** Now, I don't think we can deal with this on the phone, so I'm going to send a service engineer to see if they can retrieve your data. Can you give me your product reference number?
B: Hm? Er, yes. It's … here it is … it's SF11–003.

C: Thank you.

B: I'll be expecting a total refund *and* compensation if this can't be fixed!

C: **Unfortunately, we're not authorised to give refunds, but what I can do is send you a brand-new computer. How would that be?**

B: This is supposed to be a brand-new computer. You think I want another one of these, after what the last one did to my files?

C: Well, let's see what our engineer can do. Hopefully, it's not quite as bad as you think. Now, I've got your address here in your customer file. Oxford OX2 6BJ, right?

B: Yeah, right.

C: And it's Mr Harris, isn't it?

B: Yes.

C: Right, Mr Harris. We'll have an engineer with you this afternoon. And I'll ask him to bring a new hard disk with him. **Is that all OK for you?**

B: Er, well, I suppose …

C: Good. **Glad to be of assistance. Is there anything else I can help you with?**

B: Hm? Oh, no, no.

C: Well, best of luck this afternoon. I hope we can solve the problem for you.

B: Well, thanks. Erm, goodbye.

C: Goodbye, Mr Harris.

📼 5.3

B: Hello?

A:

B: Yeah, speaking. Is that you, Piotr? Aren't you supposed to be at the Trade Fair in Krakow?

A:

B: What?

A:

B: You haven't got a stand? Well, how did that happen?

A:

B: Maybe it's the CD player you're using.

A:

B: Well, what happened to *our* CD player?

A:

B: Damn carriers. That's the last time we use *them*! I'll play hell with them when I speak to them.

A:

B: Where's Liesl?

A:

B: This just gets worse, doesn't it?

A:

B: What's gone wrong with the brochures?

A:

B: Portuguese! Oh, no …

A:

B: That may be because I forgot to phone Tony. You remember we were going to attend the Lisbon Trade Fair originally.

A:

B: It completely slipped my mind. Oh, I'm really sorry, Piotr.

A:

B: Well, we're snowed under at the moment trying to get things ready for the Midas launch, but, look, don't worry. I'll sort something out. Can I call you back in an hour?

A:

📼 5.4

B: Hello?

A: Graham?

B: Yeah, speaking. Is that you, Piotr? Aren't you supposed to be at the Trade Fair in Krakow?

A: I *am* at the Trade Fair in Krakow, Graham. I'm just about the only thing that arrived here in one piece!

B: What?

A: Well, the stand got badly damaged in transit, so I've basically just got a table here, a few chairs and a couple of posters with nothing to attach them to! It's a complete disaster!

B: You haven't got a stand? Well, how did that happen?

A: Don't ask. Look, it's not just that. I've just tried out three of the promotional CDs and two were defective – wouldn't play at all. I don't know how many more are like that.

B: Maybe it's the CD player you're using.

A: Wouldn't surprise me. I had to borrow it from another exhibitor.

B: Well, what happened to *our* CD player?

A: I'll give you three guesses.

B: Damn carriers. That's the last time we use *them*! I'll play hell with them when I speak to them.

A: Yes, well, never mind that now. You've got to do something, Graham. **I'm working flat out** on my own here.

B: Where's Liesl?

A: She's come down with some sort of virus. I left her at the hotel.

B: This just gets worse, doesn't it?

A: Wait till you hear about the brochures …

B: What's gone wrong with the brochures?

A: The English ones are OK. The others are all in Portuguese.

B: Portuguese! Oh, no …

A: What?

B: That may be because I forgot to phone Tony. You remember we were going to attend the Lisbon Trade Fair originally.

A: And you didn't tell Tony about the change of plan?

B: **It completely slipped my mind.** Oh, I'm really sorry, Piotr.

A: Graham, you've got to get me out of this mess.

B: Well, **we're snowed under at the moment** trying to get things ready for the Midas launch, but, look, don't worry. I'll sort something out. Can I call you back in an hour?

A: OK, I'll be waiting to hear from you.

📼 5.5

A: Hello?

B: Hello, Piotr.

A: Graham! You said an hour.

B: Sorry. I got held up.

A: What's happening, then?

B: Right. I've been on to the carriers and they're sending a new stand out on the next plane. You should have that by tomorrow morning.

A: Well, at least that's something.

B: **Can you get hold of the organisers** and tell them we'll set up tomorrow at 7?

A: Yeah, sure. **I don't suppose you remembered to put another CD**

player in with the stand?

B: I've sent two – just in case.

A: Oh, right. Good. Thanks.

B: And **do you happen to have a phone number for the promotions people?** Because if those CDs are defective, I'll get them to send more by courier.

A: I've got it somewhere. Graham, **is there any chance of sending someone else out here?** Kim, for instance.

B: Piotr, you know how short-staffed we are here right now.

A: What's this exhibition costing us, Graham? $18,000?

B: You're right. **I'll check with Liz and see if she can spare Kim for a few days.**

A: Thanks. It's murder here.

B: Well, **I'll see what I can do, but I can't promise anything.**

A: Hm. And **would you mind getting some brochures to me in Polish**, seeing as I'm in Poland?

B: Yes, we're having a few problems with that – seem to have run out. **Is there any point in sending the ones we've got in Russian?**

A: No, Graham, not a great idea. Send the German ones, if that's all we've got. But **are you absolutely sure we didn't order a reprint of the Polish ones?**

B: **I'll look into it the minute I get off the phone.**

A: OK, but **could I ask you to hurry that up a bit, please?** It *is* pretty important.

B: I know, I know. **Would it help if we got a local Polish interpreter in?** I know you speak Polish, but it might help you out a bit.

A: Well, I wouldn't have much time to brief them on the product, but yeah, anything's better than nothing.

B: OK, **I'll get on to that right away. Leave it to me.**

A: I did leave it to you and look what happened!

B: Yeah, well. You're doing a great job Piotr. I owe you one!

6 Leading meetings

📼 6.1

A: Coming up on CBN Business: an interview with media king and head of News Corporation Rupert Murdoch, stock market report and Katy Alexander with the week's business news round-up. But first, suffering from boardroom blues? Tired of taking minutes at meetings that take hours? Tess Liebowitz may have the solution …

B: According to diplomat and economist JK Galbraith, 'Meetings are indispensable when you don't want to do anything.' Therefore, logically, if you really do want to do something, it's the meetings you must dispense with. But can you dispense with meetings altogether? And what would take their place? At several well-known companies they think they've found the answer.

At high-profile UK advertising agency St. Luke's, meetings are simply considered 'a ceremonial and rude interruption to people's working day'. So they've introduced meetings-on-the-move. Any member of staff can hold a meeting anytime, anywhere – in the elevator, in a local café or just sitting cross-legged on the floor. Anywhere, that is, but in a boardroom!

At Internet company another.com they've gone one step further by building a 'park area' right in the middle of the building. Staff can go sit on the park bench amongst the flowers or even play on the swings while they hold meetings! They used to have real grass too, but watering it became a problem.

At media strategy company, Michaelides & Bednash they've come up with a different solution. All employees, irrespective of status, work around one enormous central table. Meetings become unnecessary when everyone in the company is sitting just across the table from you the whole time. The working day is a constant meeting!

At the Xerox Corporation a more down-to-earth approach has proved successful. All staff, from junior management upwards, are trained in chairing skills and get an equal opportunity to use them. This breaks up hierarchies in the workplace, creating democratised meetings, where everyone can practise their leadership skills.

Finally, at Federal Express, they've been experimenting with technology. Using specially designed software, people sit around a large U-shaped table at workstations connected over a local area network. Meetings stick strictly to the agenda, are highly focused and more or less silent. Items instantly appear on the participants' screens and people simply key in their views rather than voice them. The software allows you to attach further comments and to see graphically how your position differs from the consensus. The only problem is the price – $35,000 for the fully functional system!

6.2

Extract 1

A: OK, **thanks for coming, everybody**. Erm, has anybody seen Lance, by the way? He was supposed to be here.

B: Oh, yeah, he phoned to say his flight in from Chicago had a two-hour delay. He said to go ahead and start without him.

A: Oh, I wanted his input on this one. **OK**, never mind, **let's get started, then, shall we?** Erm, so, **as I said in my e-mail, the purpose of this meeting is to** review last week's talks with the people from timeofyourlife.com and, secondly, to decide if we're interested in taking things further. **Luis is going to fill us in on the background. Luis?**

C: Yeah, thanks, Ross. Well, now, timeofyourlife is a really exciting business proposition. Basically, the idea is that ordinary people can buy a kind of timeshare in various luxury goods

that they could never afford to buy outright. What happens is you buy points online at the timeofyourlife website and you can use these points to buy, like, a Ferrari for a day, a Rolex Oyster for a weekend or a Jean-Paul Gaultier original for an evening! Neat, huh? I just love this proposal …

D: Er, sorry to interrupt, but is this going to take long, Luis? Only I have an appointment at eleven and we *have* all read the summary on this company already.

A: **Jack, could Luis just finish what he was saying?** We're looking at twenty million dollars in seed capital here. I don't want us rushing into anything. But **perhaps we could speed things up a little**, Luis. We *are* short of time and **by the end of this meeting I'd like some kind of decision on this**.

Extract 2

C: So, as you can see, the advance publicity alone is attracting half a million visitors to the timeofyourlife website every day.

A: Sorry, Luis, but **we seem to be getting side-tracked here.** This is all very interesting, but **can we go back to what we were discussing earlier?**

C: Oh, OK. Sure.

A: **Perhaps we can come back to this later**. Tell us about their logistics.

D: Can I just say something here?

A: **Hold on a minute, Jack – you'll get your chance in a moment.**

D: It's just that I thought we'd agreed we weren't investing in any more dot.coms.

B: No, Jack. That's what *you* wanted. But nobody actually agreed.

D: Tania, we've been through this. E-commerce is dead. We learned that the hard way.

B: Wait a minute. Who was it that said …?

A: **OK, OK! Let's all just calm down, shall we?** We're here to talk about this proposal we have on the table. **Tania, what's your position on this?**

B: Well, I agree with Luis that it's a great business plan. Like you, I'm a little concerned about the logistics, though. The procurement and delivery system for a business like this would be extremely complex. And the insurance costs could be prohibitive.

C: Now, hold on a second! This is all covered in the proposal, Tania. What are you saying? I thought that you were with me on this one.

A: **Luis, I think what Tania is trying to say is** she likes the idea but the figures don't quite add up.

B: Exactly.

A: OK, **maybe we should take a short break at this point**, grab a coffee and meet back here in fifteen minutes.

Extract 3

A: **OK, so just to summarise what we've said so far**. Basically, we like the timeofyourlife idea.

D: (*groans*)

A: At least most of us do. We're aware of the risks involved in a major investment

in an e-business, but we think the concept has great potential. We need to make another appointment with these people because we have some doubts about their logistics. **Luis, can I leave that one with you?**

C: Sure. I'll get right on to it.

A: We're also a little concerned about the amount of insurance a business like this would need. **Tania, can you get back to me on that?**

B: No problem, Ross.

A: Great. **I think that's about as far as we can go at this stage**. Thanks, everybody. **I'm afraid we'll have to stop it there.**

E: Hi, guys. Sorry I'm late. Tania told you the story, right? Say, did I miss anything here?

7 Information age

7.1

a

Contrary to popular opinion the planet is not getting significantly warmer. **Nor is there any real evidence that** global warming is caused by heavy industry. Over the millennia the Earth's temperature has constantly fluctuated. Between 1850 and 1940, when there were almost no CO_2 emissions, it went up by one degree. But in spite of much higher levels of CO_2 emissions between 1940 and 1979, the rise in temperature was just 0.5 degrees. And since 1979 NASA satellites have in fact detected a slight global cooling of around 0.02 degrees.

b

It's impossible **to quote an exact figure** for the number of mergers that fail, **but there does seem to be some truth in** a recent study by KPMG, which puts the figure as high as 83%. **There is, however, disagreement as to** the precise failure rate. The Journal of European Industrial Training says 70% and the American Management Association 65. Certainly, in 1997 more than $1.6 trillion were spent on mergers and acquisitions, half of which, according to the Academy of Management Journal, eventually resulted in divestment or demerger.

c

It's a sobering thought that the world's seven richest countries do indeed earn 67% of global GDP. In fact, the richest 30% of the planet gets 90% of its income, leaving the remaining 70% of the world's population to get by on just 10%. The gap between rich and poor is now such that the average income in a rich country like Switzerland is around 280 times higher than that in a poor one like Mozambique, and the world's top three billionaires are able to earn as much as 600 million people in the poorest parts of the world.

d

The figure of 120 million km² may or may not be accurate, but with systematic replanting of new trees, the real question is: how many trees do we still have left? **It's simply not the case that**, as some environmentalists claim, the number of trees in the world has halved in the last 50 years. The fact is that global forest cover increased very slightly by 0.85% between 1950 and 1994 and is expected to continue to do so at least until 2100.

e

This is simply untrue. While there was a rise between 1984 and 1992, since then there has been an overall decline, in some years by as much as 33%. Young people typically get a bad press, each generation apparently worse than the last. But in a study by journalist Mike Males, he reports that, **statistically speaking**, today's teenagers are committing fewer crimes, smoking and drinking less, less likely to get pregnant and generally far healthier than adults. In fact, **surveys show** that 90% of them are happy, self-confident individuals.

f

The truth of the matter is that IMF and World Bank loans have not helped the economy of a single country they have been given to. In the old government-controlled days of 1969 to 1980 Latin America's per capita income grew by 73% and Africa's by 34%. Since IMF intervention and the subsequent privatisation and liberalisation programmes Latin America's growth has dropped to just 6% and Africa's to minus 23!

g

This figure was first referred to back in 1979 in Norman Myers' book *The Sinking Ark*. Myers estimated that a million species would die out in the following 25 years, which works out at 110 a day. In reality, however, no one even knows how many species there are – **estimates vary widely between** 1.6 and 80 million – much less how many have become extinct.

h

The shocking truth is that, in spite of international aid, 40 million people die from hunger every year. **To put that in perspective**, it's the equivalent of the entire population of Spain disappearing or 300 jumbo jets crashing every day of the year with no survivors.

▭ 7.2

1

A: Stefan, you work for a weekly business magazine in Frankfurt.

B: Uh huh.

A: So information really is the name of the game in your job, isn't it?

B: Yes, I suppose it is. But, erm, part of the problem today is that there's just too much information out there, and not all of it is reliable. It's, er, a complete maze of information, really.

A: You can get lost in it?

B: Exactly. Actually, Reuters produced a report on this very topic: information overload.

A: Oh, yes?

B: Yes, the report was called *Dying for Information*.

A: Very appropriate.

B: Yes. It was based on interviews with 1,300 managers in different countries, so it was very thorough. Anyway, what the report showed is that two thirds of managers suffer from stress and poor health, and one of the main causes is what they're calling 'information anxiety syndrome'.

A: Information anxiety syndrome?

B: Yes, caused mostly by the Internet. Apparently, managers are getting so frustrated knowing that the information they need is out there somewhere …

A: But it could take them the rest of their lives to find it!

B: Precisely. It's driving them crazy!

2

A: Olga, you work for the Russian subsidiary of a multinational mobile phone company.

B: Yes.

A: How well informed are you about what's going on in your sister companies around the world?

B: Well, pretty well informed, I think. In fact, we regularly benchmark all our company's national divisions against each other.

A: Benchmark?

B: Yes, compare them, according to different criteria, to see who's outperforming whom.

A: Oh, I see.

B: Yes, and then the top performers in each category coach the others on how to get the same results. Actually, we estimate that just one knowledge-sharing exercise like this boosted our sales revenue by $65 million.

A: Impressive.

B: Mm. It's all part of what we call 'knowledge management', or KM. We think our most important asset is the information our employees carry around in their heads: their intellectual capital. If you think about it, so much routine work can be automated, digitised or outsourced, your knowledge – your expertise – is all you've got, really. In fact, KM guru Thomas A. Stewart has calculated that whereas the cost of a product used to be about 80% materials and 20% know-how, now it's split 70:30 the other way. And there's a Swedish insurance firm, Skandia, which actually has its very own director of intellectual capital.

3

A: Lee, you work for a financial services company in the City of London.

B: That's right, yeah.

A: I imagine it's all much faster now in these days of computerised financial markets. Does it ever get too fast? Do people start making mistakes with all this information coming at them?

B: Oh, sure. There's quite a lot of room for error with computers, I can tell you. They're a disaster waiting to happen, really.

A: Can you give me an example?

B: Well, yeah, I mean losing a fortune can be as easy as pressing the wrong button!

A: Not as easy as that, surely?

B: Oh, yeah. A few years ago the whole London FTSE 100 Index actually fell by two per cent when some trader typed £300 million into his computer instead of 30 million.

A: You're joking!

B: No, it's absolutely true. Too much pressure, basically. And, er, oh, yeah, back in the late 90s, some guy at Salomon Brothers, I think it was, made an even bigger mistake. Sold 850 million pounds' worth of French government bonds – by accident!

A: By accident?

B: Completely by accident. He leaned on his computer keyboard and sold the lot!

8 Promoting your ideas

▭ 8.1

1

Erm, well, to tell you the truth, there's a part of me that's still scared I might just **dry up completely**. I mean, you know, **your mind goes completely blank**? Makes me sweat just thinking about it. I have this nightmare where **the audience has gone deadly quiet**, and everybody in the room's just staring at me and I haven't got a clue what to say next! It's only ever happened to me once, thank god, but I still lose sleep over it in case it ever happens again.

2

Technology. Well, it's Sod's Law, isn't it? **If anything can go wrong it will**. About a year ago, I had not one, but two projectors **break down** on me. And then **my mike went funny** as well. I sounded like Darth Vader out of *Star Wars* for about half an hour until they fixed it. Completely ruined my whole presentation, obviously. I went mad with the technicians afterwards. But what can you do?

3

I always seem to **run out of time** and then have to rush the end of the talk or, even worse, **run over schedule**. Audiences hate that. I've had people tell me I overprepare, but it doesn't seem to matter what I do, I always have at least twenty minutes too much material. So, for me, every talk's a race against the clock!

4

Well, some people, older people especially, have told me that I move around too much when I speak in public

– you know, that I **pace up and down** and **wave my arms about**. They say it's distracting. They can't concentrate on what I'm saying. But for me, as an Italian, you know, it's quite normal for us to jump around, be rather dramatic. So, now I worry about trying to stand still. And that just makes me feel tense and uncomfortable.

5

What was it Franklin D. Roosevelt said? The only thing to fear is fear itself? That's the thing I'm afraid of, still, after all these years in business – fear. Ridiculous, isn't it? But fear's an absolute killer in a presentation. **Your mouth goes dry. Your heart speeds up. Your legs turn to jelly.** In my experience, the first two minutes are usually the worst. Survive those and you're in with a chance.

📼 8.2

1

Er, well, I think the most important thing to remember is that people expect you to be an expert in your field of business. I mean a real expert. That means you should **have all the technical information at your fingertips**. Which is not to say they won't want to see it all in print after the presentation as well. And if you don't cover every detail in your pitch – costings, cash flow projections, everything – believe me, they won't be slow to interrupt you to ask for it. People here seem to like PowerPoint, the whole technology thing, you know. A word of warning, though: forget the jokes. If you try to be a comedian, they just won't take you seriously.

2

Erm, I think the main thing here is to **give your presentation the personal touch**. That's what they value above everything else. You see, they're judging *you* as much as, if not more than, what you're actually talking about. But, erm, I think too many presenters worry about offending the local culture and then they end up sounding much too conservative. Don't. Be loud, be lively, be eloquent. They love all that. It's true that attention spans do tend to be a bit short sometimes and you'll get loads of interruptions, but **just go with the flow**. In any case, people will probably want to talk to you about everything all over again later.

3

Well, it's almost a cliché, but the hard sell does actually work here. And, believe me, you really can't be too assertive. In fact, they *want* you to impress them and expect you to work hard to maintain their interest. So, be fast, be slick, make sure you **have a few gimmicks up your sleeve**. They like all that stuff. And you can say as many nasty things about your competitors as you like – especially if they're funny. Humour's nearly always appreciated, and, er, you don't need to be too subtle with that. They don't want dark sarcasm, though – so nothing too negative. Wisecracks, clever remarks – that's what they tend to **go for**.

4

Erm, my main piece of advice here is: don't overwhelm them with your enthusiasm. Of course, they expect you to be highly competent and confident, but quietly confident. People'll probably have read through all the paperwork beforehand, but they'll want you to **go through** all the main points again. For the sake of formality and politeness, they'll want to hear it directly from you. But **don't get so carried away talking about your own ideas** that you forget to point out why it is their company you especially want to do business with. That's very important – creating a sense of harmony and compatibility between you and them. Oh, and a long-term commitment for them, by the way, is 20 to 25 years, not three to five, as it is in the States.

5

I suppose having a sense of humour's the main thing. In fact, you can't **do without** it really. Certainly, if you haven't made them laugh even once within the first five minutes, you probably won't be very popular. People may even **switch off** altogether. Speakers are kind of expected to be fairly entertaining as well as knowledgeable about their product or service. You don't actually have to crack jokes the whole time, but anecdotes and amusing stories seem to **go down well**. Making jokes at your own expense, especially, seems to help build rapport with an audience that can otherwise seem a bit cold and unfriendly. And don't try to wow them too much with technology. Be too techno and people'll just think you're **showing off**.

6

Being stylish seems to be what matters here – both in terms of your personal appearance and how you actually **come across** as a person. It's true that you do have to **keep up** a certain formality and your talk should always be logical and well-organised, but within those constraints you can be as imaginative and innovative as you like. In fact, unless you are offering something pretty special, something 'sexy', something unique that they haven't seen before, you'll find them very difficult to persuade. Obviously, knowing exactly who you're presenting to is always important, but here it really is essential that you **do your homework**. And, er, don't be surprised if the questions you get asked seem quite hostile. Tough questioning is all part of the business culture here.

📼 8.3

Extract 1

A: Good morning, everybody. Thanks for coming. I'm Rachel Weissmuller, area manager for the north-west division, and this is Brad Kennedy, head of our physiological research unit.

B: Hi.

A: As some of you already know, Brad and I have been working on a project of our own for some time now – a project, which we think you're going to be as excited about as we are. Brad?

B: Thanks, Rachel. Well, now, as the USA's leading chain of health clubs with over 1,000 centres in 35 states, we pride ourselves on providing the best in fitness training programs, on getting nearly a quarter million Americans off the couch and into the gym. For us, staying in shape is not just a business. It's a way of life. There's just one problem – the majority of Americans don't seem to be getting the message. According to the National Center for Health Statistics, seven out of ten of us don't take regular exercise. Four out of ten are not physically active at all! Figures recently published by the Surgeon General show that 61% of Americans are now seriously overweight. That's 122 million people! A disgraceful statistic. But, you have to admit, one hell of a marketing opportunity! The question is, how do we reach that market with something totally new?

Extract 2

A: A recent report claims that a mere 13% of Americans are satisfied with their physical appearance. And a staggering 92% are dissatisfied with their current level of fitness. So, why aren't they doing something about it? We did a nationwide survey of people who had previously shown an interest in joining a MaxOut club and then changed their minds. Full details are in the report in front of you, but this chart highlights our main findings. As you can see, 15% of respondents said joining a gym was simply too expensive. Fifty-three per cent said they'd love to join if they weren't so busy. And, interestingly, 32%, almost a third, admitted they were just too embarrassed to join a health club in their present physical condition. They wanted to get fit first! So, what does all this mean? We think the implications are clear. There's obviously a huge market for an inexpensive alternative to going to the gym for people who are conscious of their appearance but short of time. And this represents a golden opportunity to stretch the MaxOut brand and develop a new product that perfectly complements our existing business.

Extract 3

B: OK. And now the moment you've all been waiting for! The MaxOut Micro-GYM! Forty per cent of our project budget went into constructing the prototype. And it's taken 18 months to get this far with the design. But does this look cool, or what? I'll pass it round in a moment. Ladies and gentlemen, what you're looking at is the world's smallest full-body workout system – ever. The ultimate go-anywhere exercise machine. And, we believe, a significant part of this company's future. With its sleek, lightweight design, the Micro-GYM weighs just over a pound, or 450 grammes. That's less than most quality cameras. Disassembled, it fits easily into a coat pocket. The assembly itself is childsplay. You can be ready to exercise in under 45 seconds. Now, I know what you're thinking. Can something so small possibly work? But let me reassure you. The Micro-GYM offers 35 different exercises for upper body, lower body and mid-section. It can be adjusted from the five-kilo setting for gentle exercise right up to the 18-kilo setting for a real workout. In fact, it can do just about anything that much bulkier and more expensive equipment can. When you can't get to the gym, the Micro-GYM comes to you. You can get fit at home, on holiday, at the office, even in-flight!

Extract 4

A: You'll have to excuse Brad. He gets a little carried away sometimes. But we do think the Micro-GYM could be an enormously successful sideline to our main business. OK, to wrap things up. The Micro-GYM has been fully costed – a complete breakdown is included in the report. Estimated costs of manufacturing, packaging and advertising are all itemised. Product testing is still being carried out, but we would obviously need the go-ahead from you before we proceed much further with that. The Micro-GYM would probably be priced at around $35: well within the reach of most people. It has been suggested that exercise demonstrations could be recorded on video and that the product might easily be sold online. Both these suggestions would incur extra costs, but are currently being considered. The prospects for Micro-GYM are exciting. What we hope you'll give us today is the authorisation to move on to the next stage. Thank you very much.

B: Thank you, Rachel. OK, we'd like to throw this session open now for questions and suggestions. But, no, sorry, you can't take the Micro-GYM home just yet. It's the only one we have at the moment!

9 Relationship-building

 9.1

Extract 1

A: Stella! Max! You're just in time to join us in a little pre-match drink.

B: Hi, Craig. Hi, Karen. Oh, is that malt whisky? I don't know if I should. I mean, I just had breakfast!

A: Nonsense! It's just the thing to warm us up. Max, you'll have one, won't you?

C: Of course, thank you.

A: There you go. Stella?

B: Well, OK, just a drop. It *is* a little chilly this morning. Beautiful day, though.

A: Isn't it? Well, now, **we should probably be thinking of making a**

move quite soon. Unfortunately, **we can't count on the weather staying fine at this time of year**. Max, you're partnering Karen. And Stella, you're stuck with me, I'm afraid. Now, **I've arranged for us to have lunch at the clubhouse** – they've got an excellent restaurant there. So I thought we'd start at the tenth and just play the last nine holes, if that's OK with you. That way **we should be able to get round the course in a couple of hours or so**.

C: Sounds perfect.

A: And, Max, I think you'll find my game's improved a little since we last played.

C: Splendid! I always like a challenge, Craig. You know that …

Extract 2

A: Damn! I don't know what's the matter with my game today. I just can't seem to keep the ball straight. Sorry, Stella. **You must be wishing you'd been teamed up with Max**.

B: Well, you have been in two sand-traps and a lake, Craig! And this is only our third hole!

A: I know, I know. Your shot, Max …

B: Craig, **I've been meaning to have a word with you about this disposal operation** of ours.

A: Ah, **I was wondering when you'd get round to mentioning that**. Look, Stella, you know my position on that …

B: Now, Craig, listen to me. You know I want that oil platform disposed of at sea. It's by far the most cost-effective method.

C: (*coughs for silence*)

B: Oh, sorry, Max. Not trying to put you off your game. Oh, great shot! Wow, that's almost all the way to the flag! Craig, you didn't tell me Max was such a fantastic player.

A: No, I, er, look, Stella, this oil platform – disposing of it at sea. Don't you think that's a bit risky? I know it's technically possible. But there must be 130 tonnes of highly toxic and radioactive substances on that platform!

B: Craig, you're starting to sound like a Greenpeace activist, for goodness' sake! … By the way, I understand you've applied for the top job here in Scotland.

A: Yeah, so?

B: So's Max.

A: What?

B: Yeah. And the way it's looking he may well get it. Seems the board like his competitive spirit.

A: I see.

B: Of course, I could probably put in a word for you. Let's talk later. For the time being, I'd like you to concentrate on your game! I'm not a good loser, Craig!

Extract 1

A: Magda!

B: Hello, Anne. Brrr! It's a bit nasty out there tonight.

A: Horrible, isn't it? Come on in. **Let me take your coat. You managed to find us OK, then?**

B: Well, I got a bit lost coming off the ring road, as usual. Sorry I'm a bit late.

A: Oh, don't worry. Martin's still slaving away in the kitchen. Actually, he had a bit of a crisis with the starter just half an hour ago. You should have heard the language! Probably just as well you weren't here.

B: Oh, right. So Martin's cooking, is he?

A: Mm. He's quite an expert in the kitchen – fortunately for me. I can't boil an egg myself!

B: **Oh, I brought you this**. I wasn't sure what you liked, but apparently it's meant to be quite a good year.

A: Oh, thanks. **You shouldn't have**. Lovely. I'll put it in the fridge. **Come on through**.

Extract 2

B: **Oh, what a fabulous apartment!**

A: Thanks. We like it.

B: Have you been here long?

A: Um … about two years now. The whole place was an absolute wreck when we moved in. We had to do just about everything to it. **Now, what can I get you to drink?** How about a gin and tonic? That's what I'm having.

B: Yes, that'd be great.

A: Ice and lemon?

B: Please.

A: OK. **I'll be right back. Make yourself at home**.
(*pause*)

C: Hi, Magda. I'm Martin. I don't think we've met.

B: Hello, Martin. Pleased to meet you. You're the chef, I understand.

C: Oh, yes. Doing a good job of setting fire to the kitchen at the moment. I had to rescue the starter.

B: So I heard.

A: Ah, so you two have met. Good. There we are, Magda. Let me know if want more ice in that.

B: Thanks.

A: Are we nearly ready, then, darling?

C: Er, yes, I'm just waiting for the sauce. In fact, I'd better go and check on it. I don't trust that new cooker.

A: Oh, OK.

Extract 3

B: **I was just looking at some of your oil paintings**, Anne. **You've got quite a collection, haven't you?**

A: Mm, yes. Dutch mostly. Eighteenth century. They're Martin's, really.

B: **And I love the way you've done the fireplace. Was that here when you moved in?**

A: Yes, it's the original. We had to have it restored, obviously.

B: And what beautiful chairs. I could do with some of those for my place. French, aren't they?

A: Italian, actually. We bought them at an auction in Milan.

B: Oh, really? And, wow! **Look at that view!**

A: Good, isn't it?

B: You can see practically the whole city from here.

C: **Dinner's ready when you are.**
(*pause*)

C: Right, Magda, **sit wherever you like.** Now, we're having duck in a port sauce.

B: Mm, smells delicious!

C: So, **I thought we'd have a nice Spanish red**, something with a bit of body in it. Or do you prefer white?

B: No, red's fine, thanks.

Extract 4

C: **Now, there's more duck if you want it. And help yourself to vegetables.**

B: **Mm, this is absolutely delicious.**

A: It's one of Martin's specialities.

B: Mm, it's really good. The duck's all crispy on the outside and juicy on the inside.

C: **I'm glad you like it.**

B: **You must let me have the recipe.**

C: Oh, it's very simple, really. You just need the right ingredients.

A: **A little more wine**, Magda?

B: **I shouldn't really. I'm driving.**

A: **Oh, go on. You've only had one.**

B: Oh, all right, **just a drop, then.**

A: Magda, I've been meaning to talk to you about this business in Poland.

B: Oh, yes, that.

A: Do *you* know what's going on there? Because no one seems to be able to tell *me* anything.

C: Right, well, excuse me a moment. If you two are going to talk business, I'll go and see to the dessert.
(*pause*)

B: **Well, I ought to be making a move soon.** Early start tomorrow.

C: Oh, **you don't have to rush off just yet, do you? How about some more coffee?**

B: **OK, just half a cup. And then I really must be going.**
(*pause*)

B: Well, **thank you both for a lovely evening.** Martin, you're a brilliant cook.

C: I know. There's no point denying it.

B: **Next time you must come to my place**, although I can't promise you such a fabulous meal.

A: Bye, Magda. **Take care now.** See you tomorrow.

10 Taking decisions

🔊 10.1

1

Don't even think about jumping from a moving vehicle. At 70 miles per hour **the chances** of surviving **are remote.** And crashing into the mountainside at this speed will almost certainly send you straight through the windscreen. So, even though you may be scared of going over the cliff, your best chance of slowing the car down is to repeatedly run it against the crash barriers. After all, that's what they're there for.

2

Resist the temptation to run. You cannot outrun or outclimb a mountain lion. And **put any ideas of** playing dead **out of your mind**. Whilst it may work with grizzly bears, to a mountain lion you'll just look like a free lunch. **Your best bet is to** shout and flap your coat at the animal to make yourself look bigger and fiercer than you really are. Mountain lions are not proud. If you look like more trouble than you're worth, **there's a fifty-fifty chance** they'll back away.

3

Water transfers heat away from the body 25 times faster than air. So trying to keep warm is more or less futile. And while you're staying calm and conserving energy, the chances are you're dying. You have to get out. Turn in the direction you fell and use your elbows to lift yourself onto the edge of the ice. Reach forward as far as possible and kick your feet as if you were swimming. Once you are back on the ice, crawl to shore. **Do not in any circumstances** try to stand up.

4

The current world record for the long jump is just under nine metres, but most people can barely manage three or four. The chances are you can't either. To clear four and a half metres in conditions that are far from ideal you'd need a 20 to 30 metre run-up, perfect timing and a great deal of luck. Frankly, **your chances are slim.** The truck is a much better idea and it is quite possible to fall from the sixth floor and live. But don't jump out from the building unless there are balconies in the way. You'll be carried forward and miss the truck completely. Drop vertically and **take care to** land on your back to avoid breaking it.

5

The taxi could take anything from a few minutes to just a few seconds to sink. But **there's not much point trying to** force the door open because the water pressure will make this almost impossible. If the car does sink there'll be little or no air left anyway, so **forget about** trapping air inside. **By far the most sensible thing to do is** to open the window and actually let more water in. Even if you can't escape through the window, once the water pressure inside and outside the car are equalised, **there's a fair chance** you'll be able to open the door and save yourself – and maybe the driver too!

6

It's very unusual for both parachutes to fail, so by struggling with the emergency chute **there's an outside chance** you'll get it to work. But don't bet on it. You may just be wasting precious time. If you can share one of your friends' parachutes **you're in with a chance**, but just grabbing onto the nearest person **is not a smart move**. The G-force when the parachute opens will throw you apart. At 14,000 feet and falling at your terminal velocity of 120 miles per hour you've got about 75 seconds before your appointment with Mother Earth. So firmly attach yourself to the chest straps of another parachutist. **You don't stand a chance** unless you do.

7

You are 30 times more likely to be struck by lightning than to be attacked by a shark, but this is little comfort in your present position. Splashing around and making a noise will simply give the shark the idea you're in distress and easy meat. **It's a common mistake to** think the shark's nose is the best area to target. Punch it there and you are liable to lose a hand or arm – depending on the size of the shark. **You'd do much better to** strike at its eyes or gills since these are a shark's most vulnerable points.

8

When landing a light aircraft, **make sure** that the nose of the plane is six inches below the horizon. As you approach the runway the plane should be flying at an altitude of about 100 feet. If you're higher, you'll overshoot the runway completely. The optimum speed on landing is about 60 miles per hour. Go faster and you may take off again. Go slower and you'll drop like a stone. Upon landing, **it's a good idea to** brake as soon as you've gained control of the steering. By reducing your groundspeed by 50% you triple your chances of survival.

🔊 10.2

1

A: Right, as you know, our last offer to the union was a three per cent pay rise and a two-hour reduction in the working week to be gradually phased in over the next 18 months. **The ball is** now firmly **in their court**. Ragnar, do you have any idea which way they'll vote?

B: The word is they'll turn it down. In fact, they might even be considering taking industrial action.

A: A strike?

B: I don't know, Dan. It's a possibility.

A: With the current backlog of orders a strike's the last thing we need!

C: Now, let's not **jump to conclusions.** They haven't announced the result of the vote yet.

B: My sources are usually accurate, Per.

A: **Look, time is short**. If the vote goes against us, I want us to be able to come straight back with an improved offer. **So let's put our heads together and see what we can come up with.**

2

A: **OK, we've weighed up the various pros and cons. Now it's time to reach a decision and stick to it**. Our latest information is that the political situation in Somalia is worsening. In fact, it may only be a matter of days before the country is plunged into civil war. The proposal is that we should pull our people out of there immediately.

B: Now, wait a minute, Richard. **I don't want us rushing into anything. This whole issue requires long and careful consideration**. This is our biggest production plant in North Africa and we're talking about closing it down here.

A: I'm well aware of that, Hans. But **I take it we're all in agreement that our first priority is to safeguard the well-being of our personnel.**

B: Of course.

A: **Well, then, I don't see we have any option but to give this proposal our full backing**.

C: Aren't we overlooking something here? I mean it's all very well talking about flying our management team home and closing the plant, but what about our factory workers? They'll all be out of a job.

A: I'm afraid our responsibility to local workers is different, Andrea. **When it comes to the crunch**, we have to look after our European staff first …

3

A: OK, you've all seen the results of the road tests. It looks like the two-litre model has some kind of a steering problem and we may have to authorise a total product recall while we conduct further tests.

B: Isn't that a bit drastic, Simon? I mean, it's only a slight steering problem, isn't it? And it doesn't seem to be affecting the smaller-engined models.

A: Well, that's what we're here to discuss, Matt. With a safety issue like this I don't think we should take any chances, but **I'd like your input on this before committing us to any definite course of action**. Laura?

C: Hm, **I'm in two minds about it**. I mean, I agree with you that the safety of our customers must come first. But if we take the whole series off the market, I dread to think what the newspapers will do with the story. **At this stage I think we should keep our options open**. And these test results aren't conclusive, are they?

A: Well, no, but I don't think we can just **sit on the fence** here. In the long run, failing to act quickly could do us a lot of harm.

B: So what do you suggest?

A: **Well, in the absence of more reliable data, I think I'm going to have to go with my gut instinct on this one**. I'm just not prepared to put our customers' lives at risk …

🔊 **10.3**

The mighty Coca-Cola has been the world's number one brand for so long, it's hard to imagine anything threatening its position of global dominance. One of the company's own publicity brochures proudly declares: 'A billion hours ago human life appeared on Earth; a billion minutes ago Christianity emerged; a billion seconds ago the Beatles performed on the Ed Sullivan Show – a billion servings of Coca-Cola ago was yesterday morning.' Quite a claim. And one that makes a loss of consumer confidence unthinkable.

But take yourself back to May 1999. The unthinkable has just happened. Hundreds of people in Belgium and France have become ill after drinking what they claim is contaminated Coke. And when the cause of the problem cannot quickly be established, the famous soft drink is officially banned in both countries as well as Luxembourg and the Netherlands. The price you pay for being the brand leader is that customers expect quality, as Coca-Cola's CEO is the first to admit. 'For 113 years,' he says, 'our success has been based on the trust that consumers have in that quality.' Now that trust is shaken.

In fact, the four countries banning Coke only represent two per cent of the company's $18.8 billion in annual sales. But within a week consignments exported from Belgium to other countries as far apart as Germany and the Ivory Coast have also been seized by officials. Though no definite proof of contamination has yet been found, the panic is starting to spread …

🔊 **10.4**

1999 is not a good year for soft drinks companies. Though the Dow is up 25%, both Coke and Pepsi, normally well ahead of the market, are down by around 13%. Coca-Cola is not going to rush into a highly expensive product recall.

In any case, early examinations of the Belgian bottling plants find nothing unusual and an official toxicologist's report concludes that the 200 cases of sickness are probably psychosomatic.

But while Coca-Cola is deliberating over what action to take, rivals Pepsi and Virgin Cola are quick to fill the gaps left on the supermarket shelves. And Coke's refusal to react until it has conducted a thorough investigation is starting to look like a denial of responsibility …

🔊 **10.5**

This is how Coca-Cola actually handled the problem.

Initially, full-page advertisements were taken out in European newspapers to reassure the public that the quality of Coke was 'irreproachable'. This was not totally successful as the public at that time could still remember a similar contamination scare at Perrier some years before and all the talk was of pesticides on fruit and mad cow disease.

But, fortunately, the source of the Coke contamination was eventually traced to a strange fungicide on cans shipped from Dunkirk and poor carbon dioxide at Coca-Cola's bottling plant in Antwerp which makes the Coke taste a little different but does no real harm. It wasn't the Coke itself but the cans that were contaminated.

Coke took the necessary measures and, at enormous cost to the company, all 17 million cases of Coke were withdrawn. Finally, in a spectacular public relations coup, and as an apology to the Belgians who had been ill, Coca-Cola offered a free one-and-a-half litre bottle of Coke to each and every one of Belgium's ten million citizens! Coke was immediately back in the stores.

11 Branded planet

🔊 **11.1**

A: Next on CBN Business: *'Branded!'* Ruth Silbiger reports on the companies aiming to brand our lives and the 'adbusters' out to stop them.

B: The average American is bombarded with 274 advertisements a day – or seven million over a lifetime! On billboard and football shirt, TV screen and PC monitor, there's no escape from our branded planet.

The stakes are high. In 2002 PepsiCo spent nearly nine million dollars on a 90-second commercial featuring Britney Spears to be screened at the world's biggest sporting event, the American Superbowl. Sure enough, 75 million viewers watched the ad.

But were they paying attention? Celebrity endorsements like the Spears ad seem to make a big initial impact. But then what? These days, most of us channel hop during commercials, throw junk mail straight in the garbage and delete spam unread.

In the never-ending battle to keep our attention, the advertisers have tried everything. First they tried corporate sponsorship. But do we buy Vodaphone because it zooms past us at 180 miles per hour on the side of Michael Schumacher's Ferrari? Probably not.

Then they tried product placement. But when Tom Cruise walks into a GAP store in the film *Minority Report*, we barely notice. We're looking at Tom, not the clothes.

Now they're trying branded content – commercials so subtle, they look like straight entertainment; commercials so cool people *choose* to watch them. Nike's latest, a basketball skills film with a loud dance beat, was so popular MTV ran it as regular programming. The company was scarcely mentioned. But not a basketball player under the age of 20 didn't know who it was.

So how do the top brand names keep up with what's cool? In the youth market, by employing so-called cool hunters to prowl the streets, shopping malls, nightclubs and inner-city basketball courts. These cool hunters blend in with the rest of the teenagers and report back on what's in, what's out and what's going to be the next big thing.

But has all this wild consumer-spending gone too far? The Vancouver-based magazine *Adbusters* thinks so and went on CNN to propose an alternative in a controversial TV commercial that was subsequently turned down by ABC, NBC and CBS. This is what they said:

'The average American consumes five times more than a Mexican, ten times more than a Chinese person and thirty times more than a person from India. We are the most voracious consumers in the world – a world that could die because of the way we North Americans live. Give it a rest. November 29 is Buy Nothing Day.'

■ 11.2

A: … Well, it's the old exploitation argument, isn't it? Ten-year-old kids working for ten cents an hour in Indonesia to make overpriced sports shoes that sell for $180 in the West. We've heard it all before.
B: It's still a disgrace. Did you know that in the last 20 years the number of people living on less than a dollar a day has actually *increased*? So much for globalisation! Look at the profits those companies must be making.
A: That's not the point. They just pay the standard rate for the countries they're in. Did you know that in Vietnam a Nike worker gets paid more than some doctors?
B: No way!
A: It's true. And, anyway, there's a lot more to running a business than just the price of making stuff.
B: There is if you pay some adolescent pop star millions to promote it, yeah.
A: It's not just that. You've got design and development costs, warehousing, shipping, whole finance and marketing departments. These so-called anti-globalisationists – they just don't understand the first thing about how business works. Take these protesters in Seattle and London and just about everywhere else these days. They're just a bunch of anarchists.
B: Made the World Bank change its mind though, didn't they?
A: Did they? Just made a nuisance of themselves, if you ask me.
B: No, apparently, the World Bank's now finally accepting that economic growth is not enough to reduce poverty. You've got to have sustainable development as well.
A: Sustainable development!
B: It's true. The French are particularly in favour. They've got that tax now – what is it? … the Tobin tax – to stop financial speculators taking capital out of poorer countries.

A: Oh, well, the French, yes. But they're just anti-American, aren't they? Like that guy … what was his name? Smashed up a McDonald's restaurant in his tractor or something. Ridiculous!
B: He was simply saying France doesn't want any more junk food, thanks very much. Good luck to him, I say.
A: Well, that's a joke for a start. McDonald's is France's biggest restaurant chain.
B: No way! Where did you read that?
A: It was in *The Economist* the other day. They've got nearly a thousand McDonald's in France now.
B: Good god. Well, I mean that's just my point, isn't it? All these brands are taking over the world. Apparently, more people go to Ikea on Sundays than church these days.
A: Doesn't surprise me. According to this programme I watched, you can get married at Disney World and buried in a Harley Davidson coffin as well if you want to.
B: What's it all coming to, eh? You know the average American consumes thirty times more than an Indian?
A: Yeah, but that doesn't mean much. I mean, if you look at the GDP per capita, you'll find the average American *produces seventy* times more than an Indian.
B: Does he?
A: Roughly. Look, the thing is, world trade is good for jobs. And living standards. Capitalism works. Those World Bank figures prove it. The more globalisation, the more growth.
B: Yeah, but it's not quite as simple as that, is it?
A: Isn't it?
B: Well, you know all those countries that have been getting these IMF and World Bank loans?
A: Like in Latin America and Africa, you mean?
B: Exactly. Well, did you know that they were actually better off before they got the loans?
A: What? Under all those military, socialist, protectionist governments? I don't think so.
B: No, it's true. You see, there are always conditions to these loans. Like Mexico joins NAFTA, right, gets a loan provided it accepts a load of toxic waste as well.
A: Ah, yeah, but that's a different …
B: Or Ecuador gets a World Bank loan and is ordered to liberalise its markets – let capital flow in and out freely.
A: So what's wrong with that?
B: What's wrong is it flows freely all right – but only out. So they raise interest rates to 90%, sell off all their assets, anything to bring cash back into the country and it all goes to hell.
A: Well, yeah, but …
B: And look at Brazil. It owes about, what, $235 billion now?
A: Well, no one expects them to pay that back, do they?
B: They already have paid it back.
A: The whole amount? 235 billion?

B: Yeah – in interest!
A: What, you mean the interest is now as much as the loan?
B: No, now it exceeds the loan. You see, the thing is, in some places capitalism just doesn't work. Take Africa …

12 E-mailing

■ 12.1

A: This week on CyberReport Terry Lancaster takes a look at some of the biggest e-mail blunders ever made.
B: In April 2000 millions of computer users received an unexpected e-mail. The subject line was intriguing. It said: 'I love you.' Those whose curiosity got the better of them opened the message and unleashed what later became known as the Love Bug – a virus so lethal it has so far infected 45 million PCs and caused 8.7 billion dollars' worth of damage to computer networks worldwide.

Computer viruses like the Love Bug sound like every company's worst nightmare. But the real danger these days is not so much what can get *into* your e-mail system as what can get *out*. You just never know where that e-mail you now regret sending may end up.

The first high-profile blunder occurred in 1997 when employees at the Norwich Union insurance company started spreading a rumour about a competitor on their internal e-mail system. Western Provident, they said, was about to go bankrupt. Western Provident was *not* about to go bankrupt, and when the e-mails suggesting it was came into their possession, it sued. The case was eventually settled out of court for a cool £450,000.

Three years later, Londoner Claire Swire briefly became a celebrity when sexually explicit e-mails she sent to her boyfriend were forwarded to mailboxes right across the world. It might not have been so bad, had Swire's boyfriend not worked for Norton Rose, a company which gives specialist advice to businesses on effective electronic communications.

Understandably, then, when Dow Chemical discovered hundreds of X-rated e-mails being exchanged between members of staff, the company took no chances. It fired 74 employees and suspended a further 435.

But disciplining your staff electronically isn't always a good idea, as the CEO of Cerner, Neal Patterson, found out to his cost. When Patterson reprimanded 400 managers by e-mail, his criticisms somehow found their way onto the Yahoo! website – for all the world to see. Cerner stock fell by 28% within the week.

And at Merrill Lynch in 2002, the company ended up paying out $100 million when Henry Blodget, an Internet stock analyst, strongly recommended buying stock in a company he had previously described, in what he thought was a private e-mail, as 'a piece of crap'.

But perhaps the most famous business e-mails in history came to light during the Microsoft antitrust trials. Netscape CEO Jim Barksdale claimed his company never wanted to collaborate with Microsoft in the Internet browser market – until, that is, Microsoft lawyers unearthed an e-mail from Netscape president Jim Clark to a senior executive at Microsoft stating clearly: 'We do not want to compete with you.' And Microsoft, for its part, denied any attempt to push Netscape out of the market – until an e-mail from Bill Gates to AOL executives was submitted as evidence. The e-mail read: 'How much do we need to pay you to screw Netscape?' Oh, dear!

So the message is clear. With e-mail, honesty is not always the best policy. And if you must tell the truth, think twice before clicking that send button.

A: That was Terry Lancaster talking about the biggest e-mail blunders ever made. And now a sneak preview of the latest in wireless technology …

13 Making an impact

📼 13.1

1
Did you know that of the world's one hundred biggest economies only 49 are actually countries? That's right, 49. The other 51 are companies! In fact, if companies were allowed to join the G7 group of the world's richest countries, Microsoft would take the place of Canada! I think it's getting a little scary, don't you, when a corporation can outperform a nation? And maybe it's time to stop and ask ourselves: should business really be that powerful?

2
You know, the joke books of the world are probably full of more lawyer jokes than just about anything else. **One of my favourite** lawyer **jokes is**: this guy's having a quiet drink in a bar when a drunk starts shouting 'All lawyers are dirty criminals!' The man jumps to his feet and cries 'I resent that remark!' 'Why?' says the drunk. 'Are you a lawyer?' 'No' says the man, 'I'm a criminal!' But I'm here to tell you that not all lawyers are corrupt. It's just 99% of them who give the others a bad name.

3
Good morning. Erm, **I'd like to start off by thanking** Dr Jensen, Dr Tan and, er, Dr Martinez, of the faculty of cybernetic engineering for inviting me to speak today. Our company has a long history of collaboration with this university and it's always a great pleasure to address the robotics experts of the future. Erm, yes, before I begin, perhaps I could just take a moment or two to introduce you to the rest of my team, who are here with me this morning …

4
I think it was Thomas Edison **who said**: 'I have not failed. I've just found 10,000 ways that don't work.' Of course, Edison was an inventor, but he could just as easily have been talking about sales. In sales, our success rate is nowhere near as bad as one in 10,000. At least, it better not be! But we have to go through an awful lot of 'no sales' to make one sale. And the ability to deal with failure is the single most important characteristic of the successful sales professional. Could you just raise your hand if you failed to make a sale yesterday? … Just about everybody, right? Well, congratulations! You're obviously on the right track!

5
I was looking through the appointments pages **the other day** – don't we all? – **and came across this** unusual job advertisement. Here it is: 'Good hours, excellent pay, fun place to work, paid training, mean boss! Oh, well, four out of five isn't bad.' Wouldn't you like to be interviewed by that boss who admits he's mean? How powerful that little touch of honesty is. And that's exactly what I want to talk to you about this morning: honesty in advertising. And how you get people's attention when you simply tell the truth …

6
Whenever I'm asked about Total Quality, **I think of the story of** the American steel magnate, Andrew Carnegie. It seems Carnegie was doing a factory tour one day, when he stopped to speak to one of the machine operators – a grey-haired old guy obviously coming up to retirement. 'Wilson,' he said, reading the man's name badge, 'how many years exactly have you been working for me now?' 'Thirty-nine, sir,' Wilson replied with a proud smile. 'And may I add that in all those years I made only one very small mistake.' 'Good work,' mumbled Carnegie, 'but from now on, please try to be more careful.'

📼 13.2

Extract 1
In the long history of the world, only a few generations have been granted the role of **defending freedom** in its hour of maximum danger. **I do not shrink from this responsibility – I welcome it. I do not** believe that **any** of us would exchange places with **any other** people or **any other** generation. **The energy, the faith, the devotion**, which we bring to this endeavour will **light** our country and all who serve it – **and the glow from that fire can truly light the world**. And so, **my fellow** Americans, **ask not what your country can do for you – ask what you can do for your country. My fellow** citizens of the world, **ask not what**

America will do for you – but what together we can do for the freedom of man.
(*John F. Kennedy, Washington DC, 20.1.61*)

Extract 2
I say to you **today**, my friends … so even though we face the difficulties of **today and tomorrow, I still have a dream**. It is a **dream** deeply rooted in the American **dream. I have a dream that one day** this nation will rise up and live out the true meaning of its creed: 'We hold these truths to be self-evident; that all men are created equal.' **I have a dream that one day** on the red hills of Georgia **the sons of former slaves and the sons of former slave owners** will be able to sit down together **at the table of brotherhood. I have a dream that one day** even the **state** of Mississippi, a **state sweltering with the heat of injustice, sweltering with the heat of oppression**, will be transformed into **an oasis of freedom and justice. I have a dream** that my four little children **will one day live in a nation where they will not be judged by the colour of their skin but by the content of their character. I have a dream today.**
(*Martin Luther King, Washington DC, 28.8.63*)

Extract 3
These are the two great challenges of our time – **the moral and political challenge, and the economic challenge**. They **have to** be faced together and we **have to** master them both. **What are our chances of success?** It depends **on what kind of people we are. What kind of people are we? We are the people that** in the past made Great Britain **the workshop of the world, the people who** persuaded others to **buy British, not by begging them to do so, but because it was best. We are a people who** have received **more Nobel prizes than any other nation** except America, and head for head we have done better than America, twice as well in fact. **We are the people who**, among other things, **invented the computer, the refrigerator, the electric motor, the stethoscope, rayon, the steam turbine, stainless steel, the tank, television, penicillin, radar, the jet engine, hovercraft, float glass, carbon fibres, et cetera – and the best half of Concorde.**
(*Margaret Thatcher, Blackpool, 10.10.75*)

Extract 4
We are **both humbled and elevated** by the honour and privilege that you, the people of South Africa, have bestowed on us, as the first president of a united, democratic, **non-racial and non-sexist** South Africa, **to lead our country out of the valley of darkness**. We understand it still that **there is no easy road to freedom**. We know it well that none of us **acting alone** can achieve success. We must therefore **act together** as a united people, **for national reconciliation, for nation building, for the birth of a new world. Let there be** justice **for all. Let**

there be peace **for all. Let there be** work, bread, water and salt **for all. Let each know that for each the body, the mind and the soul** have been **freed to fulfil** themselves. **Never, never and never again** shall it be that this beautiful land will **again** experience the oppression of one by another …
(Nelson Mandela, Pretoria, 10.5.94)

▣ 13.3

a

What's the main problem we're facing? The main problem is cash flow.

b

It's so risky, so problematic, and yet so critical to our success.

c

It's faster, cheaper and easier to use. But, above all, it's more reliable.

d

Even if we can never again be the biggest, we can still be the best.

e

The point is, more and more graduates are fighting over fewer and fewer jobs.

f

Not only are we number one in Brazil. We're now number one in Latin America.

g

In this market, no company has outperformed us, not one – ever!

h

Not once, in over thirty years of business, have we ever had a complaint – not a single one!

▣ 13.4

1

Ladies and gentlemen, we are truly on the brink of a revolution in bio-technology. **I'm reminded of the words of** futurist and science fiction writer Arthur C. Clarke: 'People go through four stages,' he said, 'before any revolutionary development. Stage one: it's nonsense, don't waste my time. Stage two: it's interesting, but not important. Stage three: I always said it was a good idea. And stage four: I thought of it first.' In gene therapy we're about to enter stage four. **And I'd like this company to honestly be able to say** 'We thought of it first.' Thank you.

2

Uh-oh. Sorry. Looks like we've run out of time. Erm, so I'm going to have to cut it short. Er, yeah, I was hoping to show you some of the figures in our comparative study. But, erm, never mind. I think you'll find all the main points are covered in the handout. So I'll, er, I'll just leave copies here and you can pick one up on your way out. OK. So, sorry about that. That's it. Thanks.

3

Well, that just about brings me to the end of my presentation, except to say that the future of this company is now in your hands. For **if there's one central message I'd like to get across to you this morning it's this**: that this consultancy is no more and no less than the consultants who represent it. And whilst our reputation as a firm may have been damaged by the recent unfortunate events, our expertise as a team is in no way diminished. I want to see each and every one of you raising this company to new heights. I know you can. We built our reputation on crisis management, and it would be ironic indeed if we were unable to successfully manage this crisis of our own – and come out on top. Thank you very much.

4

So, how do you sum up the new Spearing Silhouette ocean cruiser? **I could tell you that** it has won just about every boat show in the USA and Europe this year, that the orders for it are coming in so fast we already have a five-year waiting list; that the first three names on that waiting list, though strictly confidential, include a famous Hollywood actor, a member of the Saudi Royal Family and one of the world's greatest sporting legends. **I could also mention that**, so impressed are they with our award-winning design, the directors of the Museum of Modern Art are actually proposing to place a full-size model on permanent exhibition. **But all that would fail to do it justice. For the fact is** that the Silhouette is in a class of its own. It is a masterpiece of marine engineering. **It is, quite simply**, the most stunningly beautiful boat ever built. Ladies and gentlemen, I give you … the Spearing Silhouette!

14 Out and about

▣ 14.1

1: Emma

A: So Emma, what's your worst flying experience?

B: Well, I think the worst one's probably flying back from Bangladesh to Heathrow. **It's quite a few years ago now, but I can still remember it**. We were at the gate, ready to taxi to the runway, and suddenly there was this terrible hammering noise from outside the plane.

A: A hammering noise?

B: Yes, **and the strange thing was** that the cabin crew just seemed to be ignoring it. But all you could hear was this bang, bang, bang on the fuselage. After a while, some of the passengers were starting to get nervous, me included.

A: **I'm not surprised**.

B: Anyway, eventually, after we'd been sitting there for about ten minutes with no announcement and the plane still not moving, I said something to one of the stewards and they went and opened the door to see what was going on.

A: And what happened?

B: The pilot got in!

A: **You're joking!**

B: No, they'd locked him out. **Seems quite funny now, but it didn't at the time.**

2: Enrique

A: Enrique, what's the worst flight you've ever been on?

C: Definitely the time I was flying from Malaga to Stansted in the UK. **This was around the time of** the terrible attack on the World Trade Center in 2001 and people were still very nervous about flying.

A: Oh, yes, of course.

C: I was travelling on business, but most of the passengers were British tourists.

A: Uh huh.

C: Anyway, we were cruising at 30,000 feet and I looked out of the window and saw this French air force fighter plane flying alongside us.

A: What? **Oh, yes, I read about this**. Didn't they think the plane had been hijacked or something?

C: Well, apparently, air traffic control had lost radio contact with our plane, so they weren't sure what was going on and they weren't taking any chances. I mean this French jet was armed with missiles and everything.

A: **Sounds terrifying!**

C: It was.

A: **So, what happened?**

C: Well, the jet was there for about ten minutes checking us out. Fortunately, the captain of our plane managed to keep everybody calm. **And anyway, to cut a long story short**, everything turned out OK. We even landed on schedule!

A: But I bet you were glad to be back on the ground, weren't you?

C: You can say that again!

3: Joe

A: Joe, have you had any bad experiences on planes?

D: Oh, yes, several. One flight I was on, I couldn't understand why they were making us go through the lifejacket drill for landing on water.

A: But don't they always do that?

D: What, on a domestic flight from Manchester to London?

A: Oh, right. **I see what you mean.**

D: I'm not sure which flight path they were planning to take but it goes nowhere near the sea. **But that's nothing compared to** one of my recent trips to Frankfurt.

A: What happened there, then?

D: Well, we didn't land in Frankfurt.

A: You were diverted?

D: No, no, the pilot just landed in completely the wrong country!

A: What, you mean he didn't know?

D: Hadn't got a clue. Just about everybody on the plane was looking out the windows and saying 'Er, look, I'm sorry to be a nuisance, but this isn't Frankfurt.'

A: So where *did* you land?

D: Luxembourg.

A: **Oh, my god! I don't believe it!**

4: Selina

A: Selina. You've flown all over the world. You must have some stories to tell.

E: Hm, quite a few. **I'll never forget the time I was** flying in Asia and the cabin crew asked me to sit on the toilet during take-off.

A: What?

E: Yeah, they wanted my seat next to the emergency exit.

A: Doesn't inspire much confidence in the airline, does it?

E: Not a lot, no. **And then, to top it all, I ended up** sitting next to a guy with a rattlesnake in a basket!

A: Good god!

E: Yes, that's what I said. Apparently, he just brought it on as hand luggage. But **erm, ... did I ever tell you about the time I was** working in Nigeria?

A: No, I don't think so.

E: Well, er, **you're not going to believe this, but way back in 1985 it was**, I was on this internal flight, right? And it was three times overbooked!

A: Three times?

E: Oh, yeah, that was quite common in those days. But **you should have heard** the arguments at check in.

A: I can imagine.

E: **Anyway, in the end**, they brought the army in to sort it out.

A: The army?

E: Yeah. **And you'll never guess what they did ...**

A: What?

E: They made everyone run round the aircraft twice.

A: **What on earth for?**

E: So they could give the seats to the fastest.

A: **You can't be serious!**

E: It's absolutely true.

A: And did you win a seat?

E: Certainly did. I came third. I was quite quick in those days!

🔊 **14.2**

a

A: Ugh, isn't it **dreadful**? And we'd got plans for the weekend as well. Thought we might have some friends round for a barbecue.

B: Well, it's always the same, isn't it? You plan anything, it **always lets you down**. And it was **so fabulous** yesterday.

C: Yes, wasn't it? Never would have thought it could **turn so nasty** in just 24 hours. But that's Britain for you, I suppose. **Heatwave** in the morning, a **downpour** in the afternoon and a **howling gale** by dinner time. Bloody weather!

b

B: I'm not sure this is quite right, is it?

A: Hm?

B: This. Is it supposed to be like that? Looks a bit **soggy** to me.

A: Hm, yes, it does a bit. It should be all **crisp** and **golden**, shouldn't it, the **pastry**? Not very **appetising** at all. And there's **not a lot of it**, is there?

B: No, I thought **it came with something else**. Like a **side salad** or something ... Ugh! **The meat's as tough as old boots** as well!

A: Oh, dear. I'd **tell the waiter to take it back**, if I were you ...

c

C: Line them up against a wall and shoot the lot of them, that's what I say.

A: We can always rely on you for a balanced and mature view, Roger.

C: Well, you know what I mean. Interfering in **policies** that have nothing to do with them. **Power-mad** they are. And who actually **voted** for them, that's what I want to know.

B: Well, I'm not sure I'd ...

A: Actually, Roger has got a point there, even if he is being a bit **right-wing** about it, as usual. A lot of these **Eurocrats** are just **self-appointed**, aren't they? They've never had to go through any kind of **democratic election process**.

C: No, and that's how half of Europe has ended up being **governed** by a bunch of **unelected civil servants** in Brussels!

d

B: No, it's not my thing at all, I'm afraid.

A: Oh, but I thought it was marvellous! And **it was so well done**. Because it must have been a very difficult **adaptation**, don't you think? All those enormous books.

B: Hm, yeah. **It went on a bit**, though, didn't it? I mean, what was it, three and a half hours? Should have had an **intermission** really.

A: Well, I found the whole thing absolutely **compulsive viewing**. And **brilliantly directed**. And the **special effects** were incredible!

B: Yes, well, they *were* good, I'll admit, but they've all got those nowadays, haven't they? I mean it's all **digital animation**, like *Star Wars* ...

e

B: I'd really appreciate it, because I'm just **snowed under** at the moment, what with all this **backlog** to deal with.

A: Yes, I'm sorry to have **dumped all that on you**. Couldn't think of anyone else I could trust. And with the **deadline** coming up so fast ...

B: It's no problem, but if you *could* let me borrow Kim for a couple of hours, I'm sure that together we could **polish the whole thing off** that much faster.

C: You **overworking** this poor boy, Suzanne? That's how she lost her last **assistant manager**, you know, Ian.

A: Oh, ignore Roger. I'll speak to Kim about **giving you a hand** as soon as we get back to the **office**.

B: Thanks.

f

C: What on earth is this?

A: You don't like it? It's one of my favourites. Lovely **bouquet**. **Fresh** and **fruity**.

C: **Smells off to me**.

A: Nonsense! It's fine.

C: Like **something with a bit more body to it**, myself.

B: Hm, that's not at all bad.

A: See? Ian likes it.

C: Hm. All right for lunch, I suppose. But it's still **too young**, if you ask me. Could do with another couple of years in the bottle.

A: Oh, don't be such **a wine bore**, Roger. Get yourself **a glass of something** else if you don't like it.

C: Think I will ...

15 Big ideas

🔊 **15.1**

Extract 1

A: **Synergy** – well, that's just the old combining your efforts idea, isn't it? We're all more effective if we work together as a team.

B: Hm, depends on the team, but, yeah.

A: And **re-engineering** – that was the big thing in the 90s, wasn't it? Improving efficiency and performance ...

B: ... by sacking half your staff!

A: Well, I think there was bit more to it than that, but, basically, yeah.

B: Same as **downsizing**, really. Cutting costs by making people redundant.

A: More or less ... delayering, restructuring ... all comes down to the same thing in the end, doesn't it?

B: Job losses.

A: Exactly.

B: First, you fire people. Then you write a new mission statement saying 'Our people are our greatest asset' and promise to give everybody more autonomy.

A: **Empowerment**.

B: Oh, yeah, empowerment. That's what they all talk about nowadays, isn't it? We're all supposed to have more control over what we do. I must say I don't feel very empowered where I work.

A: No, me neither. The boss sticks his nose into everything I do.

B: Yes, I've met your boss. Not a nice person. No **emotional intelligence**.

A: None whatsoever. In fact, his people skills are practically non-existent. He's just got the one strategy really for dealing with people.

B: What's that, then?

A: He shouts at them.

Extract 2

A: Erm, **TQM**, well, that's total quality management, isn't it? Quality circles. Getting your production and inventory and logistics right, and so on.

B: Yeah, yeah, pretty standard stuff nowadays ... like **JIT**. Manufacturing things just in time to meet customer demand. Makes perfect sense.

A: Yeah. Easier said than done, though. Now, **the glass ceiling**. Well, we've certainly got one of those where I work. There's hardly a woman who gets promoted beyond unit manager.

B: Did you know there are even fewer women in top jobs now than there were ten years ago? Apparently, at the current rate of change women won't achieve equality with men until 2270!

A: Huh! That's probably why a lot of women have got fed up waiting for promotion and started their own businesses instead.

B: Can't say I blame them. But nobody's job is really safe these days, is it? I mean more and more work gets outsourced to freelancers.

A: **Outsourcing**, yeah. What we all have to do is keep changing direction in our careers about every seven years.

B: Well, this is the so-called **portfolio career**, isn't it? Keep changing jobs. Nice idea, but, frankly, I have enough trouble doing the job I've got, thanks.

Extract 3

A: What's this **co-opetition**, then? I've never heard of it.

B: Hm? Oh, yeah, that's co-operating with the competition. You know, you collaborate with your competitors on some things … erm … whilst continuing to compete on others.

A: Sounds a bit risky to me.

B: Hm, me too. But **marketspace** – this is really interesting, actually, because the idea is that, in the end, it's pointless trying to fight the competition for the same bit of market.

A: Tell me about it. We're all making pretty much the same product for pretty much the same customers.

B: Right. And what we've got to do is stop winning a bit of market share here, losing a bit there and actually break free of the competition altogether. Create our own marketspace.

A: Innovate.

B: Not just innovate. We've got to look at opportunities *between* different industries. I've got a book on it, actually.

A: I guessed! … **Glocalisation** … I know, this is like 'think local, act global', isn't it? The world's breaking up into smaller and smaller countries. But at the same time you've got these big economic alliances developing – like the EU. With improved telecommunications, you can keep your business small and local, but the whole world's your market.

B: Yeah, that's what everyone keeps saying: 'The whole world's your market.' If only it was that simple.

15.2

These leaders have nothing at all in common in terms of background, beliefs, achievements, management style or personal characteristics. So, ultimately, all attempts to define the qualities of leadership are a complete waste of time. The one thing the leaders do have in common is this: followers. Every one of them has, or had, people prepared to follow them in one way or another. A leader is not what you are, but what other people make you. And whether or not you yourself are a leader is not for you to decide.

16 Teleconferencing

16.1

A: Ugh! **Who on earth can that be?** Where's the … the light switch! Ow! Er … hello?

B: Pete, is that you?

A: Er, yes. Who is this?

B: It's Max.

A: Max! … Max, it's … it's two o'clock in the morning!

B: I'm sorry, Pete, but this is an emergency.

A: Well, it better be, I've got to be up in a few hours.

B: I think you'd better get up right now, Pete. **All hell's broken loose here.** We're going to have to **shut down** the Hamburg plant immediately.

A: What!

B: It's the heat exchanger. We've got a leakage between the hydrogenation section and the oil heater. There's nothing we can do but stop all production straightaway. Otherwise, the whole thing could **go up**!

A: But Max, do you have any idea what you're saying? If you authorise a plant shutdown, **everything grinds to a halt**. We'll have container lorries **backed up** from Hamburg to Lübeck!

B: Pete, do you think I don't know that?

A: Tell me this isn't happening. It cost us millions last time … OK, look, I have no idea how long it will take me and Monica to get a flight, but we're on our way.

B: I think that's best, Pete.

A: I'll phone you to fix up a teleconference once we're airborne. Contact Françoise and Otto right away, will you? **There's not a moment to lose …**

A: Monica? It's Pete. Look, **I'm sorry to get you up at this unearthly hour**, but there's been a disaster at the Hamburg plant. Yeah. Better get dressed. I'll tell you about it on the way to the airport.

16.2

Extract 1

A: **OK, so we're just waiting for Otto.** Françoise, you told him when to call in, right?

C: Yes, I did. Perhaps he's still at the plant or he may just be having problems getting through.

B: Pete, where are you and Monica?

A: Just left Vancouver about half an hour ago, Max. Should be back in 13 hours or so.

C: Pete, I think we should just start.

B: Yes, I think so too.

A: OK, we really need to talk to Otto, but let's go ahead and get the meeting started and hopefully he'll join us later on … Right, well, as you all know, we've had a serious mechanical failure at the Hamburg plant and, basically, we've had to shut it down. There'll be time for a proper analysis of what went wrong later. Right now we need a rescue plan. **Max, could you first of all just fill us in on what's going on?** When can we expect to get the plant up and running again?

B: **Well, Pete, it's difficult to say at the moment**. My technicians tell me they can't get a replacement heat exchanger for at least 48 hours. And then it'll have to be fitted, of course. We're probably looking at three days.

D: Three days!

A: It's worse than I thought. And is that your best estimate? Three days?

B: I'm afraid so, Pete.

A: Well, that's that, then. But I want us back in production no later than Thursday, Max. OK?

B: OK, Pete, **I'll see what I can do**.

Extract 2

E: Excuse me, Mr Mendel has joined.

A: Otto! Thank goodness you got through. Have you been to the plant yet? What's the situation there?

F: It's pretty bad Pete. We've had to clear the whole site for the fire service to run safety checks.

A: I see. Otto, is there any chance we can rewrite our production plan? I mean, can we make sure our key customers get priority on orders?

F: **I'm already working on that**. The problem is it doesn't look as though we'll be able to meet any of the orders completely.

A: What's the stock situation?

F: Not good.

A: Oh, great. Just what I needed to hear. Don't we keep any stock in reserve for this kind of thing?

F: What, for a complete plant shutdown? No, Pete, we don't.

A: OK, OK. Well, what about transferring stock from one of our other European plants?

F: It'd take too long. And, besides, they're already overstretched as it is.

A: Right … Monica, **is there any point in us buying in traded goods** from another supplier to cover the shortfall? **Just for the time being**.

D: You mean buy product from our competitors to keep the customers happy?

A: Just for the time being.

D: **Pete, you know how I feel about buying from the competition**. How are we supposed to build a reputation with our customers if we end up selling them other people's products instead of our own?

A: It's not as if we haven't done it before, Monica. And **what alternative do we have?**

Extract 3

A: OK, now, we've got to make up this backlog of orders somehow. How about Handelsmann?

C: Er, **can I come in on that?**

A: Go ahead, Françoise.

C: Well, **I've already been on to** Handelsmann. They owe us a favour, actually. We helped them out a few years ago when they were in a similar situation, if you remember. Anyway, it looks like they may be able to do something, but probably not until tomorrow morning.

A: Well, at least that's something, I suppose. **OK, get back to them and see if we can hurry things up a bit. And get somebody in after-sales to ring round all our biggest customers** and smooth things over with them.

C: **OK, I'll see to it now.**

A: Now, Max. Are you sure this thing can't just be fixed? I mean, if I gave your technical people, say, 24 hours … Max, you still there?

B: Still here. I've just been told the leakage area has now been made secure.

A: Well, thank god for that. Anyway, OK, that's it for now. We're going to try and get some sleep. I suggest we schedule another conference call for midnight European Time. But, Otto, **keep me posted if there's any change in the situation,** won't you?

F: Will do, Pete.

A: OK, thanks everyone …

17 Negotiating deals

📼 **17.1**

The activity you just did is designed to demonstrate the critical importance in the negotiating process of relationship-building.

In your first negotiation you probably didn't think much about your opponent's interests. And why should you? After all, it was just a stranger who you'd never meet again. But by concentrating on only one objective, you reduced the whole encounter to a **single-issue negotiation** with **little room for manoeuvre**. This made it a simple **zero-sum game** – if I get what I want, you don't, and vice-versa.

In order to **win at all costs**, perhaps you became hostile and tried to pre-empt negotiation altogether by just grabbing the box off the other person. Or maybe you gave in completely, deciding **it simply wasn't worth the hassle**. Many professional negotiators act the same way if they think they are negotiating a **one-off deal**. As the negotiation **ended in deadlock**, perhaps you became desperate and **resorted to emotional blackmail**, inventing all sorts of reasons why your kid was more deserving than the other kid.

In the second negotiation, on the other hand, there was a **long-term relationship** you wanted to maintain. The circumstances were exactly the same, but the prospect of one of you 'losing' was no longer an option. By accepting the need to **reach some kind of compromise**, you were able to turn a **head-on conflict** into a problem-solving meeting. Now your main objective was to generate options in the hope that you could create a **win-win situation**, where you both got something you wanted.

📼 **17.2**

Extract 1

A: OK, **so, do I take it we're in agreement on volume?**

B: Er, well, just a minute, **wouldn't it be a good idea to talk prices before we go any further?**

A: Yes, of course. **But in principle you're happy about taking forty cases, right?**

B: Er, well, in principle, yes, if the product's as good as you say it is …

A: Splendid, that's settled then.

B: … But, **look, getting back to price for a moment**. This would be just a trial order, you understand? Sale or return. Until we see how it sells. So, **can you give us some idea of what kind of figure you were thinking of?**

A: €50.

B: €50 per case.

A: Er, no. Per pack.

B: Per pack? **There seems to have been a slight misunderstanding**. A pack is just 12 bottles, right?

A: Yes, that's right.

B: Is this meant to be some kind of joke or something? €50 per pack? That's over €4 a bottle. By the time we've added a decent margin, you realise we're looking at a retail price of €7 minimum. How am I supposed to sell a one-litre bottle of water for €7, Mr Koivisto?

A: Ms Barrett, *O-Zone* is an innovative, premium product. A pure oxygen-enriched drink. We're not talking about a bottle of Perrier here.

B: Well, that's as may be, but €7!

A: *O-Zone* is an exciting opportunity to get in at the start of a new trend in luxury health drinks.

B: Well, there's no way on earth I'm paying you €4 for a bottle of oxygenated water, Mr Koivisto. **With respect, your prices are simply not competitive.**

A: Ms Barrett, there *are* no competitors in this market. *O-Zone* is a unique product and at €4 – well, **I'm afraid that really is our absolute bottom line**.

B: So you're saying it's take it or leave it?

A: I'm afraid so.

B: Well, then, I think I'll have to leave it …

A: Wha …? Now, just a minute. You said on the phone you might want 100 cases.

B: That was before I knew your water was more expensive than Chardonnay, Mr Koivisto. OK, look, **let's set the price issue to one side for the moment, shall we?** Tell me a bit more about the product …

Extract 2

A: OK, I tell you what I'll do. If you order 250 units today, I can offer you not our usual five but a six per cent discount, free delivery and **I'll throw in 12 months' free parts and service as well.** Now, **I can't say fairer than that, now can I?** Of course, that's only if you can give me the order today. Can't hold the offer, I'm afraid.

B: Well, erm, Robert, isn't it?

A: Rob. Call me Rob.

B: Well, now, Rob, we appreciate the free service and delivery, but to be honest with you, **what we'd really like to see is a bit more movement on price.** I'm afraid **a six per cent discount is not quite what we had in mind**. We were hoping for something a bit closer to ten.

A: Ten per cent? **I don't think I could stretch as far as that.** Not unless this was a substantially bigger order.

C: Oh, come on! You'll have to do a lot better than that, Mr Hayes. You're not the only precision tool manufacturer, you know.

B: Hold on, Gavin. Let's hear Rob out.

C: Well, frankly, I think we're wasting each other's time here. We've already been offered a much better deal by Magnusson's.

B: Now, wait a minute, wait a minute. **Surely we can sort something out here.** Rob, **would you be willing to meet us halfway?**

A: How do you mean?

B: Well, if you were to offer us an eight per cent discount, **we might be in a position to increase our order**, say, by fifty units. But **we'd need to see a bit more flexibility on terms of payment**. Maybe on installation costs too.

A: Erm, well, **I suppose there may be some room for manoeuvre there**. I'd need to check. Can you give me a moment to have another look at the figures?

B: Sure. In fact, let's take a short time-out, shall we? And meet back here in, say, half an hour?

A: OK, fine.

C: I still say we'd be better off going with Magnusson's.

📼 **17.3**

Speaker 1

Make your priorities clear before you begin, that's my advice. I always say remember to check your tie. Not the one you wear round your neck, your T-I-E. 'T' stands for 'tradeables'. These are the things you'll take if you can get them, but they're not that important to you and you'll concede them if it helps you to push the negotiation forward. 'I' stands for 'ideals'. These are the things you'd really like to get and will fight to get, but not if it costs you the deal. Finally, and most importantly, 'E' stands for 'essentials'. It's not that these are absolutely non-negotiable. Everything's negotiable. But if it looks like you're not going to get your essentials, then that's the time to start thinking about walking away from the negotiating table.

Speaker 2

Well, frankly, I get a bit tired of hearing people go on about win-win negotiating. I mean, let's face it, a lot of negotiations are basically win-lose, and your opponent's interests are the last thing you should be worrying about. Buying a house, a car, double-glazing – all win-lose situations. And you'd be surprised how many business negotiations are basically one-off deals as well. In my opinion, in a win-lose situation the tougher you are – without actually being aggressive – the further you'll get. That's because your opponent takes your attitude as an indication of what's possible and what's not. And the friendlier you seem, the higher their expectations will be. It's like the old saying: **give them an inch and they'll take a mile**.

Speaker 3

'You always know who is going to win a negotiation – it's he who pauses the longest.' I forget who it was who said that but it's pretty good advice – basically, shut up! And remember that silence is very often your best weapon. It's a very difficult argument to counter. Faced with prolonged and uncomfortable silences, your opponent is liable to make another concession or give away their strategy or weaken their own position by becoming defensive. So **play your cards close to your chest**. Talk less, learn more. There's an old Swedish proverb: 'Talking is silver. But listening is gold.'

Speaker 4

I think the biggest trap less experienced negotiators fall into is to turn the whole negotiation into a debate, which it isn't. This is sometimes called 'positional negotiating'. Both sides end up arguing the whys and wherefores, rationalising their position, trying to justify themselves. It's a complete waste of time. You're not there to convince your opponent that you're right. He doesn't care if you're right or not. And neither should you. You're there to explore both sides' interests, generate options and trade concessions – preferably giving away things that mean little to you but a lot to him and receiving the opposite in return. This is 'interest-based negotiation' – discovering the needs, desires and fears behind your opponent's position and working on those. The two phrases you need most of all are: 'If …, then …?': If I give you that, then what do I get? And 'What if …?: What if we looked at this another way? What if we did this instead?

Speaker 5

The key skill in negotiating is the ability to ask the right questions – and ask lots of them. In fact, there's an organisation called the Huthwaite Research Group, who recorded hundreds of negotiations and guess what they found? 'Skilled negotiators ask more than twice as many questions as average negotiators.' So, my advice is: phrase as many of your comments as possible as questions. You don't

understand something? Don't say you don't understand – you'll look stupid. Ask a question – you'll look intelligent. You strongly disagree? Don't say you strongly disagree – they'll think you're being difficult. Ask a question – they'll think you're trying to be helpful. You have a good idea? Don't say you have a good idea – they'll wish it was *their* idea. Ask a question. They'll think it *was* their idea. Keep those questions coming and **don't take 'no' for an answer!**

■ 17.4

A: Tess?

B: Mr Logan. It's Kate and Miles to see you.

A: Ah, good. Send them right in.

C: Hi, Ronnie.

A: Kate, good to see you. You're looking great as usual. Miles come on in. Rough night, huh? Erm, sit anywhere you like. Can I get you a beer?

C: It's a little early for me, Ronnie. Do you have an Evian or something?

A: No problem. There you go. Miles?

D: Er, don't think I could face anything right now, man.

A: No, you certainly don't look as though you could. So, you two had quite an evening at the Marquee, so I hear.

D: You could say that.

C: Ronnie, you have to sign this band. You could hardly move for A&R people last night. If we don't snap them up, someone else will. I saw Jimmy Armstrong from Sony sniffing around.

A: Uh huh. Well, he usually is.

C: Yeah, and EMI were there as well. This band's hot. You listened to the demo I sent you, right?

A: I did.

C: And?

A: Well, …

C: Oh, come on, Ronnie. These guys are the best thing to come out of Ireland since U2 and you know it.

A: I wouldn't go as far as that, Kate. They sound a little inconsistent on the tape. They need to work on a clear musical identity, if you ask me.

C: Well, maybe they need a little help in that direction. We can work on that. But you have to admit the lead singer's voice is just amazing. In fact, they're musically really strong all round.

A: OK, I'll give you that. Apart from the drummer, that is, who's pretty second-rate. So he'd have to go.

C: She.

A: She? They have a female drummer? Interesting. Well, anyway, she's no good.

C: Could be tricky to fire. She's the lead singer's girlfriend.

A: Hm. I'm going off them already.

C: Ronnie, believe me, *The Penitents* are a class act. And I'm not easily impressed, you know that.

A: True, you're not. Miles, meet the woman who turned down *Oasis*.

D: Fine by me. I never liked them.

C: I thought we weren't going to talk about that any more.

A: OK, OK. Well, what do *The Penitents* look like? No, let me guess. Like they haven't eaten a hot meal for a week and cut their own hair, right?

C: Not at all. The lead guitarist looks like Keanu Reeves. The drummer's fabulous even if her drumming's a little off. In fact, they're all pretty glamorous. Ronnie, I have a good feeling about this one.

A: OK, call their manager and set something up. But not next week. I'm at the MTV awards.

C: OK, I'll do that. Oh, and by the way, you might want to tune in to VH1 at eight this evening. They're being interviewed live.

A: They are? Well, why didn't you say so before? Look, give me their manager's number, I might just call him myself this afternoon …

18 Shaping the future

■ 18.1

Speaker 1

Well, part of me thinks this post-human thing is just a lot of nonsense, really. I mean, even if you could genetically alter people to make them stronger or slimmer, well, so what? It's just like going to the gym and working out, isn't it? I don't think we're going to be creating superhumans for a very long time yet. So it's not going to make a whole lot of difference. Erm, and I've also read those stories about giving people memory chip implants to make them more intelligent. I suppose it could be done. And it would, in a way, give people an unfair advantage in exams and job interviews and so on. But, I mean, people already have an unfair advantage if they've had a better education, haven't they? So there's nothing new about buying advantages in life. To be honest with you, they'd have to be able to make me a real genius before I'd let some doctor start doing brain surgery on *me*!

Speaker 2

Hm, I don't like the idea of these 'new barbarians' living in luxury and controlling all the world's money, while the rest of us fight it out on the streets. Sounds a bit like that film *Blade Runner* to me. But, er, we're definitely seeing businesses getting more and more powerful. I mean, with all the corporate scandals we've had recently, I do think that companies are a law unto themselves – they just do what they like, really. So I suppose it's not too difficult to imagine certain multimillionaires forcing governments to do pretty much what they want. Er, I am, though, totally against the idea of getting rid of the welfare state. A world in which the fortunate and successful are helped to be even more fortunate and successful and the rest of us are just basically forgotten doesn't sound like the kind of world I would want to live in.

Speaker 3

Well, on the ageing population idea, I think it's one of those things everybody knows about but they're just kind of ignoring it. I mean I read somewhere that half the over-65s who've ever lived are alive *today*! Of course, in one way that's good because you've got all those relatively well-off older people with plenty of time to spend their cash – you know, the so-called 'grey dollar'. That's going to be good for travel and tourism, the leisure industry, and medical and pharmaceutical companies. And, being old might be a lot more fun in the future. What with cosmetic surgery, smart drugs and Viagra we'll be living it up well into our 80s and 90s! The problem is, we're going to need millions of young people to run our businesses while we're all having fun. That means increased immigration from the developing world, I think. Here in Germany we have a population of about 82 million, and seven million of those are immigrants. I think that figure could double at least in the next 20 years.

Speaker 4

Well, it all sounds like a good idea at first, doesn't it? You can take your skills anywhere in the world via the Internet without actually leaving home. But it's not really practical, is it? I mean for one thing, most jobs can't be done by telecommuting, even with things like videoconferencing and stuff like that. They've been talking about it for ages, but nobody seems to like working that way. Personally, I think you need human contact in most jobs. I know I do in mine. And I can't see professionals in the EU and the US and Japan just letting people in South-east Asia and Africa take their jobs. I mean it's bad enough exploiting cheap *manual* labour in those places already. But imagine if you also had low-paid engineers and lawyers and doctors working on the Net. The consequences for the professions could be devastating, not to mention the actual quality of service you might be getting.

Speaker 5

Well, this idea that our kids are going to be achieving a hundred times more over their working lives sounds a little improbable to me. Surely it depends on what kind of job they're doing. Everybody seems to think we all work at lightning speed these days. But, let's face it, in some jobs, things haven't changed all that much in twenty years. We're not all computer geeks. I don't think life itself is so much faster. It's just that we want so much more out of it and that's why we get so stressed trying to fit it all in. When I go on business trips to the States, it always amazes me how hyperactive everybody is. They're fixing up a time to play tennis on the phone, having lunch at their desk while they do their spreadsheets, skim the Wall Street Journal and instant message their childminder to check their kid's doing her math homework. You want to go out for a beer with them, you need an appointment! I think what they need is to come to Mexico and relax a little.

Speaker 6

I think Naisbitt is absolutely right. As we get more technological, we also want to recapture some of the old-fashioned values of a simpler, slower, more natural age. I mean the quickest way to buy a book is through Amazon, which is a marvellous service, but it cannot really compare with the pleasure of wandering around a good bookshop. I have a lot of fun playing computer games with my seven-year-old son, but I still want to take him ice-skating or play football in the park. I work for a design company and, interestingly, if you look at many of the most popular industrial designs of the last ten years or so, you find they all have an organic, retro look about them: the iMac, for example, the Nokia mobile phone, the Dyson vacuum cleaner, the Smart Car. No straight lines, lots of curves and bright colours. Soft, subtle technology. As Naisbitt says, high-tech, but high-touch.

Macmillan Education
Between Towns Road, Oxford OX4 3PP
A division of Macmillan Publishers Limited
Companies and representatives throughout the world

ISBN 0 333 95737 7

Text © Mark Powell 2004
Design and illustration © Macmillan Publishers Limited 2004

First published 2004

Designed by Jackie Hill at 320 Design
Illustrated by Mike Stones icons; Kim Williams pp73, 79;
Julian Mosedale p92
Cover design by Jackie Hill at 320 Design
Cover illustration by Mike Stones
Photo research by Sally Cole

Author's acknowledgements: My thanks are once again due to the
'usual suspects'. Chief amongst my collaborators has been the
managing editor Erika Vivers – no one is more willing to go the
extra mile to make a good job great. The author Douglas Adams
once said 'I love deadlines – I like the whooshing sound they
make as they fly by.' My publisher David Riley has had to put up
with rather a lot of whooshing. Thanks for weathering the storm.
Jackie Hill and Sally Cole have again done me proud on the
design. James Richardson and the actors on the recordings have
surpassed all expectations. Lastly, thanks to my wife Begoña. I
have no idea how popular this book will prove, but Begoña tells
me it's my best. Maybe that's a good teacher speaking. Maybe it's
just love. Actually, I'd settle for 'just love'.

The publishers would like to thank Bob Ratto, Byron, Rome;
Angela Wright, British Council, Rome; Norman Cain, IH Rome;
Fiona Campbell, Teach-In, Rome; Sue Garton, Lois Clegg and Irene
Frederick, University of Parma; Simon Hopson and Gordon Doyle,
Intensive Business English, Milan; Dennis Marino, Bocconi
University, Milan; Mike Cruikshank, Advanced Language Services,
Milan; Christine Zambon, Person to Person, Milan; Fiona O'Connor,
In-Company English, Milan; Peter Panton, Panton School, Milan;
Colin Irving Bell, Novara; Marta Rodriguez Casal, Goal Rush
Institute, Buenos Aires; Elizabeth Mangi and Silvia Ventura, NET
New English Training, Buenos Aires; Graciela Yohma and Veronica
Cenini, CABSI, Buenos Aires; Viviana Pisani, Asociación Ex
Alumnos, Buenos Aires; Claudia Siciliano, LEA Institute, Buenos
Aires; Cuca Martocq, AACI, Buenos Aires; Laura Lewin, ABS
International, Buenos Aires; Charlie Lopez, Instituto Big Ben,
Buenos Aires; Alice Elvira Machado; Patricia Blower; Valeria
Siniscalchi; Carla Chaves; Virginia Garcia; Cultura Inglesa, Rio de
Janeiro; Susan Dianne Mace, Britannia, Rio de Janeiro; John
Paraskou, Diamond School, Sèvres; Dorothy Polley and Nadia
Fairbrother, Executive Language Services, Paris; Claire MacMurray,
Formalangues, Paris; Claire Oldmeadow, Franco British Chamber of
Commerce, Paris; Ingrid Foussat and Anne James, IFG Langues,
Paris; Karl Willems, Quai d'Orsay Language Centre, Paris; Louis
Brazier, Clare Davis, Jacqueline Deubel, Siobhan Mlačak and
Redge, Télélangue, Paris; John Morrison Milne, Ian Stride, Gareth
East and Richard Marrison, IH Madrid; Gina Cuciniello; Helena
Gomm; Paulette McKean.

The authors and publishers would like to thank the following for
permission to reproduce their material: Bloomsbury Publishing Plc
for dictionary extracts from the Macmillan English Dictionary ©
Bloomsbury Publishing Plc 2002; Vicefund for extracts from
www.vicefund.com/docs/ViceProspectus.pdf; Copyright Clearance
Centre, Inc for extracts from Artful Persuasion: How To Command
Attention, Change Minds, and Influence People by Harry A Mills
(AMACOM, 2000) copyright © AMACON 2000; Random House
Group Limited for extracts from The Ultimate Business Presentation
Book by Andrew Leigh (Random House Business Books, 1999);
Macmillan London, UK for extracts from How To Argue And Win
Every Time (Pan Books, 1995); Copyright Clearance Center for
extracts from 'You have to start meeting like this!' by Gina
Imperato first published in Fast Company April 1999 Issue 23
(www.fastcompany.com); N I Syndication Limited for extracts from
'Should genetic tests decide job prospects?' by Margaret Cole,

copyright © Times Newspapers Limited 1999, first published in
The Sunday Times 24.01.99; Tribune Media Services International
for extracts from 'In a high-tech world, it's a clinch for employers
to spy on workers' by Liz Stevens first published in Knight Ridder
Newspapers 12.06.02, copyright © Knight Ridder/Tribune Media
Services International 2003; Francis Beckett for extracts from
'Creative way to better management' by Francis Beckett first
published in Financial Times 08.11.99, copyright © Francis Beckett
1999; Kogan Page for extracts from Great Myths of Business by
William Davis (Kogan Page, 1997); Gifford and Elizabeth Pinchot
for extracts from www.intrapreneur.com; Lesley Everett for extracts
from 'Dress for success and walk into a topline career', copyright
© Lesley Everett first published in The Guardian 22.06.02; McGraw
Hill Companies Inc for extracts from 'Golf and business: a perfect
couple' by Mark Nelson, taken from www.businessweek.com/
lifestyle/content/nov2001/1s2001116.3182.htm, copyright ©
McGraw Hill Companies Inc 2001; Quirk Books for extracts from
'The Worst-Case Scenario Survival Column' by David Borgenicht
taken from www.worstcasescenarios.com/mainpage.htm; John
Adair for extracts from Effective Decision-Making by John Adair
(Pan Books, 1985); Book House Publishing AB for extracts from
Funky Business by Jonas Ridderstråle and Kjell Nordström (ft.com,
2000); The Adbusters Media Foundation for extracts from 'Buy
nothing day' taken from www.adbusters.org; Guardian Newspapers
Limited for extracts from 'No Logo: Naomi Klein review' by
Katherine Viner, copyright © The Guardian 2000, first published in
The Guardian 23.09.00; The Economist for extracts from 'Going
global' first published in The Economist 06.12.01, copyright © The
Economist Newspaper Limited, London 2001; Lexicon Naming for
extracts from www.lexiconbranding.com/contact.html; Sandra
Harris for extracts from 'Deliver us from e-mail', copyright ©
Sandra Harris 2000, first published in Business Life Magazine
September 2000; John Wiley & Sons Limited on behalf of Capstone
Publishing Limited for extracts from The Ultimate Book of Business
Quotations by Stuart Crainer (Capstone Publishing Limited, 1997),
copyright © Capstone Publishing Limited 1997; Margaret Thatcher
Foundation for extracts from Speech to Conservative Party
Conference 10.10.75; Atlantic Syndication for extracts from 'Bad
spelling is the key to success' by Molly Watson, first published in
Evening Standard 10.04.01; Hilary Rubinstein Books for various
extracts taken from The Penguin Book of Twentieth Century
Speeches edited by Brian MacArthur (Viking, 1992); Random House
Group Limited for extracts from The Accidental Tourist by Anne
Tyler (Chatto & Windus, 1985).

Although we have tried to trace and contact copyright holders
before publication, in some cases this has not been possible. If
contacted we will be pleased to rectify any errors or omissions at
the earliest opportunity.

The authors and publishers would like to thank the following for
permission to reproduce their photographs: Action Plus/G.Kirk
p49; Alamy/Stockfolio p14, Pictor p20, J.Ward p27, R.Llewellyn
pp31(t), 40, 63, D.Delimont p51(m), T.Payne p52, TH Foto p58,
C.Ehlers pp74, 87, Robert Harding p84; Anthony Blake/T.Robins
p5, M.Brigdale p51(b), S.Atkinson p57; Car Photo Library p56;
Corbis/D.Turnley p6, Bettmann pp10, 21, 82, N.Rabinowitz p16,
Pandis Media p18, F.Cevallos p25, P.Corral p36, P.Ward p37,
J.Feingersh pp42, 83, Left Lane Productions p44, G.Mendel p46,
A.Schein p59, Hulton-Deutsch p69, J.Miele p71, S.Prezant p78,
D.Laine p81(t), R.F p81(b), T.Svensson p95; GettyImages/
Chabruken p13, M.Oppenheim p17, R.Brimson p22, S.Battersby
p35, R.Lockyer p47, Photodisc Blue p48, R.Melnychuk p51(t),
C.Hawkins p54, Photodisc Green p56, Amwell p62, T.Yamada p64,
D.Madison p68, H.Grey p77, J.Bradley p91, Hulton Archive pp32,
94, 97; Panos Pictures/Alain le Garsmeur p73; Photonica/F.Cantor
p90; Press Association/EPA pp39, 66; Rex Features/J.Sutton Hibbert
p60; Science Photo Library/B.Frisch p96, US Dept of Energy p98;
Vin Mag Archive p37; Zefa pp4, 84.

Cartoons on p23 reproduced with permission from the New
Yorker/© The New Yorker Collection 2000 Frank Cotham from
cartoonbank.com. All Rights Reserved; p59 Calvin and Hobbes ©
1995 Watterson. Reprinted with permission of Universal Press
Syndicate. All Rights Reserved.

Printed and bound in Spain by Edelvives SA

2008 2007 2006 2005 2004
10 9 8 7 6 5 4 3 2 1